D0051582

Quality Teaching in a Culture of Coaching

Second Edition

Stephen G. Barkley
with Terri Bianco

ROWMAN & LITTLEFIELD EDUCATION
A division of
ROWMAN & LITTLEFIELD PUBLISHERS, INC.
Lanham • New York • Toronto • Plymouth, UK

Published by Rowman & Littlefield Education
A division of Rowman & Littlefield Publishers, Inc.
A wholly owned subsidary of The Rowman & Littlefield Publishing Group, Inc.
4501 Forbes Boulevard, Suite 200, Lanham, Maryland 20706
http://www.rowmaneducation.com

Estover Road, Plymouth PL6 7PY, United Kingdom

Copyright © 2010 by Performance Learning Systems, Inc.

All rights reserved. No part of this book may be reproduced in any form or by
any electronic or mechanical means, including information storage and retrieval
systems, without written permission from the publisher, except by a reviewer who
may quote passages in a review.

British Library Cataloguing in Publication Information Available

Library of Congress Cataloging-in-Publication Data
Barkley, Stephen G. (Stephen George), 1950-
  Quality teaching in a culture of coaching / Stephen G. Barkley with Terri Bianco. —
2nd ed.
     p. cm.
  Includes bibliographical references and index.
  ISBN 978-1-60709-632-0 (cloth : alk. paper) — ISBN 978-1-60709-633-7 (pbk. :
alk. paper) — ISBN 978-1-60709-582-8 (electronic)
  1. Teachers—In-service training. 2. Mentoring in education. 3. Teachers—
Professional relationships. I. Bianco, Terri. II. Title.
  LB1731.B274 2010
  370.71'5—dc22   2010005282

∞™ The paper used in this publication meets the minimum requirements of
American National Standard for Information Sciences—Permanence of Paper for
Printed Library Materials, ANSI/NISO Z39.48-1992.

Printed in the United States of America

Contents

Foreword   v

Acknowledgments   vii

Introduction   xi

Part I: The Value of Coaching

1   Why Coaching?   3

2   Who's on First? Defining the Role of the Coach   23

3   Okay, What *Is* Coaching?   39

4   The Skills of Coaching   55

Part II: The Coaching Process

5   The Preobservation Conference   79

6   The Observation   101

7   The Postobservation Conference   123

Part III: Applications of Coaching

8   I'm Ready! How Do I Create a Coaching Culture?   151

9   Who Has Coaching Programs? How Are They Working?   171

Contents

Appendix   189

References   215

Index   221

About the Author   233

Foreword

Many daunting problems in education stem from the isolation of teachers. Teaching requires the highest concentration of adults in the workplace of nearly any profession, and, ironically, it is the most isolating. There is no such thing as excellence in teaching when in solitude. By definition, excellence in teaching is a form of communication and group activity.

A coaching relationship contributes significantly to diminishing this isolation, particularly when the coaching involves experienced and expert practitioners sharing their knowledge and skills with less experienced educators. There is an impulse in the nation toward more collaboration among educators, yet change is still taking place slowly. In most schools, teachers are judged on their work as individuals. Policies and practices encourage individualism and do not sufficiently promote collective actions on the part of teachers. New teachers end up learning their jobs by "sink or swim."

Thus, it was with great relief and excitement that I learned Steve Barkley was writing a book on the subject of coaching. Steve is a highly skilled educator and presenter, and his focus on the empowerment of teachers has always been paramount. Rather than viewing teachers as targets of reform, he equips them to be agents of reform. He values the synergy that comes when teacher and coach spend productive time reflecting, polishing, improving, and focusing their efforts toward greater rewards for student and teacher alike.

Japan has long known the exponential benefit of coaching and teaching. While Japan's school year is the longest in the world, teachers' direct contact with students is less than in the United States. Japanese teachers devote half their work time to joint planning, sharing their lessons with other educators, conferencing about students, and learning from each other. They call this "polishing the stone." American teachers should take example from this process and spend less time in isolation and more time in thoughtful collaboration.

I envision a teacher union that acts not only as an advocate for educators but also as a lobby for students. Coaching provides an array of tools for that effort. Steve Barkley played a vital role in bringing peer coaching into our teachers' negotiated contract as early as 1987. We believe in this direction so strongly that we have included peer coaching assistance, peer review, and now coaching and mentor programs in all our negotiated contracts.

These programs are hugely successful, and they may not have been without the infrastructure of knowledge provided by Steve and Performance Learning Systems. We have now leveraged those programs into new provisions that call for team transfers. Teachers no longer view themselves as individual practitioners; rather, they collaborate with other teachers—those who have been coached or are coaches—in order to transfer into low-performing schools.

The distinguishing difference about Steve's approach is that he shares with a wider audience and with the educational community work he has actually done, work he has honed over two decades. He doesn't just offer commentary on the work of others; he makes direct application of his own experience. A book by a dynamic and skilled practitioner such as Steve is vastly more actionable, valuable, and pragmatic than that of someone offering up only theoretical speculation.

Steve's experience throughout the United States and his observation of practices and patterns in other countries give him a solid basis from which he can develop new techniques and help others avoid negative findings, false starts, wrong turns, and pitfalls. His wisdom, gained from decades of distilled experience, can teach us what works and what doesn't. In this book, readers have a concentration of knowledge and experience to help them avoid the hard knocks involved in gaining direct experience on this critical theme.

Bravo, Steve. A book about coaching in teaching by an accomplished teacher coach is a book whose time has come.

—Adam Urbanski, Ph.D.

Adam Urbanski is president of the Rochester Teachers Association, a vice president of the American Federation of Teachers (AFT), and the director of the Teacher Union Reform Network (TURN) of AFT and NEA Locals. A native of Poland, Dr. Urbanski immigrated at the age of fourteen. He earned a Ph.D. in American social history from the University of Rochester. A former high school teacher and college professor, Dr. Urbanski is now an active proponent of change in education.

Acknowledgments

I would like to express my sincere appreciation and admiration to the team that helped develop this book:

Terri Bianco of TBEnterprises, who lent voice to my thoughts, collaborated on concepts, and made written sense out of my ideas, while applying her enthusiasm, support, and terrific writing and interviewing skills.

Barbara Brown of Phil Brown Fine Arts, for her stellar production management abilities and efficiency in preparing the manuscript for the publisher.

Sharon Bieganski-Negron of Blonde Renditions Creative Studio, for improving illustrations and creating new ones.

Adam Urbanski, Ph.D., president of Rochester Teachers Association and vice president of American Federation of Teachers, for his continuing support, dedication, inspiration, and kind words.

Tom Koerner, Ph.D., publisher, and the staff of Rowman & Littlefield Education, for publishing the original book and asking for an update which resulted in this revision.

My early mentors, coaches, and peers in New Jersey and beyond, who guided me as an educator, and to Joseph Hasenstab, founder of Performance Learning Systems, who trained me, inspired me, and encouraged me to bring knowledge, skills, performance, and heart to the profession of teaching.

I would also like to express great appreciation to the following educators, coaches, and administrators who shared programs and experiences and contributed their thoughts to the context of this coaching book: Barbara Carroll, supervisor, teacher, and coach, Cranford High School, Cranford, New Jersey; Karen Bailin, teacher and coach, Cranford High School, Cranford, New Jersey; Joseph Corriero, Ed.D., member, Cranford Board of Education,

Cranford, New Jersey; Mary Jo Scalzo, Ph.D, director of curriculum instruction and assessment, Oakwood City School District, Dayton, Ohio; Judy Hennessey, superintendent, Oakwood City School District, Dayton, Ohio; Debbie Smith, educator and coach, Oakwood City High School, Dayton, Ohio; Judy Sheehan, curriculum resource director, Winter Park Tech, Winter Park, Florida; Cheryl Jones, supervisor and Reading First teacher, coach, School District of Hillsborough County, Daytona Beach, Florida; Cindy Petree, educator and coach, Stillwater High School, Stillwater, Oklahoma; Marilyn Katzenmeyer, Ed.D., leadership development coordinator, Tampa Bay Educational Leadership Collaborative, University of South Florida, Tampa, Florida; Jean Linder, Ph.D., University of South Florida, College of Education, Tampa, Florida; Sheryl Williams, reading coach, Alturas Elementary School, Alturas, Florida; Donna L. Behn, Ph.D., director of curriculum and instruction, Hartford Union High School, Hartford, Wisconsin; Dan Roskom, educator and lead coach, Hartford Union High School, Hartford, Wisconsin; Valerie Maxwell, math specialist, Appoquinimink School District, Middletown, Delaware; Hara Blum, reading specialist, Brandywine School District, Wilmington, Delaware.

I would also like to acknowledge those who have contributed to the 2010 revision of this book. They have chosen to take risks to improve their own teaching and that of many others through dedication and hard work in various coaching programs throughout the world. My hat's off to them, not only for persevering in the development of their programs and the people who benefit from them, but also for sharing this journey with us and all who read this book: Marie Costanza, director of Career in Teaching Program, Rochester City School District, and Adam Urbanski, president, Rochester Teachers Association, Rochester, New York; Mellissa Alonso, Cheryl Jones, and Mary Vreeman, K–3 Reading First program, and Lynn Dougherty-Underwood, secondary reading, Hillsborough County, Florida; Mike Miller, former director of professional development, and Gretchen "Boo" Rayburn, instructional coach, Salem-Keizer High School, Salem, Oregon; Darlene Fisher and the dedicated and international leadership team of the Enka Schools in Istanbul, Turkey; Debbie Coffman, Karen Taylor, and the entire instructional facilitators core team at Arkansas State Department of Education in Little Rock, Arkansas; the team at the Center of Professional Development and Lifelong Learning at the Instituto Pedagogico Arubano in the Caribbean island of Aruba, including director Ingrid Kuiperdal, Earl Euson, Diana Goedhoop, Ergisela Hato, Rosemarie Amalia Hoen, and Ava Thode; former principal Dr. Tom Higgins and current principal Judy McNeil, lead teacher Suzanne Schott, Social Studies Department chair Beverly Titlow, and Gifted Department chair Hester Vasconcelos, Walton High School, Marietta, Georgia. Thanks also to Wendy Staley, teacher specialist at Washington County Public Schools in Washington County, Maryland.

A special thanks to Dr. Jim Knight and his team at the University of Kansas Center for Research and Learning for their dedication to the art and science of coaching and for their support and acknowledgement of my own efforts on behalf of furthering the value of coaching in education.

And finally, I would like to thank all the teachers, coaches, principals, administrators, colleagues at Performance Learning Systems, and students who have shared their experiences and the benefits of coaching with me over the years. You have served as the inspiration and the motivation to create this book.

Many thanks to you all. Be sure to spread the word: Wow!

Introduction

When I wrote the first edition of this book in 2005, reading coaches from Reading First funding were in place in many elementary and a growing number of secondary schools. Technology and data coaching positions were also being created. Beyond that, however, coaching remained an intriguing concept, often confused with mentoring and, in some areas, believed to be a passing fad or "flavor of the day" for staff development training. Many resisted the concept of one teacher observing another in the act of teaching; administrators often wondered why a coach might be needed. Thankfully, much has since changed.

Just as life coaching, executive coaching, and other forms of professional coaching have grown in popularity and acceptance, coaches for educators are found in almost all schools today, in many different roles, funded by various programs. Reading coaches, math coaches, instructional coaches, administrative coaches, potential specialists, behavior specialists, instructional facilitators, and mentors provide one-on-one coaching to enhance and streamline teaching skills, for the benefit of teachers and students.

The primary impetus for including coaching as a way to improve teaching skills stems from solid research by Bruce Joyce and Beverly Showers, developed in *Peer Coaching: A Strategy for Facilitating Transfer of Training* (1984) and later updated in their 1996 article "The Evolution of Peer Coaching." The study by Joyce and Showers showed a vast discrepancy between what teachers learned in professional staff development and how it was later applied in the classroom. By simply adding coaching and feedback to the training process, the transfer to the classroom was elevated 75 to 90 percent.

Research bears out the value of coaching. To me the real proof comes from my own observation of the evolution of the early coaching programs, covered in the first edition, to the scope and breadth of what's in place today, both in this country and abroad. A relatively small cadre of reading coaches has grown to include instructional coaches and content-specific coaches; the value and impact has shown up in improved student learning.

As I travel around the country and the world, I am continually reinforced in my assessment that coaching remains a key ingredient to successful teaching. Coaching empowers teachers with skills to communicate, lead, and reactivate, and it enhances their love of teaching, which in turn motivates students.

When I began teaching in 1971, I participated in an experimental student teaching program at East Stroudsburg State University in Pennsylvania. My first experience was to teach a class of eighteen fourth graders. What a kick!

Much later I realized how fortunate I was: as I taught those fourth graders, a master teacher, another student teacher, and a graduate intern were in my classroom to observe and support me. These thoughtful and experienced professionals observed my teaching every day for 180 days. As soon as a class or a lesson was completed, I received immediate feedback and encouragement.

Without the support, feedback, questions, and acknowledgment of these early coaches, I may not have succeeded in that first year. And, who knows? I may not now be spending my professional life consumed by a passion for teaching, training, presenting, writing, and coaching educators in the fine art of teaching students.

Based on our hands-on experience of success and growth of teacher coaching that has taken place since the first edition, this revision of *Quality Teaching in a Culture of Coaching* offers more ways to develop rapport and trust between a coach and the teacher being coached.

We stress the importance of continual celebration of effort in teaching and in coaching, and the book offers further examples from successful teachers. Everyone enjoys the well-being that comes from a celebration of effort. From my "coaching post" at the back of the classroom, I often find myself exchanging smiles with a teacher whose endeavors have been rewarded by an enthusiastic response from his or her students. This nonverbal communication from the teacher speaks volumes about the pleasure a minicelebration can create. Think of how energizing it is when someone you trust and respect is there to observe and celebrate your success. Teachers working in isolation miss these magical moments, even one of which goes a long way to support teacher perseverance when achievement is stalled. Providing teachers with opportunities to celebrate is a key benefit of coaching.

Coaching is not an evaluation process. It is a supportive process designed to assist and motivate those who want to improve their teaching skills, enhance their careers, and better serve students. To accomplish this, a coach observes a teacher to determine the specific skills and performance patterns the teacher wants to develop, then offers immediate feedback and debriefing on what was observed.

Is this snooping? Not at all. Most athletes and performers rely on feedback so they can adjust accordingly. Often a video camera rolls as they perform. A school I visited showed me an elaborate setup with expensive underwater video cameras recording strokes and movements made by members of the swim team. Wonderful idea; it vastly improved the swimmers' performance. I asked to see where and how the teachers were being videotaped. I was told they were not.

What's up with that?

A camera can be easily set up in a classroom, a faculty room, or in any place where a teacher, administrator, sports coach, or staff member chooses to work on a technique, strategy, communication skill, or behavior he or she wants to fortify or improve. Cameras are portable, digital, inexpensive, and can run by themselves. There is no better feedback than seeing yourself in action.

Imagine having a library of CDs or podcasts showing educators teaching various subjects at different grade levels using highly creative techniques, all available to other teachers—new and veteran alike. These digital recordings would capture creative and effective lesson plans and also provide viewers with motivation, inspiration, and ideas for professional improvement. This equipment should be a basic investment in every school building—and, no, I do not work for a video company.

Coaching has, thankfully, caught on throughout the United States and in other countries around the world; however, there remains a critical shortage of opportunities for teachers to receive feedback on how they teach. We are updating this coaching book in response to its warm reception by educators in pursuit of viable coaching programs.

When I left teaching to become a full-time instructor with Performance Learning Systems, Inc. (www.plsweb.com), an international educational services company, I delivered their graduate courses and professional staff development training. I continue to deliver countless presentations to educational associations, to state departments of education, and now at international conferences.

I train teachers, principals, administrators, and others in the art and performance of great teaching, and I love every minute of it. Since my beginnings as an educator, I have benefited from coaching. I have been videotaped countless times. I scrutinize my performance patterns and teaching techniques, and others scrutinize them along with me. Ego and self-consciousness take a back seat as the importance of delivering instruction takes precedence.

I experience the tremendous boost a culture of coaching provides professional educators. I am heartened by the personal and professional benefits coaching gives these educators and by the passion for learning inspired in students by their newly skilled teachers. Coached teachers are fiercely self-aware about their practice. They reflect on how they can strengthen students' desire to learn and achieve. They are deeply grateful for the coaches who clearly desire their success.

The first version of this book was printed nearly twenty thousand times and has been used in coaching programs, in book study groups, and as a text for training in the art of coaching. This revised version of *Quality Teaching in a Culture of Coaching* continues to outline the why, who, what, and how of a sound coaching program. We have included concrete examples, opportunities to practice specific skills, a clearly defined coaching process, coaching applications for a wide array of school professionals, and up-to-date, real-life anecdotes, and quotes to pepper it all up.

We are pleased to reissue the book with its updates and ideas to offer you a framework and an inspiration to incorporate a culture of coaching into your own educational environment.

I

THE VALUE OF COACHING

1

Why Coaching?

Certain themes and patterns emerge as we talk with teachers, principals, and directors of coaching programs underway both in the United States and internationally. One person speaks to the evolution of the coaching program from an initial content-specific focus, such as reading; another to a program that embraces overall teacher performance.

Others—many, in fact—point to the value of coaching to ease the isolation faced by many educators. Some speak of the initial resistance to coaching that later becomes central to the school's culture. Many point to the vast improvement in teaching and the statistics that reflect student success. Still others share how coaching has permeated their personal and professional lives in positive and dynamic ways.

Let's listen in . . .

"Once you embrace the language, communication skills, and concept of coaching, it's in everything you do and it impacts every relationship," says Mary Vreeman of Hillsborough County, Florida. "You find yourself applying the techniques of coaching in whatever teaching or administrative position you achieve."

Mary should know. She is now an assistant principal at Crestwood Elementary School in Hillsborough County, Florida. Before that, she and colleague Cheryl Jones were pioneers in the initial reading coach program in Hillsborough County that began in 1999. They liked the program so much they wrote a book about it! *Instructional Coaches & Classroom Teachers: Sharing the Road to Success* (Jones & Vreeman, 2008) is an excellent book exploring the role of coaching from the eyes of the teacher in a thorough, informative, and lighthearted way.

What began as a K–2 reading coach program in 1999 has expanded to include K–5. Reading coaches attend monthly small-group area meetings, in addition to their whole-group training sessions, to delve into topics that "bubble up," says Cheryl Jones. "What's changed since we began," Cheryl reflects, "is a real movement toward collaboration among the teachers and reading coaches. We have become closer, and our monthly area meetings allow time to share concerns, to celebrate, and to debrief one another."

Meanwhile, in the Arkansas State Department of Education, educators found that it is one thing for teachers to work with students, quite another to successfully coach adults. Arkansas' program of instructional facilitators, as their coaches are called, started with the formation of focus groups around the state in 2004. The program has successfully expanded ever since.

"What we kept hearing over and over was how these Instructional Facilitators needed to achieve buy-in from those they were coaching," says Karen Taylor, K–12 literacy specialist and a moving force in the Arkansas state coaching program. "They needed to learn how to work with adults, to learn how to be team leaders."

Debbie Coffman, associate director of professional services in the Arkansas Department of Education echoes that sentiment. "The Instructional Facilitator is someone who will help teachers with their instruction as far as the pedagogy, but we also needed more training to work with teachers on performance—how to achieve the highest yield in student learning, ways to problem solve, and room to practice techniques that best reach their students."

Not dissimilar was the discovery found in the schools in the Caribbean island of Aruba. "Our in-service training sessions were not resulting in real implementation of innovations in the classroom practices," says Ingrid Kuiperdal, codirector of the Instituto Pedagogico Arubano, which launched its coaching program in 2006. "We sought a coaching program that could support our way of thinking and that looked at the needs of the teachers."

At Walton High School in Cobb County, Georgia, coaching has replaced evaluation as a method of performance assessment. "The state's evaluation system checks mediocrity," says Suzanne Schott, lead teacher at Walton High School. "It is not a real learning document. When we have people grow through the years with coaching, the assessment from that model shows they actually improve every year. It's living proof, not a checklist that says you're okay, you're average, and that's okay. We are moving away from a traditional evaluation model to one where coaching is the norm."

Beyond that, Walton High found coaching an effective tool for collaboration and for mitigating the isolation of teaching. According to former Walton High School principal Tom Higgins, "Collaboration is the best way to leverage the talent in your building. To provide professional learning on a continual basis, we structured effective and frequent ways for teachers to learn from each other."

In places as diverse as the Enka Schools in Istanbul, Turkey, and the Salem-Keizer School District in Oregon, the challenge of overcoming resistance to change and a teacher's tendency to be guarded about the prospect of being coached by peers has been identical. Clarity of roles and the development of trust become paramount. Is someone a mentor or a coach? Does the coach get to evaluate me? Why do I need this other teacher coaching me?

"Our biggest challenge comes with the cultural differences about *sharing*," says Darlene Fisher, director of Enka Schools in Turkey. "Our international teachers seem more accustomed to it, while the local teachers have a different perspective. Developing a culture of coaching itself is helping us overcome this challenge," she adds.

"You can never have a second chance at a first impression," says Gretchen "Boo" Rayburn, instructional coach at Salem-Keizer School District in Salem, Oregon. Partly due to the method of funding, the district's initial Title I coaching program had what Boo calls "a deficit, fix-it model. If there was a coach on staff, it meant you were struggling."

Since then, Salem-Keizer has obtained federal funding to broaden the coaching program and enjoys the mind shift that has occurred. Per Mike Miller, retired principal and former director of professional development at the district, "There was an initial trepidation on the part of teachers. Now I have to ensure that principals allow the coaches to keep doing what they do and not be distracted, because they have had such a positive impact."

Success stories such as these abound across the country and around the world. Coaching has proven to be one of the primary tools of staff development for teachers and administrators alike. Coaching provides a vehicle by which to achieve goals, improve strategies, and make a difference for students and colleagues. With coaching, teachers discover—usually for the first time—how to reflect on their teaching in ways that add value to their methods and an enhanced level of professionalism. They see and hear themselves as educators. They get opportunities for receiving direct feedback on how they interact with their students. They increase their ability to design lesson plans that focus on specific strategies they want to implement to reach *all* their students.

The resulting support and feedback from colleagues has a bonus effect—teachers at the same school develop a synergy of creativity. When administrators and teachers together undertake a coaching program, it gets even better. Schoolwide collegial support develops. Students receive the benefit of an improved teacher in their classrooms; administrators receive the respect and support from an admiring and productive staff. All receive the caring and support for each other. A quality learning experience occurs for students and throughout the learning community.

THE GIFT OF COACHING

But why coaching? How does coaching create this synergy, this support, and these successes? Let's start by saying what it's not. Coaching is not about fixing someone. No one is broken, and no one needs fixing. It's not about giving advice, providing "constructive criticism," making judgment, or providing an opinion.

Coaching is a relationship between two equals committed to an ideal of personal and professional improvement. Improvements might be learning new strategies, getting unblocked or unstuck, developing skills to re-evaluate beliefs or values that affect professional outlook. The person being coached—the coachee—takes ownership of his or her own improvement. Therein lies the power of coaching.

Each person being coached is committed to his or her own achievements. Those being coached know what it is they need to work on, and thus there is relevancy and consequence to doing the work, achieving the goal, succeeding. In committing to coaching, coachees commit to their well-being and skill as professional educators.

A coaching relationship provides the opportunity for reciprocity of gifts of knowledge and skill, caring and support, feedback and celebration. In the coaching relationship, people being coached are the ones in charge; they have the agenda, the commitment, and the specifics of what they want to know or learn about their skills as a professional. Nothing gets discussed that the coachee does not want to discuss. The relationship is focused on achieving the results desired by the coachee.

The coach, in turn, ensures that the coachee always steers toward the goal, the achievement, the fulfillment, and the success. Sometimes the coachee has questions; otherwise, the coach asks the questions. The person being coached usually has the answers when given a forum to discover them for him- or herself.

Yet as the person being coached goes through the process of coaching, the coach achieves his or her own level of success. Imagine how the coach must feel when the teacher being coached exclaims that the goal was reached or that the process, strategy, or lesson plan really worked. Feedback received from the coach serves as "feedforward," moving the teacher or administrator along in a way that achieves success. The coach reaps rewards when the coachee excels.

A culture of coaching improves teaching and improves student learning. Teachers once entered a classroom, closed the door, and taught primarily on their own, doing the best they could, relying on their years of education and experience. They were there to impart knowledge and see that learning occurred. Those days are long gone. Teachers now are not only charged with helping students learn in a world drowning in new information and technology but are called upon to serve as social worker, nutritionist, counselor, whistle-blower, cop, nose-blower, and more.

We all know teaching has changed. Like all other professions, the need for support from colleagues, coaches, and mentors is long overdue. We pay athletes, performers, television personalities, business executives, and other professionals millions of dollars to perform with quality, effectiveness, and assurance. Each of these professions has an array of coaches, in one form or another, providing what the coachee needs.

Teaching is no different. In fact, it is more important that educators receive support to do their very, very best. After all, there are children's futures at stake.

COACHING WORKS

Research shows that teachers' skill development markedly increases when opportunities for practice and feedback are provided. To be maximally useful, such feedback must be specific and descriptive. The addition of coaching to teachers' staff development greatly enhances their implementation of skills in class.

Educational researchers Bruce Joyce and Beverly Showers, in their book *Student Achievement through Staff Development* (2002), point out that staff development training often assumes that once teachers learn and develop a skill, they will automatically use it in the classroom. Yet their research reveals it isn't a sure thing that learned knowledge and skills will transfer. However, you can expect to have a noticeable increase in transfer when coaching is added to a teacher's training.

Training or coaching that provides transfer of skills into instructional settings is crucial for learning. Table 1.1, "Transfer of Learning by Types of Training," developed by Joyce and Showers, illustrates the increased transfer of learning when a coaching component is added. This table shows a relationship among types of training and the percentage of participants who will accurately use a developed skill and achieve a desired outcome.

Table 1.1. Transfer of Learning by Types of Training

Training Provided	Skill Development	Accurate Use in Class
Theory/Knowledge	5%	0–5%
Theory/Modeling	50%	5%
Theory/Modeling/Practice and Feedback	90%	5%
Theory/Modeling/Practice/ Feedback and Coaching	90%	75–90%

Source: *The Coaching of Teaching* by Joyce and Showers (1993)

Figure 1.1 shows the five steps that take place for internalization of learning, according to Joyce and Showers.

Joyce and Showers consider *knowledge* the awareness of educational theories and practices, new curricula, or academic content. It includes the exploration of theory or rationale through reading, lectures, and discussion. An outcome has been achieved when the knowledge—awareness—has been achieved.

Modeling demonstrates discrete behaviors and skills; *practice* includes implementation of those behaviors or skills, such as the ability to deliver questions, use pause time, engage students through eye contact and inquiry, and so on. *Observation* occurs in the coaching process, as does *feedback*.

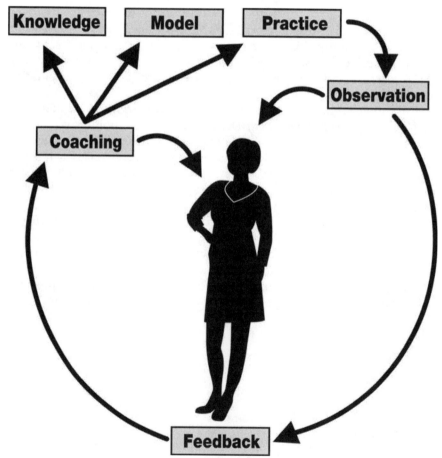

Figure 1.1. Learning a Skill

The reality of teaching in a classroom, of course, is vastly different from a training session where teachers learn and even practice new skills or techniques. According to Joyce and Showers, while practicing skills will certainly increase their use in the classroom, coaching and feedback provide the most significant leap in transfer of learning for the one being coached. Training is valuable, but unless teachers can bring the new skills into the classroom, there's little chance they will continue to use the skills in their daily teaching strategies. A separate, metacognitive learning experience eventually transfers to teaching behavior patterns that are natural and effective.

Beyond transfer, the feedback provided by coaching is extremely beneficial to the coach. Coaches can see confusion or omissions when watching others teach more easily than they can recognize it in themselves. Therefore, they learn in the process too.

Let's be real. Coaching goes on all the time. Teachers constantly support and reinforce one another. Teachers share confusion over new standards, support each other in complex lesson planning, and seek advice when discipline problems crop up.

While teachers and administrators use conferences and meetings to get ideas and support from fellow professionals, the more common exchange is from one to another. Teachers seek out teachers for support, and administrators seek out administrators for support—the operative word here is "support."

The human need to share, to improve, to seek help is ever present, even in the hectic schedule of an educator. Why not capitalize on this need by following a process designed to improve the quality of teaching and learning? Coaching invites diversity of style and approach. It improves teaching, confidence, and raises the bar on professionalism.

HAROLD, QUALITY, AND THE EMERALD BUS

Improving the quality of life for teachers improves the quality of life for students and thus the quality of learning. A quote I like to use, because it defines quality for me, is from William Glasser, M.D., author of *Choice Theory, The Quality School, The Quality School Teacher*, and *Choice Theory in the Classroom*. In his article "Quality, Trust, and Redefining Education," Glasser (1992) says, "While quality is difficult to define precisely, it almost always includes caring for each other, is always useful, has always involved hard work on someone's part, and when we are involved with it, as either a provider or a receiver, it always feels good. Because it feels so good, I believe all of us carry in our heads a clear idea of what quality is for ourselves" (p. 37).

I like his description, as I can immediately identify quality as I work in school districts around the country. Quality is not only visible in a school's environment; it is apparent in the way students and teachers interact, in the excitement of the students, in the faces of teachers and administrators, and in the teamwork of the staff.

We often speak of quality products and quality service in the consumer world, but what about quality experiences in teaching and learning? As an educator, parent, or administrator, don't you want to work in an environment where quality is achieved, both in teaching and in learning?

When I speak to various groups, I often share an incident that illustrates a quality experience. In a concrete way, this story identifies the components of Glasser's quotation about quality.

I arrived at the Atlanta airport on a Sunday night. It was late. My plane had been delayed, and I still had to rent a car and drive to a hotel near the school where I was presenting the following day. I was tired, and after I took the tram and then the escalator from the plane to the terminal, I realized there was a huge line of people ahead of me waiting to rent cars. Discouraged and resigned, I moved to the end of the line.

After a few moments, I noticed a sign on the wall over a computer. It said "Welcome Emerald Plus Cardholders." I recalled I had an Emerald Plus card. It was bright green, and I found it immediately in my wallet. While this was in my "early" computer days, I nevertheless went up to the computer, saw a slot about the size of my green plastic card, and popped it in. Boom! Up on the screen appeared the words "Welcome to Atlanta, Stephen G. Barkley!" I sheepishly looked back at the line, slightly embarrassed that someone might have seen this.

Beneath that greeting were two words: "Rent" and "Return." I clicked on "Rent," and up came another screen showing pictures of four cars. I picked the red Corsica, and out dropped a set of keys and a printed rental agreement! Feeling very cocky but trying not to show it, I sauntered past the long line of people, jingling my keys ever so slightly.

I went outside to catch the bus to the car rental lot and saw a big green bus pulling away. I waved, and, to my surprise, the driver turned the bus around and came back to get me. He jumped out of the bus and grabbed two of my bags; I took the other two, showed him my keys and my rental agreement, climbed aboard, and plopped down, relieved.

Next the driver picked up the bus intercom and began speaking. Now, it's one o'clock in the morning, I'm the only person on the bus, and he says in a booming voice, "Welcome to Atlanta, Mr. Barkley. I'm Harold, your Emerald Flyer for the day!" Arriving at the parking lot, he unloaded my two bags. I got the other two, and he approached me and said, "Your keys are in the trunk. Your rental agreement is on the dashboard. Have a *wonderful* stay in Atlanta."

Wow. I realized then that I had more energy at one o'clock in the morning than I had had three hours before. That energy came from the *quality* in the experience.

This story highlights the four aspects of quality described by Glasser. Certainly Harold the Emerald Flyer showed that he *cared*. I can attest to the fact that helping with luggage is not in the typical job description of a rental-car bus driver.

Next, the experience was *useful*. The computer network system that generated a set of keys and a rental agreement was extremely useful to me. It meant I could get on my way sooner, get more sleep, and be more alert in my presentation.

Harold *worked hard*, as did the folks who made sure that when I got to the parking lot, there actually was a clean red Corsica there, the keys fit the car, and everything ran as it should. That takes hard work on the part of many people.

Finally—and probably the most telling trait of quality—it *felt good*. It felt good for the provider and the recipient, for Harold and for me.

Coaching adds quality. It adds quality to the level of teaching as well as to the school environment. It shows *caring* on the part of the coach—he or she cares that the teacher or administrator succeeds. It is *useful*, as it adds quality to teaching and to student learning. It takes *hard work* to change, practice new skills or strategies, commit to improvement, get feedback, and recommit. And it feels good. It *feels good* to improve, to change, and to succeed; it feels good to have someone in your corner, coaching you to high achievement.

We'll work with some of Glasser's theories in chapter 3. For now, let's look at the idea of quality when considering a coaching program at your school or district. Begin with the idea of adding coaching to your life by asking questions about quality. Ask where the quality is in your school, your faculty relationships, and your interaction with students—and build on that.

Look to coaching to make it easier to have a school that's caring, to make its programs useful, and to set up an environment where hard work feels good. Quality circumstances produce positive energy. Quality permeates the school system—how the cafeteria works, the moods of educators, the productivity of students, the look of the hallways.

GETTING TO WOW

Quality means going "above and beyond" the norm. I learned about a teacher who gave out Cs to those students who completed a project successfully. To get a B they had to go beyond the project; to receive an A they needed to go above and beyond. In no job do you get promoted for merely doing what you are asked to do. If you're a dishwasher, you don't get promoted for washing the dishes. You get promoted if you wash the dishes and also polish the sink.

Peer coaching and working collaboratively with colleagues greatly improves the motivation for teachers to go above and beyond the rote elements of teaching into a realm Tom Peters (1994) describes in *The Pursuit of WOW!*

Achieving WOW, to me, is achieving quality. Ask yourself: When does a student achieve a WOW? On how many Fridays can a teacher add up the WOWs he or she received from students? Also, WOWs do not necessarily come from an entertaining presentation or activity. They are not entertainment. They are experiences of quality when a student feels exhilarated by a learning situation. How many opening days of school have WOW quality—for students or for teachers?

Some opening-day WOWs I have witnessed include teachers who dress in costume to represent historical characters for history class. Or they come as the main character of the first book students have to read in English class.

A math teacher brought single dollar bills to school on opening day and handed them out to each student. He told them if they passed math, they could keep the dollar. If they didn't pass, they had to return the dollar—with interest compounded daily! You can bet they learned about interest very quickly.

A special-education teacher in Georgia learned her class that year would be held in a portable trailer. The first day of school she dressed with curlers in her hair, slippers on her feet, and licorice on her teeth so it looked like they were missing—making the point they were located in a trailer, away from the main school building. After a few minutes of students gawking at her, she took off the bathrobe to reveal a beautiful sequined dress, high heels, and classy jewelry. She told the children their trailer was like Cinderella's magic pumpkin: all sorts of magic occurred there, and they were going to have a year of wonderful, magical surprises.

If teachers wow kids, someone has to wow teachers now and then, too. The need for excitement and motivation that applies to students presumably also applies to teachers—maybe even more so. Teachers typically start school by going over classroom rules, because administrators start their year with rules for teachers and students. Administrators talk about "have tos" instead of "going tos": "We have to meet standards this year"; "We have to make up for last year's snow days"; "We have to provide more discipline."

Imagine the quality that would result in telling teachers, "We're going to have a great year!" "We're planning an exciting parent-teacher day." "We're going to get a new computer network system." "We're going to have a lot of fun this year!" "We're going to give you support by providing you with a professional coaching program this year."

Coaching introduces quality to a relationship. Because coaches support the success of teachers—just as teachers support the success of their students—teachers gain the experience of having someone in their corner rooting for them. That's a quality feeling. Wow!

THREE OUTCOMES OF COACHING

Embedded within the coaching process are three outcomes enjoyed by the person being coached—the teacher.

Celebrations

The first outcome of coaching is *celebration*. Celebrations are opportunities to give colleagues recognition. Teachers are practiced at gleaning acknowledgement and reward for their efforts from their students whenever possible—the little girl who draws a picture of the teacher, the middle school student who delights in getting the correct answer, or the high school student who admits the teacher was right. Yet there are days upon days and months upon months without any sign of recognition for teachers who are in continuous motion, juggling mandates and parent conferences, technology and teaching, security and safety issues.

In the coaching relationship, each milestone, each achievement, any new learning, and every success or perceived failure is recognized through some form of celebration of effort. It is simply wonderful to have someone in your corner cheering you on, so that even when the coach is not physically present, the teacher delights in saving up the news to share with his or her coach. Collecting wins throughout the day or the week reinforces success and tends to create more success.

While a teacher can certainly acknowledge his or her own efforts, a steady diet of celebrating yourself, by yourself, can become an effort rather than a reward. You can raise your right hand up over your head and bring the left hand up to clap it for a single "high five," but it's certainly not very rewarding and frankly looks a little silly!

Recognition adds quality to a teacher's life, and it boosts self-confidence to try new things, to open up to new ideas, and to be proactive in the classroom and the faculty room. Celebrations offer teachers their own WOW experiences, lending quality to whatever they tackle next.

Examples of Celebrations

Here are some opening-day celebrations or WOWs I've heard about from teachers. One principal rented a red carpet and invited the parents of students to come on the first day of school. The teachers walked into the school along the red carpet as the principal, students, and parents applauded them.

Another principal provided coffee and donuts at a local racetrack. The principal wanted to accelerate learning, so he had the owner bring out some race cars and had drivers take the teachers on a lap or two at high-speed acceleration. They got the point—quickly.

At a high school in Florida, football players each picked a teacher they wanted to honor. During a home game, the players wore their regular home uniforms, and the teachers each wore the away uniform of the player who had picked them. Number forty-eight on the halfback, for example, corresponded to number forty-eight on Mrs. McGyver's jersey. The teachers jogged out onto the field behind the players, to the applause of the fans and the team.

The point is that these simple, inexpensive WOW events create quality. They generate motivation and excitement. They celebrate the profession of educators.

But every day cannot be an opening day at school. That's where coaching comes in. A key component of any coaching program is celebration. Achievement, improvement, and success need the closure of a celebration to lock in the success, to show caring and support, to reward the hard work, and, of course, to feel good. Celebration says the coaching process works. The coach celebrates the coachee's ability to set a goal and fulfill it. The coachee acknowledges the coach's support by his or her success.

Options

The second outcome of coaching is *options*. Who are the greatest teachers? The greatest teachers are those with the longest list of options at their disposal. They are not great teachers because they know what to do; they are great because they always have something else to try. They never give up. If one thing doesn't work, they try something else.

Teachers don't always know what is going to work in a given situation. Instead, they have a long list of strategies, and they are always experimenting. Being a great teacher means you don't run out of experiments before the year is over.

Coaches can provide feedback on strategies or experiments tried as well as help the teacher brainstorm new strategies, new options. Coaching can greatly reduce a teacher's stress. As coach and coachee confer, interact, and develop mutual support and trust, more options are discovered, alleviating the stress of not knowing what to do next.

Conscious Practice

The third outcome of a coaching program is *conscious practice*. Being observed and supported by a coach rather than an "evaluator," a teacher will try different techniques with a focused consciousness, knowing he or she is safe from judgment and criticism.

MULTIPLE TYPES OF COACHING

Coaching takes on different forms depending on the desired outcome. All educational coaching focuses on a specific approach aimed at improving the skills and performance of teaching and increasing student success. Some coaching focuses only on skills, other types look at theory, instructional techniques, or behaviors and attitudes displayed by the educator.

Outside the field of education—and sometimes within it—there are life coaches, business coaches, executive coaches, dating coaches, health coaches, and an array of coaches in specific industries, such as sports, entertainment, finance, and spiritual practices. The approach used depends on the ultimate result desired.

Instructional Coaching

In education, the term "instructional coach" has come to mean a specific focus on teaching techniques. Dr. Jim Knight, a research associate at the University of Kansas Center for Research on Learning, spent more than a decade studying instructional coaching. In *Instructional Coaching: A Partnership Approach to Improving Instruction*, Knight (2007) more or less coins the term "instructional coach."

"The theory behind what we do is the partnership model," says Jim in an interview. "It is based on empirical evidence that there are certain teaching techniques that work. The areas we address in instruction are identified as the 'Big Four': classroom management, content planning, instructions for learning, and assessment for learning" (Knight, 2007).

Most instructional coaches are classroom teachers hired to either serve exclusively as instructional coaches or to augment their teaching with coaching practice. A rigorous hiring and interviewing process typically occurs, and often the job is full time.

While instructional coaching can be content specific, its focus more often falls to the delivery of learning—communication, leadership skills, well-planned lessons. Video documenting serves as a primary tool to provide feedback, and instructional coaches often model specific performance patterns to teachers as a learning mechanism.

Technical Coaching

Technical coaching (Garmston, 1987)[1] is said to assist teachers in applying staff development training in the classroom. It relies on the concept that objective feedback can improve teaching performance. Technical coaching is generally given following staff-development workshops on specific teaching methods, such as learning styles or cooperative learning.

The intent of technical coaching is to impart a specific strategy the teacher can apply immediately in the classroom. While this approach has tremendous value in that regard, it has a few problems. Foremost is the perception among those being coached that this process is more like an evaluation than a coaching session.

Whether or not the specific strategy or behavior shows up in the classroom is often recorded on assessment forms. The form may judge the practice as having occurred "thoroughly" or "partially"; as having been "missing"; or as having been "not needed"—giving the air of a formal evaluation. The process also lends itself to coaches' giving their coachees unsolicited "advice" that can lead to defensiveness. To succeed, technical coaching requires accurate, specific feedback about the technical strategy being coached. If the topic of a staff-development workshop was the use of pause time when asking questions, for example, the technical coaching approach would be to look for how the teacher applied pause time—that and only that.

Challenge Coaching

Challenge coaching (Garmston, 1987) involves a group effort. A team forms to resolve specific and ongoing problems—thus the word "challenge." Unlike other forms of coaching, the team may consist of noneducators called in to provide their perspectives and expertise to help resolve a problem. This team approach in a coaching environment requires mutual trust among colleagues as they focus on solving the problem together, whether it involves the curriculum, instructional techniques, logistics, school structure, classroom management, or any other issue.

The challenge coaching process begins with identification of the problem. For example, a group of fifth-grade teachers might be concerned about the amount of homework required and time needed to grade papers. A small group of coaches and the fifth-grade teachers facing the problem meet to brainstorm solutions and develop action plans. The group may explore staggering assignments, for example, or teaming up on grading. Unlike technical and collegial (discussed next) coaching, which include one-on-one interaction, challenge coaching consists of a group working together to deal with the problem.

Collegial Coaching

Collegial coaching (Garmston, 1987) focuses on giving teachers time and support to think metacognitively about their work in a safe atmosphere with plenty of support. Its intent is to improve teaching practices, enhance relationships with colleagues, and increase professional communication about teaching practices. The underlying notion—backed by research—is that a teacher will acquire and deepen teaching strategies, habits, and reflection about his or her teaching when given an opportunity to develop and practice these skills with feedback from peers.

Collegial coaching usually includes a dyad of teacher-to-teacher, administrator-to-teacher, administrator-to-administrator, or other pair. The person being observed names the specific focus of the coaching desired—a specific technique to practice, or a behavior to correct. The coach observes both the teacher and the students in the classroom, gathering the data he or she needs to give objective and specific feedback.

While a technical coach may judge a teacher's performance, the collegial coach helps the teacher analyze, interpret, and judge for him- or herself how decisions affecting student learning and professional achievement are met.

The collegial coaching process is the focus of this book. The skills identified and practiced apply to all coaching formats.

TWO COACHING BELIEFS AND THE SUSAN BOYLE SYNDROME

Two beliefs can build a successful coaching culture:

Belief number one: Everyone working in a school should be observed once a week and receive feedback.
Belief number two: The most skilled and professional educators should receive the most coaching.

Why would we have a belief like number two? Simple. Coaching generates more options for teachers that are already good or great.

The farther up the ladder of success one goes, the more coaching is needed. This is what I call the Susan Boyle Syndrome. Susan Boyle was raised in West Lothian, Scotland. By the age of twelve, she knew she wanted to become a professional singer. She had a singing coach and at the age of forty-eight, she was accepted as a contestant on a reality television program called *Britain's Got Talent*. On April 11, 2009, Susan stood on a stage before Simon Cowell, the show's host; two other judges; and a full house. When she sang "I Dreamed a Dream" from *Les Miserables*, Susan stunned the judges and the audience. Her powerful voice was golden! In short, she brought down the house. Susan received a standing ovation and a unanimous nod and encouragement by the judges to participate in the *Britain's Got Talent* contest later that year.

Susan Boyle's audition was streamed on YouTube and watched over 100 million times within nine days; it became the most watched video of the year. Suddenly, Susan Boyle was internationally famous. Part of that global interest was triggered by the sharp contrast between Susan's powerful, golden voice and her plain, almost frumpy appearance and somewhat less-than-professional demeanor on stage. No one expected this forty-eight-year-old woman from an obscure village in Scotland to achieve such fame—least of all Susan herself.

Immediately, then, Susan had a need for additional coaches. She needed a clothing coach and a makeup coach. She needed a media coach to handle the press. A financial coach soon joined the team, as Susan's first CD was released and instantly became the number-one best seller on charts around the globe. No doubt amid this flurry of attention, there was a coach just to handle the psychological impact of instant success.

As with anyone who has worked toward honing skills and professionalism, Susan needed more coaching, not less, as she progressed. She modeled for others how success must be managed. Likewise, the most skilled and professional educators in a school can serve as role model for others. This person models for others the ideas that

- constant improvement is part of the profession;
- it's okay to be coached as a successful professional;
- coaching is an opportunity to learn new strategies, to come up with creative lesson plans, to increase one's bag of tricks, and to avoid doing the same things year after year;
- coaching doesn't mean you need fixing (You're not broken. You just want to improve and get better at what you do.);
- you gain a solid return on the investment of teacher education by learning every day better ways to teach.

Coaching offers even the most skilled professionals opportunities to improve and gives them recognition—someone cares. Skilled professionals—great teachers—need acknowledgment and recognition. In many vocations, the more you do, the more you're ignored. You are taken for granted. Good people—great people—need recognition too.

GOOD TO GREAT

In chapter 2, we will explore the differences between mentoring and coaching. It is my firm belief, however, that schools should not engage in a mentoring program unless they also have a coaching program in place.

A mentoring program is usually developed to assist new teachers to come aboard, learn the ropes, and improve what they do. A coaching program, in contrast, can be applied to new teachers, tenured teachers, and anyone in between.

Good teachers, beginning teachers, and those who are struggling all benefit from coaching. Good teachers want to be great teachers, and coaching provides them the tools and information to become great teachers.

In the coaching process, teachers are observed once a week. Beyond observation, good teachers should be videotaped once a week too. Yes, a coach can provide specific feedback from observation, but in seeing and hearing yourself in action you will immediately identify techniques to en-hance, and others you should leave on the cutting-room floor.

The combination of coaching and videotaping is powerful because a teacher's successful experience can get in the way. He or she may have an ex-cellent lesson plan and be good at delivering it. Yet without an observer—a coach and a video camera—the teacher may never stop to ask whether the activity was worth the time the teacher and the students spent on it. Maybe the activity was fun, but was it worth the effort?

When good coaches observe good teachers, synergy causes improvement to develop exponentially. Each builds on the other's input and desire to instill learning in students. The coach keeps the teacher focused on the outcome desired. The coach understands the teacher's thinking because the two have interacted in their conferences and interviews. The coach is there to offer specific and focused suggestions for improvement.

The problem is not that we do not have enough good teachers. The problem is we have way too many. There is too much "good teaching." This good teaching has become totally acceptable and some teachers have been doing this same good job for years. Good has become marginalized. To cre-ate a major improvement in learning within a system or a district or even a state, we need programs that will move large numbers of good teachers to become great teachers.

We are always talking about improving student performance. We want them to exert more effort. We say we know they have the potential if only they'd "apply" themselves. Yet isn't the same true for teachers—for all hu-mans, really? Once we achieve a certain level of knowledge or skill, we tend to use it over and over, staying within our comfort zone. Learning more skills is a skill in and of itself.

There is an old expression, "Well, you have to give 'em an 'E' for effort" when someone applies him- or herself and falls short of full success. Yet it is in the effort that improvement occurs. The more effort expended, the more able one becomes in skills and performances, multiplying ability to achieve success. Too often, when students—or teachers—make a less-than-perfect effort, it is accepted as "good enough." In today's world, that kind of mediocre achievement no longer works, if it ever did.

Rafe Esquith (2003), winner of the American Teacher Award, inspires and challenges us to rethink the way we educate our children in his award-winning book *There Are No Shortcuts*. He cites a poem given him by Charles Osgood of CBS News called "Pretty Good," which describes the various ways a student goes through school making efforts that often fall short of the mark, but are "pretty good," so he moves on to the next less-than-perfect achievement. "5 plus 5 needn't always add up to be 10," says Osgood's poem, "A pretty good answer was 9." Being used to mediocrity in achievement throughout school, the student in the poem learns when looking for a job that "pretty good" is not good enough. He sees that, "Pretty good is, in fact, pretty bad."

Teachers, too, can fall into a pattern of doing just what's needed, what's "pretty good" or "good enough." Coaching can move good teachers to become great teachers. It provides the strongest return on the investment of teaching. Coaches may cause discomfort at times. However, great coaches create an environment where the coachee is comfortable with discomfort. Discomfort is actually the key to growth and change. When good teachers become uncomfortable, that discomfort gives them impetus to improve, to wake up and get out of their box; it stimulates positive change. Coaching only struggling teachers misses the point of who could be coached, and often eliminates the opportunity to coach good teachers to greatness.

SUMMARY

As we will see in chapter 2, coaching takes many forms, and its applications are endless. What I want to convey here is the true value of coaching—that it creates quality. It moves teachers from good to great. While technical and challenge coaching have their place, collegial and instructional coaching results in creative synergy. Research is solid in support of coaching's effectiveness in teacher improvement. (At the end of some chapters in this book there are Research Shows sections that provide research supporting information in that chapter.) Coaching motivates teachers to practice their profession consciously. It increases their options, and it affords them opportunities to celebrate, locking in their achievements, goals, and successes.

Isn't it nice to know that a process that includes celebrations is an important, effective, and valuable part of quality teaching?

RESEARCH SHOWS

Beyond transfer, feedback provided by coaching is extremely beneficial to the teacher. Coaches can see confusion or omissions when observing others teach. We easily recognize in others what we cannot see in ourselves; in this process, learning goes both ways.

Other research findings underscore the value of a peer coaching relationship:

- The ultimate goal of any staff development effort is the transfer of new learning to the teacher's active repertoire (Joyce & Showers, 2002).
- Joyce and Showers also reported in 1990 that 80 percent of teachers who had received coaching implemented new strategies versus only 10 percent of the teachers who received instruction without follow-up coaching.
- "What new teachers want in their induction programs is experienced colleagues who will take their daily dilemmas seriously, watch them teach and provide feedback, help them teach and provide feedback, help them develop instructional strategies, model skilled teaching, and share insights about students' work" (Johnson & Kardos, 2002, p. 13).
- Following peer coaching, teachers report substantial increase in the use of skills and strategies to support instructional change (Bowman & McCormick, 2000; Dougherty, 1993; Kohler, Crilley, Shearer, & Good, 1997; Wineburg, 1995).
- Teachers rate learning from other teachers second only to their own teaching experiences as the most valuable source of information about effective teaching (Smylie, 1989). Teachers value learning from their colleagues more than from university professors, administrators, consultants, or specialists (Morrison, Walker, Wakefield, & Solberg, 1994; Raney & Robbins, 1989; Smylie, 1989).
- Teachers who received peer coaching after attending training workshops increased use of specific skills more than did teachers who only attended workshops (Heberly, 1991).
- Collegial self-reflection—in which teachers are trained in observation, interview, and analysis skills and then observe and write portraits of each others' teaching—increases self-awareness, critical thinking, collegiality, and interdisciplinary teaching (Harriman, 1992).
- Jenkins and Veal (2002) conclude that benefits accrued in coaching of beginning teachers far outweigh the additional time required.
- Those who receive on-going support from instructional coaches also receive encouragement to try new methods of instruction, which improve their quality of teaching. (Joyce & Showers, 2002).

NOTE

1. Robert J. Garmston's article "How Administrators Support Peer Coaching" in the February 1987 issue of *Educational Leadership, 44*(5), 18–26, © 2008 by ASCD, is adapted with permission. Subsequent references to this source are cited parenthetically in the text. Learn more about ASCD at www.ascd.org.

2

Who's on First?
Defining the Role of the Coach

Peer coach, mentor, protégé, principal, evaluator, supervisor, curriculum coordinator, educator, administrator, union representative, director of staff development, site-based administrator, reading coach, chief academic officer—who *are* all these people? Academia is awash in titles and programs, and while titles vary from district to district, certain roles are similar in their purpose, function, and intent.

The primary distinction I want to make is among the roles of coach, mentor, supervisor, and evaluator as shown on the continuum in figure 2.1.

COACHING AND MENTORING:
TWO DIFFERENT ROLES

The terms "coach" and "mentor" are often used interchangeably, yet the person in each role takes a different approach and has a different intent in similar situations. Mentors are assigned to assist another who has less

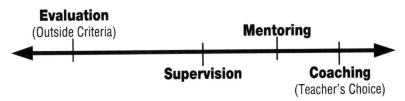

Figure 2.1.   Evaluation/Coaching Continuum

knowledge or experience. This person is in essence a protégé to the mentor, which *Webster's New World College Dictionary*, 3rd Edition, defines as "a person guided and helped, especially in the furtherance of his or her career, by another, more influential person" (Neufeldt and Guralnik, 1997, p. 1081). A mentoring relationship can come about when an executive takes an entry-level manager under his wing, or when a tenured educator is assigned to help a beginning teacher.

A "beginning" teacher may be a recent graduate, or an experienced teacher new to a state or district. It might be a teacher assigned to a new department or a teacher in need of additional support. In any case, the role of mentors is to guide, teach, tutor, and help mentees—showing them the ropes and imparting knowledge and experience.

The term "mentor" comes from Homer's *Odyssey*. Odysseus, king of Ithaca, went off for ten years to fight the Trojan War. While he was gone, he entrusted the care of his household and his son Telemachus to Mentor, who played the role of a long-term babysitter and tutor. Eventually Telemachus and his father were reunited, and Mentor's reward was that his name has come to mean a trusted advisor, teacher, and wise person.

Mentor has now gone from Homer to the homeroom, as many school districts have mentoring programs, with participation often mandatory for beginning teachers. A mentoring program usually outlines specific tasks for the mentor. Mentors may be charged with providing knowledge about how the district works. They might be technology mentors or mentors for curriculum-oriented issues. Some help with moral development and others with technical competence.

A coach may do some of these tasks as well; however, a coach is usually someone *chosen by the one who wants to be coached*. There need not be a difference in abilities, skill, or knowledge between the two. A tenured teacher can coach a tenured colleague; teachers coach administrators and vice versa. Administrators can coach principals and vice versa. Coaching tends to be more empowering than mentoring and stems from a partnership of support and development.

A distinction between mentor and coach often shows up in subtle ways. Let's say a new teacher brings questions to a more seasoned teacher early in the year. Since this is not an official mentoring arrangement, the teacher with experience would probably offer willing assistance, in essence, coaching the new teacher.

Now let's say this same experienced teacher becomes the other's official mentor. In their first official meeting, the mentor mentions to the new teacher that he or she has been arriving at school too late every morning. The mentor had been aware of the other teacher's lateness but, in her thinking as a coach, she never mentioned it, as the new teacher never brought it up. As a mentor, however, she has a responsibility to share that observation—she's moved a notch to the left on the continuum as illustrated in figure 2.1.

Again, articulating the roles allows both coach and mentor the opportunity to work with teachers in an atmosphere of trust.

The difference between mentor and coach can be equated to the semantic difference between the words "help" and "assist." Helping implies that someone cannot fare well alone, that outside help is needed. Assisting someone implies that the person is already quite capable and needs assistance to pull together a skill, knowledge, or behavior. Coaching acknowledges the coachee's capabilities. It empowers this individual to bring strengths to fruition. Its focus is on the "good to great" model described in chapter 1. A coach might say, "You have strengths; let's discover and fine-tune them, get them out into the classroom."

Mentoring can empower a person to achieve; however, it is based on the assumption that one who seeks mentoring needs help in some regard, whether to develop, or to change a skill or behavior, or to simply understand protocols. There is a lack somewhere which assumes a deficit. Often someone will turn to a mentor when he or she lacks understanding, when support is required in a specific way, or when there's trouble. Schools assign mentors to beginning teachers because it's likely that they will need to iron out problems or will otherwise need help.

In many districts mentors only work with beginning teachers for a limited time. New teachers come into a school and are each assigned a mentor. The mentors show the new teachers the ropes and then leave them on their own when it appears they are comfortable in their teaching roles. If in the future a teacher needs support or has trouble, a new mentor—or possibly a coach—is called in, implying that the teacher is now doing something wrong and needs the "help."

Mentoring is highly useful for teacher orientation, and mentors have been instrumental in helping new and beginning teachers familiarize themselves with what's expected of them and how things work. Mentors increase the competence of beginning teachers to become a part of the professional staff; mentoring truly works in that regard. But what happens next? I believe that mentoring should segue into peer coaching—that a school or district that has a mentoring program also needs a coaching program.

The Rochester City School District's ongoing and successful mentoring program has been around almost as long as Homer's *Odyssey*! Started in 1987, the program enlists highly successful teachers to serve as mentors to other teachers. New York State mandates mentoring programs for beginning teachers, called *interns* in the Rochester program.

Beyond mentoring brand new teachers, the Career in Teaching Program, headed by its director Marie Costanza, offers mentoring for professional support, mentoring teachers anytime in their career. The program also offers, for example, intervention, where an administrator might recommend mentoring for a struggling teacher and submits a recommendation to a review panel.

After review, the teacher is notified and at that point can decide whether or not to be mentored.

Over time, the Rochester program has become a blend of mentoring and coaching. It began in the 1980s, instigated by the dynamic and eloquent president of the Rochester Teachers Union, Adam Urbanski. Hearing of a Peer Assistance Review program in Toledo, Ohio, Urbanski investigated the model, mulled it over, and then presented it to the superintendent of schools in Rochester. (See the foreword of this book authored by Adam Urbanski.)

The Peer Assistance Review, essentially a coaching process, remains a part of Rochester's mentoring program. Here, teachers review other teachers' skills and abilities, with the full support of the teachers union and the district. Almost from the beginning the peer review process has been successful, has changed the district's way of evaluating teachers, and is now widely accepted as a model program.

When asked why a union leader approves of a program aimed at "fixing" teachers, Urbanski shared the simple truth, "No one knows good teaching versus bad teaching better than teachers themselves." And if there is a need to improve the performance of teaching, he added, "There is absolutely no question that we as educators can do that for ourselves, or we can leave it to others less knowledgeable to do it for us." When asked if there was resistance or controversy about teachers looking at other teachers, Urbanski noted, "Peer review is only controversial where it doesn't exist."

Obviously the choice was made to continue peer review and expand it to mentoring and coaching. Mentors emerge from teaching ranks, as Costanza and others in the Career in Teaching Program strongly believe mentors have to be practitioners to be successful. Teachers flock to apply for the role of mentor and undergo a thorough scrutiny, meeting very specific and strict qualifications. To achieve mentorship, a candidate must have seven years of teaching and six solid references from colleagues, administrators, and his or her union. Candidates are interviewed by a governing panel, and scored; if qualified, *then* they go through an intensive training program for mentoring and coaching to see if they make the grade.

Once a mentor, the individual goes to classrooms, videotapes lessons, and engages in classroom conversation. Mentors have collegial circles, and research skills they want to improve. "It's really more than mentoring," admits Costanza. "We open the whole gamut of professional development and are constantly there to support both teachers and mentors, whether they are struggling with teaching or working on improving themselves as mentors."

Does it work? Since 1987 Rochester City School District has enjoyed a teacher retention rate of from 82 to 88 percent. Teachers apparently like the support and the ability to support others. And the students? "Teachers will do well only if students do well," says Urbanski. "Our role is to focus on student success and that makes teachers more successful. One way to do that is through peer review, mentoring, and coaching." (Forms and materials used by the Career in Teaching Program in Rochester are found in the appendix.)

At Hartford Union High School District in Wisconsin, there are two distinct programs in place: collegial coaching and mentoring (the latter is for beginning teachers, referred to as "initial educators"). The mentoring program is mandatory for these initial educators in their first year only, unless program directors decide that a teacher be mentored for another full year. Mentors in this program are department chairs and focus on administrative matters and curriculum for teaching content.

The opportunity for collegial coaching exists within the mentoring program, both for the first year of teaching and then on an ongoing, voluntary basis. Teachers participating in the coaching program receive various incentives to continue with coaching, depending on how often they participate in a coaching observation session. The incentives include such things as tuition vouchers, compensatory days off, flextime, and attendance at national conventions—even free lunches!

The purpose of this coaching program is to *improve student achievement, professional success, and self-esteem*. Coaching can occur in class or through review of materials and videotapes. The program stresses that coaching is not evaluation, and that any materials, comments, observations, or suggestions made to the person being coached "become the property of the teacher being coached." Coaches assist teachers with classroom management, instructional strategies, motivation techniques, stress and time management, or any other strategy, technique, behavior, or attitude the coachee wants to improve.

The coachee-focused aspect of this program points up another key difference between coaching and mentoring. Whereas mentoring focuses on the knowledge of the mentor, coaching focuses on the one being coached. That person is asked what he or she wants to know, to accomplish, to improve— what does the coachee want the coach to observe?

Those being coached might also indicate how, when, and why they want feedback. The coachees reveal weaknesses or areas where they want to improve and ask for coaching on those issues only. The funnel is not open for coaches to pour in their own knowledge. The coach asks the questions; the coachee discovers the answers.

Another difference between coaching and mentoring is that in most school mentoring programs, mentors are assigned to teachers—the teacher has no say in the choice. In collegial coaching, the person being coached chooses who comes into his or her classroom, establishes the reason the coach is there, and determines what he or she wants the coach to observe. The choices are all in the coachee's court.

Mentoring and coaching each have their own purpose and strength; each is important in the professional development of teachers. Relationship is paramount. Mentor and coach need to establish a level of mutual trust. And communication is key.

The issue of trust is a big one. More and more schools are implementing mentor programs that pair beginning teachers with experienced colleagues.

Principals realize that mentors are crucial to the survival, effectiveness, and satisfaction of beginning teachers and that they help to create a trusting environment quickly.

Yet the principal is also inevitably involved. New teachers have difficulty having to seek advice or help from mentors, while at the same time trying to appear competent to their new "boss," the principal. A new teacher is often excited and challenged about all he or she is learning, yet also cautious, fearful, or vulnerable. There are ways to set up a mentoring program that do not create this situation, as you will see.

FOUR MENTORING MODELS

When setting up a mentoring program, I recommend that the mentor, teacher, and principal meet to establish norms for working together. They should identify how they will work with one other and how they will communicate. The following diagrams show four different models for how this can occur; there are undoubtedly others.

Model 1: Two-Way Communication

In the Two-Way Communication Model, shown in figure 2.2, communication exists between the mentor and the teacher, and separate communication takes place between the principal and the beginning teacher. By agreement, there is no discussion between the mentor and the principal about the teacher.

The model assures the teacher that nothing he or she shares with the mentor will get back to the principal; instead the mentor offers the teacher

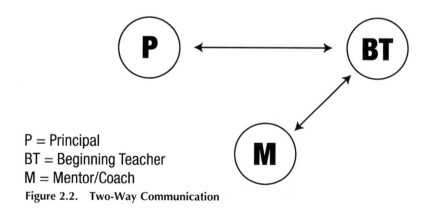

P = Principal
BT = Beginning Teacher
M = Mentor/Coach
Figure 2.2.   Two-Way Communication

opportunities to learn and correct any initial weaknesses without the principal's knowledge. Some beginning teachers feel more open to sharing weaknesses and are willing to ask a mentor for help if they know that no information is shared with the principal, who ultimately will be doing the teacher's evaluation.

For example, a principal might tell a new teacher that she will be expected to work with a team of teachers to implement a student conduct program. The teacher may not fully understand the program, yet may be hesitant to share her ignorance with the principal. Instead, she would turn to her mentor for insights and receive the information she needs without fear of repercussion or a negative evaluation.

The Two-Way Communication Model assumes a basic level of trust; it addresses the needs of the principal and the school system as well as those of the teacher, who moves through the insecurity.

Model 2: The Silent Mentor

In the Silent Mentor Model (figure 2.3), the mentor does meet with the principal, but only *listens* to the principal's concerns and doesn't discuss the teacher at all. This procedure provides the same safeguards for the teacher as in the first model—freedom to be open with the mentor and yet security that no information will be passed to the principal. It also allows the mentor to understand issues or desires raised by the principal and to pass them on to the teacher in a productive fashion.

For example, if a principal expresses a concern that a teacher is not connecting learning activities to district assessments, the mentor would listen carefully and decide how best to work with the beginning teacher to accomplish the principal's goals. The principal would not pry into how the

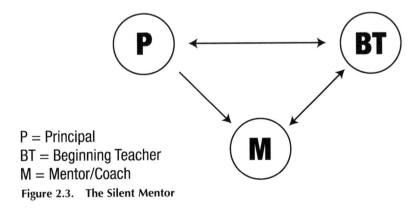

P = Principal
BT = Beginning Teacher
M = Mentor/Coach

Figure 2.3.   The Silent Mentor

teacher was faring, but would simply explain to the mentor what was to be improved—or say something positive about the teacher's ability to learn and work in the new situation.

This model encourages the mentor to earn the trust of the teacher. Trust of the principal often develops in the hiring process, yet teachers also need to trust mentors for the program to succeed.

The teacher and the principal continue to interact, as do the mentor and the teacher, but the mentor can decide how to best help the teacher. The mentor serves as a buffer between teacher and principal, and lends a helping hand without the principal's direct involvement.

Model 3: Positive Reinforcement

As in the Silent Mentor Model, the mentor in the third model, Positive Reinforcement (figure 2.4), has meetings with the principal regarding the teacher. In this model, however, there *is* discussion between mentor and principal about the teacher, but the mentor's comments focus *only on the teacher's positive growth.*

Notice in figure 2.4 the line between the principal and mentor is shown as a dotted line. This indicates that only "good news" is shared with the principal. The principal can express areas that might need improvement, but the mentor continues to reinforce only what is positive.

For example, the principal may comment to the mentor that the teacher needs to implement lesson plans in more depth. The mentor might reply, "John has just completed a great unit on the environment. You might want to take a look at it." The mentor focuses the principal's attention on the teacher's improvement and accomplishments.

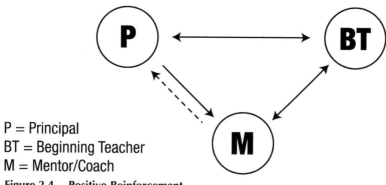

P = Principal
BT = Beginning Teacher
M = Mentor/Coach

Figure 2.4. Positive Reinforcement

Model 4: Full Communication

The Full Communication Model (figure 2.5) provides for the most open trust of the four models, and it is the one I believe principals, teachers, and mentors alike should choose as their model. It assumes that everyone is convinced that the teacher's success is the goal. If the principal sees a behavior or omission in teaching technique, this model offers a forum to address it in a positive light. The principal serves as a supportive coach or mentor, working as a team with the teacher and mentor to ensure the teacher's success in the classroom.

All three people collaborate and openly discuss the teacher's progress. The teacher is empowered to provide new ideas, giving the principal-teacher-mentor relationship a strong base from which to operate. The process leads to improved morale, motivation, and performance by the teacher, enhancing student learning as a result.

An Example of Full Communication

A teacher at Hartford Union High School in Hartford, Wisconsin, relates having two girls in his sophomore English class whose behavior often creates disruption in the classroom. They talk, giggle, and leer at the teacher, making him feel intimidated.

In his meeting with the principal and his mentor, the teacher shares his feelings without concern he will be chastised for not using better classroom management skills. Rather, his colleagues collaborate with him, and together they develop strategies to deal with the situation. This gives him ideas he can use with the two sophomores and with others. He discovers more options, boosting his confidence and motivation. As the teacher employs these strategies in his classroom, the other students as well as the

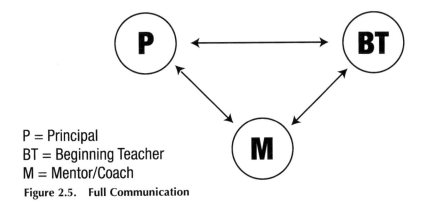

P = Principal
BT = Beginning Teacher
M = Mentor/Coach

Figure 2.5. Full Communication

teacher are relieved of the disruption, the two girls are quieted, and more learning occurs.

This fourth model, Full Communication, is closest to coaching as opposed to mentoring. A shared emphasis on the success of the person being coached can occur whether the person is a new teacher, a long-term tenured educator, an assistant principal, or administrator.

The most significant similarity between coach and mentor in this model is the nonevaluative nature of the relationships. As in most mentoring programs, mentors in the Full Communication Model are not given evaluative responsibilities. The principal may offer suggestions for ways the teacher might improve, but no evaluation takes place. The fourth model differs from coaching in that teachers being coached or mentored do not pick their own mentors.

In short, no one is being judged here. Mentor, principal, and coach support the teacher, whether to learn the ropes of a new school or situation, with ongoing professional development.

EVALUATION

An evaluator uses a skill set entirely different from that of either mentor or coach. Criteria on which one person evaluates another are controlled and come from outside the relationship between teacher and principal. Evaluators work for "the system," such as a school district or state. Their task is to protect the system from incompetence. Minimum competencies are defined by the system, and the evaluator ensures that a teacher meets them.

Yet are evaluations useful in effecting change? Because the evaluation criteria come from outside the relationship of teacher and evaluator—the principal or administrator—little direct connection to the teacher's individual goals, innovation, leadership, and skill set exists. Moreover, evaluations by themselves are seldom motivating or even helpful in identifying improvement.

Stephen Sawchuk (2009), in his *Education Week* article "Grade Inflation Seen in Evaluation of Teachers, Regardless of System"[1] claims, "The evaluations . . . appear to have failed as a method for offering professional development tailored to individual teachers' needs. Seventy-three percent of the teachers surveyed said their evaluations did not identify an area for development. Only 43 percent said the evaluations helped them improve."

A number of schools have begun to shift from a process that evaluates or judges teachers to one that encompasses coaching and peer review to measure teacher growth and improvement. The experience, success, and issues raised by this important shift among a few of these schools are described in the coaching programs featured in chapter 9.

Regardless of the evaluative system in place, whenever an evaluator who serves as a principal or administrator also wants to be considered a coach, it can threaten to impair trust in the relationship. Evaluation is judgment; coaching offers support and encouragement. A teacher, who might be working on a skill or behavior targeted for improvement, becomes intimidated if the "coach" now raises the proverbial red pen in the role of evaluator, judging the very performance they were working to improve.

"I" Messages: Evaluation and Assessment

I often do an "I" message activity when I'm training coaches to see the differences between the feeling of being *evaluated* and that of having one's skills *assessed*. I ask participants to pair up and decide who will be partner A and who will be partner B. Partner A notices something about partner B's appearance. It could be clothing, eyeglasses, height, color of hair, or shape of nose.

Partner A then tells B what he or she noticed by beginning a sentence with the word "you": "You look great in red." "Your eyeglasses are broken." "You're sure tall!"

They do this a few times each, and then I ask them how it felt. I hear comments such as "self-conscious," "like a guinea pig," "embarrassed," "defensive." Because the sentence begins with a "you," it automatically implies judgment and evaluation. They hear the other person's opinion of who they are or how they appear, whether or not it matches their own opinion or is complimentary, it creates self-consciousness, discomfort, and can be insulting.

They do the exercise again. This time partner A notices something about B's appearance, and shares what was noticed, beginning the sentence with "I": "I like you in red." "I always wanted to be tall like you. How tall are you?" (They can also ask questions.) Then A and B switch roles.

When prompted as to how they felt, individuals say things like "good," "important," "complimented," "cared for," "noticed." When I asked them why, they said it was because the other person took responsibility for what they noticed and their opinion about it. The questions didn't come across as judgmental, and therefore they didn't feel self-conscious or uncomfortable; it was just the other person's opinion.

Evaluation uses an indirect "you" message; it puts people on the defensive, on guard, and makes them ill at ease, even when they receive positive or complimentary evaluations. An evaluation judges a person based on criteria developed from someone else's set of beliefs, opinions, or ideas about correct ways of teaching.

In a coaching model, the process is focused assessment. When a coach assesses someone, personal thoughts and feelings surface. It is not the cold objectivity of evaluation. A coach notices, or is asked by the teacher to ob-serve, certain behaviors about the coachee's teaching. The coach then asks the teacher for permission to share personal observations. The coachee has the option to say yes or no.

The coach's feedback is given as an implied or direct "I" message: "I saw—or felt or heard—this when you implemented that strategy or re-flected on your behavior." Hearing an "I" message, coachees can respond more openly and freely. They are not burdened by the coach's judgment or evaluation. What the coach noticed or felt is simply what was noticed; it's not right or wrong.

Principals often take on a coaching role, helping a teacher to improve performance. In my experience, principals feel they are evaluating 60 per-cent of the time and coaching 40 percent. Teachers, however, feel it's more like 95 percent evaluation to 5 percent coaching. It's all in perception. The teacher's perception is that the principal is evaluating, not coaching, and the principal thinks the opposite. They're both telling the truth in terms of their *perceptions*. When I introduce a coaching program to a school district that includes principals and administrators as participants, I find that the perception of evaluation quickly wanes as they learn the value, behaviors, and skills of true coaching.

To make the principal's role clear, you can establish the following crite-rion. If a teacher invites the principal into his or her classroom, it's coaching. If the principal comes without invitation, it's evaluation or supervision.

This model requires that trust connect those who take on these roles. Teach-ers want their evaluations to be fair, and many researchers feel there should be an inter-rater agreement when evaluating—that is, the teacher would receive the same evaluation regardless of who came to evaluate, because the criteria would be standard. Most schools lack such a standard, however, so when the principal or outside evaluator changes, scores change as well.

Typically, an evaluation is based on minimum competencies, and edu-cators are graded on whether they meet those competencies. This practice undermines the trust level and the professionalism of teachers—they don't like to get good grades for doing the minimum, which goes against the goal of moving from good to great teaching. Once an evaluation is completed, the score sheet—not the evaluator—dictates the teacher's future efforts. The evaluator does not make suggestions for improvement; coaches do. They are separate from the evaluation instrument.

SUPERVISION

Stranded in the middle of this continuum is the supervisor. While this may often be the principal, there are several people in a school who might have the title of "supervisor." Supervisors are responsible for evaluation based on a set of criteria, such as state guidelines, school board policies, and union contracts. They are also responsible for satisfying the desires, motivations, and goals of the individuals on their teaching staff and for teacher growth. These responsibilities require supervisors to act as coaches. In short, where an evaluator might just evaluate and a coach just coach, a supervisor might do both.

Given differences in purpose, philosophy, skill, and attitude, it is possible to do both, but difficult. The teacher often doesn't clearly understand the supervisor's role, so the trust level is low. A supervisor may or may not be effective in conveying his or her concern for a teacher's best interest. The supervisor may refer to it as "our" evaluation session, when in fact it is the teacher's evaluation. But how does the teacher perceive it?

Often supervisors or principals play all the roles on the continuum. A principal or an administrator may do an evaluation, supervise, mentor, and coach. Human nature being what it is, however, when teachers have their own weaknesses—and everyone knows their weaknesses—they certainly never want to reveal them during evaluation sessions when their careers and future may be at stake. On the other hand, when someone comes in to coach, teachers may be more willing to focus on their weaknesses, as the coaching process itself is not tied to career judgment.

Because teachers become confused about how to behave when someone walks into their room unless they know the person's role in advance, I often suggest that the principal or supervisor literally wear different colored hats depending on the role they're playing—evaluator, supervisor, mentor, or coach. When the teacher sees the hat color, he or she knows which "role" just walked into the room.

Another idea is for the principal or supervisor to copy the figure 2.1 continuum, laminate it, and carry it around, pointing out to the teacher with a pen mark where he or she is on the continuum at that moment.

Clarity in roles should be replicated by teachers as they work with students. They should change "hats" whenever they are changing roles so that students know who they are dealing with and what to expect. The teacher as a coach makes suggestions for improvements; the teacher as an evaluator grades tests.

SUMMARY

The purpose of all roles associated with education is to teach students. In the process of teaching, a teacher needs constantly to change gears, improve, learn, change, grow, and adjust. Mentors help teachers learn the ropes and untie difficult knots along the way. Principals or supervisors, in their roles, ensure that teachers are up to standards—that they are in fact performing well and if not, are working on ways to improve. Coaches work on the side of teachers to help them be and do all they are capable of, by addressing specific issues teachers need and want to work on.

All roles are interchangeable as long as everyone knows who's on first—the role each is playing and why. That knowledge builds trust and paves the way for teachers to improve their skills in a safe environment. Ultimately, the students benefit.

In chapter 3, we'll take a look at exactly what coaching is—how it plays out in terms of improving skill, knowledge, and behavior. Also, we'll look again at the issues of trust and quality and at how both principal and coach can interchange roles to support the one being coached or evaluated.

RESEARCH SHOWS

Four Types of Coaching

A survey of mentors at Pennsylvania High School Coaching Initiative found that

- administrators, mentors, and coaches noted "substantially increased student engagement" in their schools;
- there was more discussion among teachers about professional issues and instruction, as well as more interest in collaborative planning;
- mentors played significant roles in strengthening the capacity of coaches and the ability of school leaders to support instructional coaching;
- mentors were instrumental in helping coaches resolve challenges that interfered with their work;
- mentors promoted a better use of data in the districts and consistency in improved instructional strategies and curriculum.

Research shows the benefits of a comprehensive peer mentoring program go beyond merely reducing the rate of attrition (Villar & Strong, 2007). The researchers found that at the end of the first year, teachers with mentors are as productive as fourth-year teachers who had not had a mentor.

Trust

- Research shows a relationship exists between the degree of collaboration among colleagues in a school and the level of trust attained (Tschannen-Moran, 2009).

- "When high trust allows for candor and the open exchange of information, problems can be disclosed, diagnosed, and corrected before they are compounded" (Tschannen-Moran, 2009, p. 229).
- Research shows while peer observation is seen as an essential ingredient in successful staff development, it is most likely to make a difference when an atmosphere of trust and collaboration exists (Dunn and Villani, S., 2007).

NOTE

1. Copyright *Education Week*, June 10, 2009, by Stephen Sawchuk. Reprinted with permission from Editorial Projects in Education.

3

Okay, What *Is* Coaching?

We've looked at the various roles in coaching, but what exactly is this thing called "coaching"? Coaching creates an opportunity for two individuals to enter into an ongoing dialogue and relationship, the focus of which is to improve skills, techniques, and behaviors that lead to professional and personal success.

Coaching is a profound and dynamic practice used in sports, in personal relationships, by business entrepreneurs, in marriages, and wherever support, feedback, and a mutual commitment to change and growth are desired. This book focuses on coaching *and* teaching, where a coach supports a teacher's efforts to improve his or her teaching skills and furthers student learning. Coaching is tied to an educator's professionalism and to students' achievements.

Coaching in the private sector consists of a professional relationship in which the coach is paid by the one coached for his or her services. In teaching, coaching focuses on improving professionalism, and the coach provides this service as part of a coaching or mentoring program established by the school or district or through a peer relationship with a fellow teacher.

Friendship might occur in the process, but coaching is not about making friends. A friend might support another friend without necessarily working toward improving that person's behavior. On the other hand, a coach focuses on allowing the coachee to commit to positive change and then supports that person in the effort to accomplish that change. Coaching for educators has a specific focus—improving teaching. Coaching is not just limited to two people supporting one another in their profession. As we shall see later in this book, when carried out with quality, coaching follows a well-defined process and utilizes finely tuned verbal skills and questioning techniques to achieve the desired outcome.

Supporting someone willing to make changes, guiding them toward stretching and improving, giving them useful feedback, and otherwise jumping into their life requires a high level of trust from both parties. This type of coaching provides a type of professional staff development training that uncovers ways to improve specific techniques or behaviors through observation and feedback. The coaching process is meant to give a coachee sufficient skill and practice so that transfer occurs and skills and techniques become ingrained.

Coaching also gives those being coached an opportunity for conversation with other like-minded professionals. It provides a forum for the development of collegial relationships that enhance self-esteem and professionalism.

In *Motivating Students and Teachers in an Era of Standards*, Richard Sagor (2003) makes the following observation concerning what motivates educators:

> The classroom teacher's need for belonging is often overlooked in schools. School administrators occasionally and incorrectly assume that because teachers are granted considerable autonomy within the walls of their class rooms, they don't have a professional need for collegiality and community. In environments where workers have come to feel like members of high performing teams and regularly get to enjoy the camaraderie of their coworkers, higher levels of performance are invariably produced (Senge 1990; Senge 1999). It is imperative that teaching be restructured into a more collaborative and collegial endeavor. (p. 9)

Voilà coaching.

INSTANCE OF ONE

Research shows that learning occurs best when a relationship is involved. Think about a time when someone taught you something quickly. Choose a task, a skill, or an action you were taught, one time, and that you never forgot. You were immediately successful, and you have known how to do it or use it from that time forward. Examples might be tying your shoes; riding a bike; washing dishes; or, later in life, understanding an equation, setting up a computer, using pause time effectively in the classroom.

In these instances, there is typically someone present—someone with whom you have a relationship. You were taught in a safe environment. The consequences of what you were learning were real to you, and you may have experienced an emotion. In short, the experience was probably a positive one with the person teaching you basking in your success right along with you. That is the true nature of learning and the true nature of coaching. *The coach succeeds when you succeed.*

Three outcomes of a coaching process include the opportunity for celebration and personal recognition, the opportunity for developing a wider array of options, and the opportunity to participate in "conscious practice." Let's use the model in figure 3.1, developed by William Gordon, to show how these coaching opportunities occur.

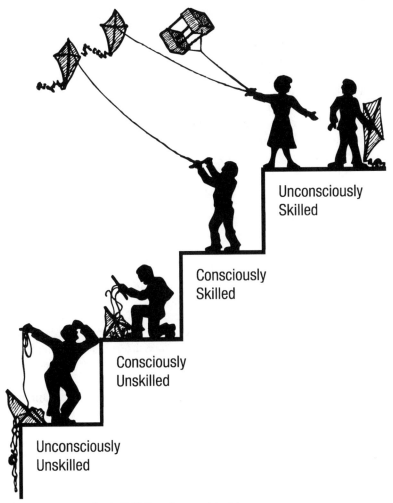

Figure 3.1. Gordon's Skill Development Ladder

Gordon's model is called a Skill Development Ladder. In it he identifies the process one goes through when beginning a task not previously undertaken. We all go through various stages when we are learning something new, trying to grasp a new concept or technology, or going to a new location and meeting new people—all require a process that has us moving up and down the ladder of skill development. Once we get the hang of things, we operate naturally and successfully, until the *next* time we are up against something new.

For our example, let's use the basic teaching technique called "pause time." The teacher takes a three- to five-second pause after asking a question, after calling a student by name, and again after a student has answered a question. Likewise, pause time can be used when a teacher puts forth a new idea or concept.

Pausing when asking a question benefits teacher and student alike, as we shall see later. When putting forth a new idea, it is often beneficial to pause and allow the thought to linger in the air a little before the students absorb it. In our fast-paced world, we often move from thought to thought quickly. Pause time allows thinking and learning to take place.

At first, pausing may seem awkward, contrived. It's hard enough for a teacher to keep track of the questions as students are answering them, how much time remains—even the students' names—much less mentally counting out three or five seconds!

Enter Gordon's Ladder. On the lower rung you see a teacher—let's call her Becky. Becky has never heard of pause time, never used it, and never thought about it. This teacher is Unconsciously Unskilled in that technique. She hasn't a clue.

On the next rung, Becky now knows that pause time is a valuable tool that should be used in her classroom. She has learned that at least three seconds of pause should occur after a question is posed and before the teacher calls on a student by name. After calling the student's name, there should be another three-second pause. Jumping in too fast or moving to the next person too quickly undermines a student's self-esteem. Time is needed for the student to form a thought and respond without teacher interference.

Pausing after a question is posed also allows the teacher time to review the question for its appropriateness and understandability, determine who to call on, and assess who might likely know the right answer. Pausing three seconds after calling the student's name gives the teacher time to decide what would constitute a complete answer.

Once the student answers the question, the teacher should pause five seconds. This gives the student time to elaborate, ask questions, make a student-to-student exchange, and build confidence in the process. Less vocal students, when given that breathing space, can feel comfortable contributing as well. Pausing helps learning, and that's what Becky wants to do.

So, while she is aware of its value and knows something about the technique, Becky isn't skilled in its use. In fact, she may have been using it, but now that she is *conscious* of the technique, it suddenly feels uncomfortable, unnatural. She is Consciously Unskilled, and is on the second rung of Gordon's Ladder.

In Becky's case, at the Consciously Unskilled level, she posed a question for the class and then she paused, her arm in midair and her body very still, as if suddenly frozen. She counted in her head and looked a little silly, and yet she really did know what to do—even though she may have done it hundreds of times in the past. She may be conscious of what she's doing, but the new knowledge about the skill and her actual behavior has not meshed—it's not yet internalized or natural. Thus, she comes across as awkward. This happens to many of us when learning a new sport or task that requires the combination of knowledge and performance. We know the *what* of it but not the *how*. It's easy to become frustrated and, because we're conscious of our lack of skill, even embarrassed.

Enter Becky's coach. This is where the coach provides feedback, support, and celebration, and serves as Becky's "cheerleader," helping her practice in a safe environment without concern about how she looks the first few times out. The coach can make the coachee feel comfortable with his or her discomfort, because the mutual goal continues to be the improvement of teaching. If one goes through a little discomfort to get there, well, so be it.

When I first began teaching, I asked my coach for feedback on my presentation skills and my ability to engage students. She pointed out that I tended to keep my hands in my pockets when I was talking. Worse, I jingled my keys and pocket change around, creating a distraction that lessened student engagement.

To remedy this, we agreed that she would observe me teaching and that whenever I put my hands in my pockets, she would make a gesture of putting her finger on her forehead. That would signal to me to take my hands out of my pockets.

I began the lesson, and after a while, sure enough, my hands were in my pockets. I saw her signal, and boom! Out came the hands, flying up into the air. That seemed a safe place, so I continued talking and moving about the room with hands held wide and high. Muttered comments from students indicated perhaps I had had too much caffeine that morning!

This stilted behavior is typical of anyone who becomes conscious of a new skill. We experience what is called a "learning dip," shown in figure 3.2.

The Learning Dip

Discomfort using a new skill causes confusion, and learning suffers a little at first. With continued observation, support, celebration, and feedback

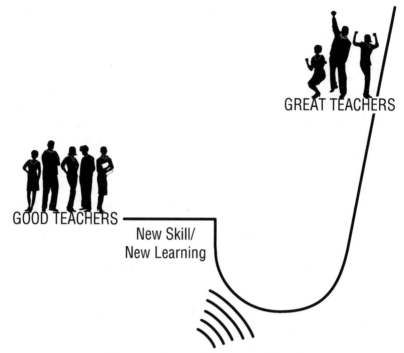

GREAT TEACHERS

GOOD TEACHERS

New Skill/
New Learning

The coach provides support and
guidance during this difficult time.

Figure 3.2.   The Learning Dip

from a coach, the skill level climbs to a higher level, and more options become available to the teacher.

Once a coachee has practiced a skill and has it internalized, he or she moves up to the Consciously Skilled rung on Gordon's Ladder. The coach's observation and feedback is also crucial on this rung of the ladder. The skill can be accomplished so long as the person is thinking about it, aware of it, practicing it in his or her head. In our example, Becky may pose a question, think about pausing three seconds, and then call on the student. She knows the *what* and the *how*, so long as she *consciously* thinks about it.

This works, however awkwardly, and at this level the teacher has, in fact, accomplished the new skill. Yet to have the skill or behavior become smooth and natural, to have it internalized so that there is no thinking about it, a teacher needs to have more conscious practice and feedback. Here is where the work really begins.

At this juncture, the coach can provide the observation, support, feedback, and cheerleading to get the teacher through whatever skill, situation, difficulty, or other aspect of education that caused him or her to face the curve of learning or, in our example, the learning dip. We call it a "dip," as one often goes "down" into awkwardness and frustration before moving up into natural performance or discovering the solution. A boost at this time will start us moving to a point where we go beyond where we were when we started. That is where a coach comes in.

Too often teachers resist going into this learning dip. It's uncomfortable and takes time, so, sadly, many teachers arrive at knowing a skill and then rest there. They have become good at what they are doing, and that seems to suffice. These teachers move laterally to the platform of "good teaching." Good teaching then becomes socially acceptable, the norm. After that—after they have segued to the flat platform—making positive changes or improvements becomes all the more difficult.

With some coaching, support, and practice, however, a teacher learning something new can move to the Unconsciously Skilled rung of Gordon's Ladder; he or she can become a great teacher. At this level, the skill has become ingrained. It is used naturally and well. In our basic example, no longer does Becky have to be concerned that she is not providing enough pause time. She no longer thinks about it, counts seconds, or otherwise feels awkward doing what she knows works best.

With her coach, Becky has been observed doing the skill, she has practiced it, she has received feedback from her coach (and also, ideally, from a video disk [VCD]). She has practiced so often that it is ingrained in her. She does it without thought. This rung is where teachers want to be—skilled but unconscious of the skill or behavior, so that it is a natural part of their performance and does not get in the way of teaching or student learning. I've often said teachers do their best work when they're unconscious!

I grant that our example of pause time is basic, chosen to underscore the process of Gordon's Skill Development Ladder. Yet the same process applies for more complex teaching skills as well as other techniques, such as creating and delivering a math lesson that reaches all learning styles; incorporating content learning into a high school field trip; using the right voice intonation to ensure better classroom management; and, for administrators, facilitating a meeting, interviewing a potential employee, or prioritizing action plans.

An example from coaching to improve facilitation can be found within the Hartford Union High School coaching program in Hartford, Wisconsin. Here a teacher wanted to facilitate presentations given by students. She wanted specific feedback on her *facilitation* skills and her ability to keep students engaged. While she had teaching skills down pat, her skills at facilitating—moving the discussion along neutrally, with little or no input—tended to be awkward. She was at the Consciously Unskilled level. Her coach observed her facilitating, and she accomplished the skill, yet her body language indicated she was "biting her tongue," having difficulty not speaking or leading the student discussion.

In another example, a technical education teacher at Hartford asked his students to create race cars out of blocks of wood. They had to first design a car on a computer using specifications, and then create physical cars using saws and other machinery. Later students would compete in a race with their cars. The teacher wanted to ensure he was focusing on *all* students in the room, despite their variety of tasks. This was a new project, and he wanted to make sure he was as "there" for them in a group as he was in a single-focus lesson plan. His coach confirmed that he was.

In figure 3.3 you will notice an addition to Gordon's Skill Development Ladder. Based on my experience with educators and administrators, I found a need to add another element, or rung, to Gordon's Ladder. Perhaps it's the place where one could put a can of paint on a real ladder. I call this category Unconsciously Talented. It refers to some professionals who just seem to be talented without any thought about what they are doing. Through years of trial and error, they have developed strategies or behaviors that cause them to be successful. They are unconscious of their talent. They cannot explain to others what it is they do.

Here the person exhibiting the skill or behavior does so without benefit of any specific process of skill development or coaching. He or she can perform moves or work through teaching strategies seemingly without effort. Such educators do not know either the *what* or the *how* of their actions; they simply perform them.

Are these, then, the "great teachers"? Certainly they are good teachers, yet they lack abilities that are inherent in the Unconsciously Skilled teacher. They possess skills and strengths that cause them to be successful, yet they are unable to identify these strengths and apply them to other situations.

Unconsciously
Talented

Figure 3.3.   Unconsciously Talented

They cannot mentor others very well due to this lack of self-knowledge. Unconsciously Talented teachers would struggle to relate, for example, how they accomplished something, because they may not be aware of what they did. More importantly, because they remain unaware of the skills they do possess, they have difficulty being coached for improvement.

In order to improve their teaching and ability to benefit from a coaching relationship, coachees must ask to be coached on specific skills or behavior development. The Unconsciously Talented person wouldn't know what to ask for. The role of the coach in that situation would be to break down the skills so that the Unconsciously Talented teacher goes down the ladder to the Consciously Skilled level, becoming aware of the skills he or she already knows—so as to articulate them to others or to improve upon them—and then move back up the ladder.

A note of caution here: the Unconsciously Talented coachee may be coaching-avoidant, as the move to being conscious while doing may prove uncomfortable or interfere with performance. Moreover, the coachee may not understand the improvement value of the coaching.

So, from my viewpoint, great teachers are Unconsciously Skilled teachers. Unconsciously Talented teachers are also great teachers, but they lack an understanding of their need to grow, change, improve, and enhance their professional teaching abilities. Once coached by breaking down their skills to specifics—making them Consciously Skilled for awhile—Unconsciously Talented teachers would ultimately become ideal coaches for other teachers and would serve to improve student learning.

TRUST

Coaches are judged by the performance of those they coach, whether teachers, administrators, staff people, or other professionals. In education, the success of the coachee becomes tied to the success of the coach, much as the success of a basketball coach is determined by the success of the players. A coach supports performance.

Paramount in any coaching relationship is trust. Trust means saying what you're going to do and then doing it. When looking at the various roles of evaluating, supervising, coaching, and mentoring, we saw that trust is crucial to success of the process. Someone who coaches you can never come across as an evaluator, judge, or supervisor; doing so damages the coaching relationship. Trust serves as the foundation of the relationship between coach and coachee.

This does not mean that principals cannot be assigned the role of coach. In many cases, they are. Administrators can give up their supervisory role and serve as mentor or coach if they agree to the boundaries involved in coaching. A principal must agree to play the part of a coach when coaching, and be able to switch into the role of supervisor when supervising. It's perfectly all right to switch back and forth.

The difference in these roles is that when principals (administrators, supervisors, or evaluators) evaluate, they look for weaknesses that need attention and improvement. Either the principal identifies the weakness, or the teacher comes forth and shares it. In coaching, a coachee asks to be coached on a specific skill or behavior.

The principal and teacher can opt to switch into a coaching relationship and work on the weakness, but that work does not then become part of an official evaluation. Once a teacher is professional enough to express to the principal what he or she wants to work on, the principal can assume the teacher is competent enough to teach. Teachers with that much ability to reflect, self-knowledge, and commitment to improve teaching don't need evaluation or supervision and can benefit from coaching.

When the principal provides coaching, he or she works with the teacher, not for "the system." If the principal is effective as a coach, he or she should then be able to evaluate the teacher later and see an improvement. The weakness or challenge should have been overcome. Once again, the improvement of the coachee reflects the success of the coach. It's to the principal's advantage to coach and create improvement. If, however, principals change behaviors in midstream—switching from coach to evaluator without warning—then all bets are off. Trust is broken, and the coaching relationship will be damaged and, very likely, ineffective thereafter.

QUALITY AND COMPLIANCE

Why do we make such a fuss over the distinction between evaluating and coaching? Research on how the brain operates in its highest level of productivity suggests that when people are empowered, they take ownership of their own learning and effectiveness.

The third edition of Susan Kovalik's seminal book *ITI, the Model: Integrated Thematic Instruction* (1997) explores eight elements that need to be present in order for the human brain to learn and operate at its best:

1. Absence of threat
2. Meaningful content
3. Choices
4. Adequate time
5. Enriched environment
6. Collaboration
7. Immediate feedback
8. Mastery

All eight are present in a coaching environment. In an evaluation, most of them may not be. The teacher usually receives little choice about the time, place, or specifics on which he or she will be evaluated. A time constraint usually exists, as the principal walks into the room unexpectedly, and the teacher hastens to get to the "good" part of the lesson or presentation. The teacher may become uncomfortable, as he or she is taken off guard, and may feel vulnerable, if not actually threatened. Often little collaboration or immediate feedback takes place, and the content may be meaningful only to the evaluator or the system. Since the teachers have no say in what is being evaluated, the evaluation lacks meaning for them.

In a coaching relationship, two people work together in a *collaborative,* trusting, and, therefore, *enriched environment.* Initially they meet in an environment where trust develops and an *absence of threat exists.* This place might be the teacher's classroom, where he or she feels safe. *Collaboration* occurs as the coach and teacher work together on what the *teacher chooses* to improve. Since it's something the teacher really wants to know or be able to do, it holds *meaning* for the teacher. *Adequate time* exists to practice, receive *immediate feedback,* and thus create an opportunity for *mastery.*

In short, in a coaching environment, the coachee is fully engaged. The brain operates at its optimum in terms of learning about oneself and performing most productively.

UNIVERSAL MOTIVATION

In coaching, there also exists a need for motivation. In the third edition of *The Quality School: Managing Students without Coercion* (1998), William Glasser, M.D., identifies five universals that motivate people:

1. Survival
2. Belonging
3. Power
4. Freedom
5. Fun

Let's look at Glasser's motivators in terms of teaching and coaching.

Survival

Survival motivates people when they approach something new, make a change, take on a new task, or move to a new location or job. The motivating factor is to *survive*: to learn the ropes, do the right thing, find one's way, avoid getting lost. A beginning teacher is in a state of survival, and so too is a teacher new to a school, or a newly hired principal. All need to take on new "worlds" of people, tasks, rules, and events. The need to survive in their new situations motivates their behavior.

Belonging

The need to be accepted by others motivates—to be included, to receive approval, and to be liked. Once people realize they are going to survive in their new surroundings or job, they become motivated to join others. They may sign up for a committee or volunteer for a task after school. They want belonging and approval, so they are motivated to put their best foot forward when someone is evaluating or observing them.

Power

Things start to look up for the new teacher. After surviving an initial learning curve and being accepted, people begin to experience a sense of power. They know how to do what they need to do! They can even excel! This gives them a sense of personal power, and it also puts them in a position where others begin showing more respect or asking for advice. A sense of power comes from competence.

Freedom

Now things are cooking! The survival period is over, people seem to have been accepted and have a sense of competence and power. Now what? Now they are motivated by flexibility; they belong, and they enjoy the freedom they can earn by their competence and ability to survive. They have freedom to choose: choose lesson plans, choose themes for the school year, and choose to collaborate with other teachers. A sense of freedom inspires people. They take real ownership of their work, which leads to creativity and quality.

Fun

Now the new teacher or newly hired principal begins to have fun. When the motivation is fun, people jump out of bed to come to work. They already enjoy a sense of power and freedom (they've long since surpassed survival and belonging), and now they just want to enjoy what they do. They use all their resources—intelligence, social skills, creativity, research, camaraderie, and knowledge—to make every day enjoyable. Days go by quickly and agreeably. Students now respond to the new teacher with enthusiasm, and their motivation spreads to others. Likewise, the new principal, at the motivation level "fun," inspires and he or she imparts enthusiasm to teachers who, in turn, spread their motivation to their students.

In my experience, when heavy-handed bosses or systems impose strict standards on others, people are typically motivated only by survival and belonging. They want to meet the criteria (survival), and they want their work to be accepted (belonging). In short, they comply with what is being asked of them. That's about all.

When there is collaboration, when coaching is taking place, when people are allowed to take ownership of their own learning and their own professional improvement, they are motivated by power, freedom, and fun. A sense of belonging shores up coaching, and coaching leads to increasing feelings of competence and power. Tremendous freedom results in an environment where one can explore behaviors and techniques without judgment. It's fun to improve; it's really fun to have a coach—your own personal cheerleader—willing to give you feedback and support. When that occurs, walls come down and people are willing and able not only to comply with what is needed but to exceed the norm and produce quality work.

Evaluations are necessary to track progress and comply with various mandates and even federal laws. And when the environment fosters the empowerment of those being evaluated by collaborative and collegial coaching, quality, and overall productivity, enjoyment of teaching increases. The brain comes to life in the absence of threat. When choices, collaboration, and immediate feedback are available, a teacher can comply with what is required, and enjoy power, freedom, and fun in the process. Here's where teachers and students alike can experience a WOW day; celebrations are in order, and both morale and student learning are sky high.

Coaching requires relationship. It requires trust. Coaching is brain based—it empowers teachers to be more productive and creative. Coaching becomes essential to support teachers learning new tasks or new skills, moving them from the awkward Consciously Unskilled level of performance to a level where the skill comes naturally, without thought or concern. Coaching requires the motivation of survival, belonging, power, freedom, and fun.

FIERCE CONVERSATIONS

Coaching really entails conversation. Susan Scott, a coach of many years to CEOs from some of the largest international corporations, encapsulates her ideas about coaching in her book *Fierce Conversations*.[1] By "fierce," Scott does not mean threatening or cruel. Rather she takes the original meaning of "fierce" and synonyms from *Roget's Thesaurus*: "robust, intense, strong, powerful, passionate, eager, unbridled, uncurbed, untamed." Wow! Imagine the possibilities of that!

When was the last time you had an "untamed" or "robust" conversation? How often have you had conversations with coworkers or family members that were bland, meaningless, or significantly less than "fierce?" Evaluations are often bland and meaningless to the person being evaluated; many conversations are depleted of meaning and lack authenticity. They just fill a void. Scott's contention is that conversation *is* the relationship. The level of the conversation between people—its intensity, power, unbridled nature—reflects the level of the relationship.

In coaching, the conversation between the coach and the coachee forms the basis of the relationship. Communication creates the trust—saying what you will do and then doing it. It uncovers the coachee's agenda, vision, and beliefs. It helps explore options and strategies, tactics, and the focus of the teaching, along with the personal and professional development of the individual.

SUMMARY

In many ways, coaching is a unique relationship in which both parties feel privileged. It consists of a supportive and nurturing dialogue between two people, yet it also asks one to stretch, grow, and improve. This may or may not be a comfortable task, yet the coach provides the tools, techniques, and guidance to make it possible.

Coaching becomes particularly useful when a teacher learns a new skill or behavior. As we saw in Gordon's Skill Development Ladder, discomfort, awkwardness, and even a little intimidation can occur at certain rungs on the ladder. As a teacher progresses, the coach cheers the coachee on. Coaching increases the coachee's ability to persevere and succeed as he or she climbs up the ladder to utilize skilled teaching strategies.

Substantial research shows how the brain lights up when learning and empowerment occur. Coaching allows a coachee to achieve quality, as opposed to simple compliance. The coaching relationship utilizes many of the elements of brain-compatible learning and working techniques, allowing people being coached to excel at their own pace within a safe environment of learning.

Coaching also opens up possibilities for teachers to work together as a team to help individual students. It paves the way for a new kind of school where students belong to the whole school—or at least to a focus group of teachers who share in the success of each student. While many schools may give lip service to this kind of teaching atmosphere, coaching can ensure that it occurs.

Coaching is a means to an end. The end result is an improved teacher and thus improved teaching. It is a professional relationship that causes positive actions to occur.

In chapter 4, we'll explore ways in which your conversation—your communication—with your coach and with others can move from bland to fierce, gaining momentum and meaning at each step of the way.

RESEARCH SHOWS

- Research shows a relationship exists between the degree of collaboration among colleagues in a school and the level of trust attained (Tschannen-Moran, 2009).
- "When high trust allows for candor and the open exchange of information, problems can be disclosed, diagnosed, and corrected before they are compounded" (Tschannen-Moran, 2009, p. 229).
- "Only in an atmosphere of trust will peers freely admit their failings to each other and be receptive to suggestions for improvement" (Koballa et al., 1992, p. 43).
- "Coaching exists in name only unless the coach and the person being coached share trust and a sense of purpose" (Caccia, 1996, p. 19).

NOTE

1. Adapted from "Questions for One-to-Ones," from *Fierce Conversations* by Susan Scott, copyright 2002 by Fierce Conversations, Inc. Used by permission of Viking Penguin, a division of Penguin Group (USA) Inc.

4

The Skills of Coaching

The coaching process includes a series of conversations between coach and coachee. Initially, the conversation takes place in what we call a "preobservation conference." After the person being coached has been observed in a classroom; while preparing a lesson plan, conducting a meeting, reflecting on his or her growth and improvement; or in other situations where the coachee wants feedback, it is followed by a "postobservation" conference. We explore the postobservation process later on in the book.

The purpose of the initial conversation—the preobservation conference—determines what the coachee wants the coach to observe, what specific feedback he or she seeks, or what behaviors or techniques the coachee wants to improve or enhance. If this is to be done in a way that serves both the coach and the coachee, certain coaching skills must be in place. This ensures that the process is effective and creates the essential ingredient of trust between the coach and the person being coached.

AGENDA SKILLS FOR COACHING

People behave in certain ways for their own reasons, following their own agenda. Likewise, individuals will change their behavior for their own reasons. When a coach comes to understand what goes on in the coachee's mind, a communication strategy can be developed that will be congruent with his or her self-interest.

Agenda skills for coaching described here help coaches discover their coachee's agenda as well as provide techniques to ensure a trusting relationship. While you may recognize and even use some of these skills, I have adapted them to a coaching relationship because, as we shall see later, beyond uncovering a person's agenda, the coachee must also reveal his or her vision, mission, or the beliefs behind his or her strategies and behavior.

Open-Ended and Closed-Ended Questions

The first two Agenda Skills are Open- and Closed-Ended Questions. These questioning skills help you find the coachee's agenda—what he or she thinks and intends, what is wanted or needed, and his or her reasons for behaving in certain ways.

When asked an Open-Ended Question, the person being asked has the opportunity to express what's on his or her mind, to explain what he or she considers important. These questions allow a wide range of responses and provide the opportunity for sharing thoughts, feelings, or ideas freely. They are useful in learning the story behind the facts, the reasoning, the assumptions, or the background of a situation, or the source of a piece of information.

Closed-Ended Questions, on the other hand, limit the length of a person's response to a few words. They elicit yes/no or short responses. Think of the TV cop shows where people ask for "just the facts." Closed-Ended Questions are useful in gathering data. They are helpful when a precise piece of information is required. They focus directly on a specific point and limit the opportunity for the person to elaborate.

Asking Closed-Ended Questions is efficient. Yet the Open-Ended Question may be even more efficient; while the response may be longer, a less pointed inquiry encourages the coachee to explain the reasoning and assumptions leading up to a response. This paves the way for more open, fierce conversation between the coach and the coachee.

A Closed-Ended Question controls the direction of communication. The person asking can control where the conversation goes. In the Open-Ended Question, the answer controls the direction—the person is given the leeway to respond fully and leads the direction of the conversation.

The continuum in figure 4.1 shows how the environment—the circumstances leading to the purpose of your questioning—influences whether a question is closed (where the question controls the direction) or open (where the answer controls the direction).

Examples of Closed-Ended Questions a coach may ask a coachee follow:

- "At what point did you notice that most of your students were with you?" (The answer to this Closed-Ended Question would be a specific time or incident; a short response, e.g., "Right after we hung the posters.")
- "What emotions did you feel when Olivia made that smart remark?" ("Angry, frustrated"—a short, specific response.)
- "Would you like to rehearse alternative responses?" ("Yes." "No." "Not now." "Maybe.")

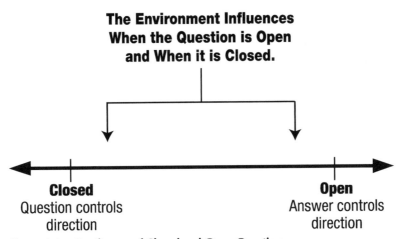

Figure 4.1.   **Continuum of Closed and Open Questions**

- "Did you know that gesturing with your open hand is perceived as more friendly than pointing?" ("You don't say!")
- "Did you know that you have excellent eye contact with all students in the room?" ("Thank you.")
- "Where can I sit that would make you feel most comfortable?" ("In the back." "By the window." "On the left side of the room.")
- "Did you notice that when you moved close to Toni's desk, she got back to work?" ("Yes!")
- "At what point in your lesson did you feel the most successful?" "Why?" (Closed-Ended Question followed by an Open-Ended Question.)
- "What strategies in your lesson would you like to improve?" "Why?" (Closed-Ended Question followed by an Open-Ended Question.)
- "In what areas do you want to be coached?" ("Engaging students." "Rotating my teaching style." "Going over homework assignments." "My new math lesson." "Eye contact." "Gestures and body language.")

As mentioned earlier, Open-Ended Questions allow maximum latitude for the other person to share, elaborate, and express. As you read through the Open-Ended Questions that follow, imagine how you might answer them, noting what they might lead you to reveal about your background, beliefs, and feelings.

- "What are your strengths as a teacher?"
- "How would you know if your lesson was successful?"
- "What have you considered as areas of growth for the year?"
- "How do you think coaching will benefit your teaching?"
- "If there were no curriculum, what would you be teaching?" "Why?"

- "How would you describe a 'good' lesson?" "A 'great' lesson?"
- "If you were a student, what kind of teacher would you like to have?"
- "How could I be the most help to you?"
- "What do you feel contributed to your success today?"
- "Imagine it is the end of the school year. What would you want to say about the year?"
- "If you could change anything, what would you change in education?"

You may have noticed most Open-Ended Questions begin with "what" or "how." They may also begin with "why," although a word of caution is necessary here. Questions such as "Why did you do that?" and "How could you have handled him differently?" can work against you, because they often might trigger a defensive response rather than elicit information. Even if the question is delivered with neutral or positive intonation, *why* and *how* questions may be linked in people's brains with the assumption they have done something wrong, that they're in trouble, especially if asked by someone they consider an authority figure. As a coach, you want to be a collaborator, not an authority figure. Ask *why* questions about positive issues to avoid implying that something is "wrong."

Here's an example of a *why* questions with a positive outcome:

Coach: "Why did you open with the song from World War II?"

Teacher: "I thought it would be unexpected and capture the student's attention."

Coach: "It looked to me as if it did just that. Several students laughed and were singing along. That's very brain compatible: music, fun, nonthreatening."

Repeating a positive pattern assures the coachee that the *why* questions are meant to uncover his or her thinking, not point to a problem in delivery. Also, the attitude and positive body language of the coach adds to a successful outcome of the conversation.

While the idea of Closed-Ended and Open-Ended Questions may seem fairly straightforward, people tend to pose only Closed-Ended Questions. As in any skill, practice is necessary to internalize asking these two types of questions. Research shows that twenty to thirty trials of a new skill or procedure are necessary to achieve comfort and control (Joyce, Wolf, & Calhoun 1993).

Practice

See if you can change the following Closed-Ended Questions into Open-Ended Questions. Phrase them in your mind or jot them down here. Suggested examples of how these can be changed are found at the end of this chapter:

- "Do you think your lesson will turn out well?"
- "Did you think the students were interested?"
- "Give me another reason."
- "What are you going to try now?"
- "What part would you change?"
- "When does it end?"

By learning to ask good questions and make statements appropriate to a coaching situation, you will learn to formulate dialogue that stimulates thinking, reveals a person's agenda, and generates more understanding. Understanding generates trust. Make a point to use Open-Ended Questions throughout your day. Begin the sentence with "what" or "how" or a gentle "why." Remember you want a broad-based response, so the question should be phrased to encourage the other person to share the background, their feelings, and then intent—to tell, as radio commentator Paul Harvey said, "the *rest* of the story."

Yes, it takes longer to listen to the responses to Open-Ended Questions. Yet in the long run, you will have gained valuable knowledge about the coachee and your next encounter can be more in-depth. You can start where you left off. A certain amount of trust will have been built—an openness that allows you to "cut to the chase" a lot sooner.

Another tip: Word your questions so the answer is neither right nor wrong. "What did you notice?" "What do you want to have happen?" The coach accepts all answers; there is no reason to judge any response.

Remaining Congruent

Whether you are asking Closed-Ended or Open-Ended Questions, your tone of voice, body language, and the way you phrase a question have a tremendous impact on others. Positive, congruent intonation and body language leads to more authentic communication.

Imagine you are standing before a dog. You lean forward, your finger pointed at his muzzle. Your voice is stern, your left hand is on your hip, and you say in a low, menacing voice, "You are such a good dog! You are the best friend I've ever had. I am so glad you're in our family."

The dog will crouch, looking sheepish and unhappy. Next you kneel down, look the dog in the eye, smile, adopt a cheerful, nice tone, and say, "You are a bad, bad dog! You drive me crazy the way you track in mud. I'm not happy with you." The dog will wag its tail, lick your hand, and otherwise "smile" at you. Dogs are experts at reading nonverbal body language and voice intonation, while the verbal meaning may be lost on them.

Research has shown that in all exchanges between people, most of the message is communicated nonverbally through voice intonation (38 percent) and facial expression and body language (55 percent)—a total of 93 percent nonverbal! The least part—7 percent—is communicated verbally through words (Philpott, 1983; Wiener & Mehrabian, 1967). Nonverbal cues should confirm the verbal messages they accompany. If they contradict the words spoken, then the communication becomes incongruent, and that erodes trust.

Much of our communication is nonverbal, so it becomes necessary for coaches to observe and attune themselves to interpreting the body language of their coachees.

Imagine a teacher standing in front of a classroom. She is clutching a messy stack of papers, her posture is slouched, she looks a little unkempt, and her facial expression indicates she is tired, maybe even bored. Students pile into the classroom, and the teacher says, "Welcome! I am glad to see you. We have an exciting lesson planned for today."

Students sense the incongruence intuitively, even if they do not recognize it cognitively. If what we say and what we do don't match, we become less believable and less effective. Why would this teacher's students participate or engage in the lesson, or even behave well in class, when they know she doesn't mean what she says, or if she does mean it, she doesn't behave as if she does? We "get" incongruence because missed messages are disturbing and do not make for a quality experience.

When we communicate or interact with people, we usually have certain intentions in mind; however, sometimes our behavior does not line up with our intentions. Despite good intentions and a good plan, a teacher might fail to reach her students if her body language or voice contradicts her words.

The only way she—or any of us—would recognize incongruence in our behaviors or intentions comes from feedback. Without feedback, the teacher is likely to attribute the students' response to something other than her actions. Her students' behavior may provide the feedback that tells her the intentions she had for the lesson were not getting through; then again, the students may not let on and she will have no way of knowing that she was incongruent and therefore not very believable.

This is another situation where videotaping a lesson can be invaluable. If the coach has learned a teacher's intention and the areas in which he or she wants to be coached, the coach can video while observing the lesson and focus on that specific behavior. Watching the taped lesson, the teacher should be able to see how her voice, body language, and expression did or did not communicate her good intentions. The behavior and its effects can be explained and described, but a video provides a far more powerful impact, particularly when the coach and the teacher view and debrief it together.

So, what if the coach feels this teacher appeared unenthusiastic? Is she tired and just doesn't feel like being cheerful, motivating, or dynamic? What then? Well, I'll let you in on a little magic trick that you can use in your own teaching and share with your coachee: *you fake it 'til you make it.* That's right. Conjure up an emotion or an image that will give you a shot of energy. Recreate the feeling or anticipation of a WOW experience.

Think about what you intend to have happen, imagine it happening, get excited, and a magical thing occurs. You actually begin to feel the excitement! Our emotions tend to be reflected in the way we walk, move, or hold ourselves, and our bodies naturally respond by adopting the pose of someone who's excited and motivated. You'll find yourself standing up straighter, your shoulders squared, your breathing more relaxed, a smile on your face. You're there! You're awesome! You rule!

This is not make-believe. It actually stems from work in the art and science of neurolinguistic programming (NLP), developed by researchers John Grinder and Richard Bandler in the 1970s. NLP relies on emotional expression and body language to achieve intended results. Try it sometime. You may find it's a great tool to get you through some tough times when your intentions may be sound, and your behavior can't quite catch up. We'll learn more about NLP in chapter 6.

Confirmatory Paraphrases

Another important Agenda Skill consists of the Confirmatory Paraphrase. This is a statement by the coach that summarizes what the teacher just said; it indicates the coach is listening, thus creating alignment and trust between both parties, and it also allows the coach to begin using the same language as the coachee.

The Confirmatory Paraphrase also indicates if the coach has heard and understood the coachee. If the coach has taken the time to frame a good Open-Ended Question, he or she needs to listen carefully to the answer. As you actively listen, you will hear not only the words but also the underlying feelings and attitudes, and be able to discern the fact and intentions. A successful exchange of question, answer, and Confirmatory Paraphrase builds a strong communication link, good rapport, and trust.

When the person being coached makes a statement, which of the four underlying mental states are being revealed?

- An attitude or feeling
- A fact
- An implied or expressed intent
- A commitment

Consider the following example: A teacher says, "When Sarah came in late, I really got upset." As a coach, you might use the following Confirmatory Paraphrases to respond to that statement:

"You became angry." (Confirms attitude or feeling.) "She is often late." (Confirms fact.)

"Next time, you want to handle the situation differently." (Confirms intent.)

"You want to handle her differently next time." (Confirms commitment.)

In most dialogues, you may wish to confirm feelings first, get the facts straight second, establish intent third, and in appropriate circumstances, establish commitment to the intention last.

Once again, to determine feelings or attitude, look at the body language and listen to voice intonation. Something to note here: an attitude can be either appropriate or inappropriate; a feeling is what it is. In other words, an underlying reason exists for an attitude, yet a feeling remains just what the person feels. It's neither right nor wrong, appropriate or inappropriate. It's just what's so.

As coaches, we can flush out emotion by gently and objectively confirming what we heard (even if we "heard" it nonverbally) in order to bring what is going on to the surface. Practiced use of paraphrasing can get to an underlying attitude that may have caused the emotion, and this in turn can lead to empathetic understanding, trust, and an enhanced coaching relationship.

It's important when paraphrasing to avoid parroting back what the other person just said, even when you are learning to use his or her vocabulary. In other words, if you say exactly the same thing it might come across as mimicry.

Also avoid problem solving when paraphrasing. How can we solve a problem before really finding out the scope of it? Real value comes when the coach draws meaning from what has been said and then paraphrases it back as a neutral statement, not as another question.

Coaches let the other persons know they heard the facts expressed. If they pick up a feeling or attitude, they want to confirm that they "heard" it accurately. If they learn from the coachee that they did not hear the fact or the feeling, attitude, or intention correctly, this gives the coachee the opportunity to clarify, thus providing new information.

These are examples of introductory words in a Confirmatory Paraphrase that reflect fact or attitude or feeling:

"You feel . . ."
"You're saying that . . ."

"You're suggesting . . ."
"Your point is . . ."
"The problem is . . ."
"So what you're feeling is . . ."
"What I hear is . . ."
"What this says to me is . . ."
"You're saying you're frustrated about . . ."
"You're pleased that . . ."
"You want to . . ."
"You're upset about . . ."
"You're feeling vulnerable . . ."
"So what you mean to say is . . ."
"I'm hearing your exuberance and . . ."

The next example shows how using a Confirmatory Paraphrase (CP) can further uncover the other person's agenda:

Coach: "What gets you excited about teaching?" (Open-Ended Question)

Teacher: "I've been thinking about teaching for a long time."

Coach: "Your goal has always been to teach." (CP of fact)

Teacher: "Well, no, actually, my goal was to be a social worker. I worked with low-income families for several years but it was really difficult, so I decided to do something else."

Coach: "You were frustrated and that led to a career change." (CP of feeling)

Teacher: "Exactly. I knew there were things these families could do that they weren't doing to improve their lot in life, and one of those things was getting a good education. I decided to be a teacher to see if I could help more people become educated and improve themselves. I value education, and I wanted to make a difference, especially to low-income families."

This coach now knows a whole lot more about the coachee than just what excites her about teaching. She revealed her background, values, and motivation for teaching. The coach can focus on these values and beliefs to provide feedback that will have meaning to the coachee and guide her in maintaining her motivation and intent. Notice that the Confirmatory Paraphrase that missed the mark opened up the conversation to uncover the agenda.

A Confirmatory Paraphrase of intent restates an action to be taken. It focuses on future behavior. Confirmatory Paraphrases, incidentally, provide a great tool in parent-teacher conferencing as well as in coaching situations. The key to success in using a Confirmatory Paraphrase of intent is to be *very* specific about the intention. "You'll try to do better next time" just isn't specific enough. You need to name the behavior or action the coachee intends.

It's also important for a coach to simply and objectively confirm the intent that was uttered, not use it as authority or it will smack of supervision. Here's an example:

You have observed a teacher coaching. You noticed three students who did not understand the lesson. From the teacher's behavior, it becomes clear he was unaware this had occurred. When you tell him later about these three students, the teacher replies, "I see your point about missing those three kids." Then you could respond with your Confirmatory Paraphrase of intent: "Next time you will check to see that all students understand the lesson before moving on." This restates the action to be taken.

While the above example accurately depicts how to use a Confirmatory Paraphrase of intent, a coach may feel uncomfortable making such a statement to a colleague. Someone who possesses some authority over another generally uses it more than a peer would. A teacher might use it with students, for example.

Examples of beginnings words for Confirmatory Paraphrases of intent:

"Next time you . . ."
"You will . . ."
"Your intention is to . . ."
"You plan to . . ."
"Then we are in agreement that . . ."

In a coaching situation, establishing equality, trust, and avoiding even the semblance of evaluating or supervising remains important. So, in coaching, we can use a Confirmatory Paraphrase of commitment. A Confirmatory Paraphrase of commitment states the belief or value behind the coachee's intention. As we shall see later in this chapter, it becomes vitally important that the coach bring to the surface the coachee's beliefs, values, or visions in order to proceed in the relationship effectively. These things are an important part of the teacher's motivation and purpose.

The Confirmatory Paraphrase of commitment in the previous example might be stated as either of the following:

"It is important to you that your lesson be understood by all your students."
"You want all students included in the learning process."

A conversation might sound like this:

Coach: "What do you hope will be the outcome of today's lesson on the election process?" (Open-Ended Question)

Teacher: "We read and hear so much about corruption in politics that I want the kids to really appreciate how well the system does work."

Coach: "You believe in our electoral process and want to instill that belief in your students." (CP of commitment)

Examples of statements that lead into Confirmatory Paraphrases of commitment include the following:

"It's important to you that . . ."
"So you believe that . . ."
"You want to . . ."
"You think [feel, believe, are convinced] that . . ."

The Agenda Skills are also powerful to use with students, colleagues, parents, and anyone with whom you converse in your personal and professional life. With any skill, of course, practice makes perfect. As you go about your day, notice how often a Closed-Ended Question could be changed to elicit more information. Practice rephrasing your questions as Open-Ended Questions. When you listen to others speaking, listen for the fact, attitude, feeling, or intent behind what they say and practice paraphrasing back, confirming what you heard said and, perhaps even more importantly, what was not said. You will be surprised how you can enhance and strengthen communication.

Finally, if you find yourself "out of sorts," notice whether your nonverbal behavior is congruent with your intention. See if you can correct your mood by conjuring up positive emotions that will assist you in focusing on what you really want and intend to do—your vision.

VISION, MISSION, BELIEFS, VALUES

Most people in the field of education gravitated there because they had a vision about or a belief in improving the lives of students, making a difference, imparting knowledge to others. Time, circumstances, and the maze of bureaucratic mandates and protocols can erode these visions and beliefs, and educators begin teaching from only the curriculum instead of from their beliefs and vision of learning. They begin to lose their power, freedom, and fun, as described by William Glasser, M.D. (1998), in *The Quality School: Managing Students without Coercion*, discussed in chapter 3. They simply survive in the company of others whose visions are also blunted by joining the BMW Club—the Bitching, Moaning, and Whining Club.

Nobody likes being in the BMW Club, yet once people become dues-paying members, peer pressure and agreement keep them locked in the clubhouse. They are in a comfort zone. Probably the most important aspect of a coaching program is the opportunity it provides to rekindle the vision of educators—to release them from the BMW Club and empower them to, once again, teach with their vision, allowing their mission, beliefs, and values to drive every decision.

Including a coaching program in your school creates a culture where it becomes socially unacceptable to belong to the BMW Club, like smoking cigarettes in the building—as indicated in figure 4.2.

Those who remain in the club will find themselves outside with the smokers. Beginning teachers are susceptible to recruitment by the club because they are anxious to belong. With coaching, teachers are recruited to join a different club that brings power, freedom, and fun to their professional lives.

Good teachers—great teachers—survive testing requirements, standards, state governors, and negotiation with parents. Teachers are treated to a daily parade of outrageous styles, tattoos and piercings, secret cell calls and texting, shocking lyrics, and more. Teachers in today's school compete with the culture for the attention of the young. Even great teachers—*especially* great teachers—need support to stay focused on what's important: that the students learn and improve in the midst of it.

So what constitutes the visions, missions, beliefs, and values that we are trying to discover in coaching sessions? And why is it important to do so?

Most corporations, civic organizations, and nonprofits adopt a vision and mission statement and develop core values that are periodically revisited and fine-tuned. Their *vision* provides a picture of the future—Where do we want to be? The *mission* defines why the organization exists. Core *values* represent the organization's beliefs, what makes them do what they do? *Goals*

Figure 4.2.   Ban the BMW Club

are developed from the vision and mission statement and are achievements that would create the future an organization desires while keeping its mission intact. Goals translate into *strategies* that outline the activities or game plan to reach the goals, often described in broad, directional priorities.

For example, if the goal of an organization is to *gain more recognition within the community*, a strategy might be to hold an open house or arrange for a community picnic. Strategies, then, break down to specific tactics— How will we go about implementing this strategy? One tactic might be to send out a mailer about an open house or a picnic; another tactic might be to contact the media and send a press release. *Operations* become the way these tactics will be carried out.

Here's another way to look at goals and strategies:

A CRUSADER'S TALE

You are a crusader who wants to capture a castle for your king. The castle was won by someone else in a previous battle, but the victor has since abandoned the castle. When he left, he burned the bridge over the moat. The moat is now infested with hungry, man-eating sharks.

Your *vision* as a crusader is to place your king's flag on the rampart of the castle, claiming the castle for your king; you have that pictured in your mind as a successful outcome. Your *mission* as a crusader is to do the king's bidding, and he wants the castle. You *value* adventure and making things right, so this is important to you. You *believe* that you are the person for the job and that the king deserves the castle.

Your *strategy* is to create a new bridge into the castle with the resources you have.

Your *tactic* is to attach a strong rope to a hook that you will catapult to the top of the castle wall; once the hook grabs, the rope can be climbed and hence provide a temporary bridge to get inside. Once in the castle, you and your men will build a bridge that can be pushed out over the moat.

To accomplish this tactic, you find a hook, attach a rope, and catapult them into place. You have carried out the *operation* successfully. You did it!

Now you and a few of your men perform another *operation*. You grab tools, shimmy up the rope, careful not to dangle your feet in the shark-invested waters. Once inside, together you rebuild a bridge and move it into place across the moat. The rest of your crusaders cross into the castle using the new bridge and together you claim the castle for the king. Your strategies worked; the goal was achieved. Bravo!

Breaking down the various aspects of an organization's focus into parts keeps people moving toward their goals. Why should teaching or coaching be any different? Take a tip from them and use their model. The same areas of focus apply to education and teaching and thus to the coaching of teachers.

A graphic of the breakdown of vision, mission, beliefs, strategy, tactics, and operations—called Goals for Preconferencing—is found in figure 4.3.

In coaching, the coach and coachee strive to pinpoint a specific focus for a coaching session. To get to there, they first identify their vision—the imagined picture of the future. The vision points to the end result, guided by the mission and beliefs that drive it. A coachee's vision, mission, and beliefs are revealed by asking three types of questions—creative, evaluative, and personalized—which are designed to elicit a teacher's vision from a balance of perspectives:.

Strategy involves a broad plan; a teacher's strategy might be his or her plan for responding to a recently adopted board-of-education curriculum or state-mandated course of study. In coaching, it might entail an overall approach where the coach provides the teacher with a roadmap to incorporate the strategy while remaining true to the teacher's vision. Tactics involve lesson plans as specific components of the overall strategy. Operations call for the execution of the tactics—the teacher's teaching skills and behaviors that will impart learning.

This same process might work in the development of strategies in school board and faculty meetings. If schools are to be successful in achieving their vision, mission, and beliefs relating to society and the education of students, there must be agreement and alignment among school personnel—at the administrative and instructional levels—as to the nature of the vision, mission, and beliefs/values of the school system.

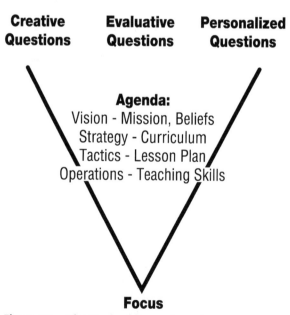

Figure 4.3. The Goals of Preconferencing

Empowering Questions: Creative, Evaluative, Personalized

To accomplish this alignment, the coach must be skilled with Open-Ended Questions and Confirmatory Paraphrases. He or she must also ask empowering questions that are creative, evaluative, and personalized. (See figure 4.3.) To uncover a teacher's creativity, ask questions that encourage the coachee to explain what creativity means for him or her. Questions formed to elicit information as to what the teacher values are evaluative questions. If the teacher and coach have had prior sessions, personalized questions can be introduced.

All questioning moves and shifts depending on the answers received, so the questioning might start by encouraging a teacher to talk about creativity and shift as he or she says what is valued.

Creative Questions allow the teacher to move away from the immediate and into his or her imagination in order to generate ideas. They might include the following:

"Share some ideas you have considered for this lesson."
"What do you think would happen if you . . . ?"
"What other options do you have?"
"Where will your creativity show in this lesson?"
"If you could wave a magic wand over your classroom before this lesson began, what would you have the wand do?"

Evaluative Questions encourage the teacher to respond based on his or her values rather than intellect. Here the coach digs for the underlying belief, value, or mission the teacher carries. The question may often be followed by a "why" to uncover the value behind the answer.

"If you were to hire your replacement, what three traits would be most important for that individual to possess?"
"How does this behavior fit with your beliefs?"
"How do you think the lesson went today?" "Why?"
"Judging from the students' responses, how do you think the lesson was received?"

Personalized Questions indicate that the coach has been listening. They may be based on the teacher's previous responses, for example:

"You said before that you appreciated humor in your students. What did you discover about that today?"
"I remember what you said about working in your previous district, and you seem to like it better here. What are the differences to you now?"

One word of caution about Personalized Questions: Coaches should avoid dropping into the role of friend. A friend may make assumptions in favor of, and certainly will back, a friend, whether it helps or not. A coach personalizes the question based on past conversations and events with the focus on success rather than support only. Personalized Questions when appropriate can help reveal more about what the teacher thinks and feels. They can also underscore the trust and serve as a nudge to continue to stretch and improve.

So how does one develop good Creative, Evaluative, or Personalized Questions or statements? Typically, asking Open-Ended Questions improves the chances of eliciting the desired information, although that is not always the case. The coach can also use cue words to trigger answers and thoughts on a specific topic. Cue words signal to the coachee what kind of thinking or what emotion is called for.

Cue Words for Creative Questions

Examples of cue words for Creative Questions include what I call "idea" words. Here are examples with the idea cue word italicized in each question:

Ideas—"What other *ideas* have you had?"
Goals—"And your overall *goal* in this lesson is . . ."
Options—"What are your *options* here?"
Changes—"Describe *changes* you want to make."
Ways—"In what *ways* can you improve this lesson?"
Possibilities—"What other *possibilities* might we look at?"
Opportunities—"This may lead to a lot of *opportunities*. Let's explore that."

The cue words to elicit creativity might contain predictive idea words:

Predict—"*Predict* the outcome of your meeting with Dan."
Hypothesize—"If you reorganized the lesson this way, what would *happen*?"
Consequences—"What are the *consequences* of doing the homework assignment first?"
Affect—"In what ways would this strategy *affect* your students?"
Effect—"What might be the *effect* on your career?"
Happen—"What would *happen* if . . . ?"

Or your questions might contain words that imply action:

Apply—"How would you *apply* this to your personal life?"
Build—"Let's *build* on that idea."

Design—"Can you show me a *design* that allows more kids to see it?"
Compose—"What could you *write* that would give you what you want?"
Create—"How will you *create* this?"
Produce—"How could this be *produced* differently?"
Build—"What else can you *build* into this?"

Cue Words for Evaluative Questions

Examples of cue words that elicit a coachee's evaluation of the situation include the following:

Evaluate—"As you *evaluate* the situation, how did you think it went?"
Value—"What do you *value* about this process?" "Why?"
Belief—"What *beliefs* underscore what you just told me?"
Opinion—"What's your *opinion*?"
Believe—"What do you *believe* was going on?"
Judge—"How would you *judge* my performance?"
Decide—"What made you *decide* to do it that way?"

Evaluative Questions may also include some words that involve analysis:

Analyze—"Let's *analyze* why you felt that way."
Reasons—"What were your *reasons* for changing that?"
Factors—"What *factors* influenced your decision to do this?"

Other ways to elicit what the coachee values may have to do with insight cue words:

Insights—"What *thoughts* or *insights* did you have about that issue?"
Inference—"What did you *infer* from his remark?"
Connection—"What *connections* would you make between this situation and the last?"

Cue Words and Phrases for Personalized Questions

Personalized Questions reflect back to what was already discussed. Some phrases that draw on recollection are as follows:

"*Remember* when we . . . ?"
"The *last time* we discussed this, you said . . ."
"In our *last* coaching session, you were trying to . . ."

Phrases that show the coach understands the person:

"Your *strength* has always been . . ."
"I know *you feel* strongly that . . ."
"Well, I know *you value that*, so it makes sense to me that . . ."

Without getting bogged down in semantics, know that using cue words is an excellent way to frame a question or statement to help the coachee focus on what is being sought. The point is for the coach to guide the teacher into creative, evaluative, or personalized thought processes.

Sample Conversation

Let's peek in on a preobservation conference—a coaching session where the teacher and coach determine what they want the coach to observe in the observation phase, in the classroom, or elsewhere. This comes from an actual session with Sheryl Williams, a teacher from Polk County, Florida. I am seated next to Sheryl, taking notes as she talks so that she can see what I am writing.

Notice my use of Open- and Closed-Ended Questions or paraphrasing. See if you can identify where I am seeking her values, her creativity, or where I make the question more personalized. Look for cue words that I use to elicit her thinking. While I am still seeking her agenda—what she wants observed—my primary focus remains on developing Creative, Evaluative, and Personalized Questions to help Sheryl bring to the surface her values, vision, beliefs, and mission as a teacher.

Steve: "Hi, Sheryl. What's up?"

Sheryl: "Hey, Steve! I'm feeling very creative today. I want the kids to have fun at school. I'd like to give them a 'wow' experience!"

Steve: "What do learners having fun look like or sound like for you, Sheryl?"

Sheryl: "Good noise. Chatter. Sidebars, discussions. The kids coming up with their own ideas. Lots of interacting, conversation."

Steve: "Learning is occurring when there's noise in the room."

Sheryl: "It is."

Steve: "What did you want me to look into or observe?"

Sheryl: "Well, as you know, Steve, I like math lessons. I think they are interactive. I'm going to introduce graphs to my students tomorrow."

Steve: "What ideas have you had for the lesson?"

Sheryl: "The students will be given crayons, and I'll be showing them how to make graphs. They collect data from one another."

Steve: "What is your role in the lesson and what task have you given the students?"

Sheryl: "I'll give them two statements which explain *x*, *y*, and the title. They'll put it all together so everything is on the graph."

Steve: "What happens then?"

Sheryl: "I'll ask them to determine how it all fits together, what it tells them."

Steve: "You're giving them activities, then debriefing the lesson."

Sheryl: "Yes. And I want them to get a sufficient amount of practice too."

Steve: "What do you believe is important about practice?"

Sheryl: "Practice will internalize it for them. I can tell them all I want, and if they practice, they'll get it. I am a firm believer in practice."

Steve: "You value practice as much as standard teaching."

Sheryl: "Yes, I do. These kids are active, and I want them to be able to use that energy to learn."

Steve: "This sounds like a lesson designed for things you've said you like about learning: interaction, movement, and opportunities for students to help one another, practice, and inductive learning. How will you decide you have succeeded in this lesson?"

Sheryl: "Students will be able to label a graph, write two comparative statements, and walk away with an understanding of how to chart data."

Steve: "What percentage of kids will tell you if you've succeeded?"

Sheryl: "100 percent."

Steve: "You're going for all of them?"

Sheryl: "That's my intention, yes."

Steve: "Good for you. What role would you like me to play?"

Sheryl: "Well, there is a student named Billy who sits in the back. He's an awesome student if I grab him and get him involved. Notice if I grab him, if he comes around, and if he brings others with him. Sometimes it's Billy's class more than mine! I want it to be my class."

Steve: "How about if I come in with a focus on Billy, jot down where you are in the activity, and notice what Billy is doing at each point? Will that work?"

Sheryl: "That'll work."

Steve: "How long should I be there?"

Sheryl: "Come in at 10:00 A.M. and stay for thirty minutes."

Steve: "Here's a chart I might use. I will bring several colored pens, take notes and change pen colors every ten minutes so you get a map of what happened when. Would that help?"

Sheryl: "That's good. Note in each section what Billy is doing, okay?"

Steve: "Will do. Tell me your goal for Billy today."

Sheryl: "Today, I'd like to have him be successful early on and be motivated by that success."

Steve: "What's your goal for Billy six months from now?

Sheryl: "What I'd like to see Billy do is work to his potential, to get into the lesson instead of disrupting the class. He can be a great leader, negative or positive. I'd like him to be a positive leader. He's a smart boy and could be an A student."

Steve: "With your vision and intention, Sheryl, I'm sure he will be."

There is no specific recipe for using the Creative, Evaluative, and Personalized Questions. Each question may be peppered with elements of other types of questions. The job of a coach is to work with the teacher's vision—to first uncover it, and then to keep focused on it so that everything the teacher does is driven from a place of greatness, excitement, and enthusiasm.

LISTENING SKILLS

The most important skill a coach can have is the ability to really listen. All the correctly worded questions make no difference at all if there is not also a listening component. Listening builds the relationship; listening allows for nuance and nonverbal communication to be "heard"; listening allows for clarity; and listening ensures trust.

The gift of empathy—being able to think someone else's thoughts and feel someone else's feelings—can be indispensable to a trusting coaching relationship. This represents the ultimate level of listening. Stephen R. Covey (1990) identifies five levels of listening in his highly acclaimed book, *The 7 Habits of Highly Effective People* (p. 128):

1. Ignoring: making no effort to listen.
2. Pretend listening: making believe or giving the appearance you are listening.
3. Selective listening: hearing only the parts of the conversation that interest you.
4. Empathic listening: listening and responding with both heart and mind to understand a person's words, intent, and feelings.
5. Attentive listening: hearing without evaluating.

Again, paraphrasing back what the person said in terms of fact, attitude, feeling, or intention goes a long way toward assuring the coachee that the coach was indeed listening and understanding.

The Confirmatory Paraphrase shows the coachee that the coach understands what was said. When people being coached hear that their feelings were so easily understood (that is, the coach paraphrased back "You are upset because . . ." or "You're feeling excited about that . . ."), it helps them temper or defuse negative feelings and accelerate positive ones.

The coach also listens to gain clarity on all sides of a problem or issue. A coach listens and checks meaning by restating what a coachee said. Restating what was said also encourages the coachee to hear what he or she said, and this often leads to new ideas ("So, your plan is to . . ." or "As I understand it, you plan to . . .").

The coach also listens with neutrality and does not convey his or her response through body language or facial expression. A neutral listening style combined with an obvious interest encourages the coachee to continue talking, particularly if an Open-Ended Question has been asked.

Also, the coach listens to be able to summarize what was said, possibly with a confirmation of intention. This often serves as a springboard to further discussion, a signal to move on ("These are the three things you plan to do . . . " or "So far we have decided that . . .").

The skills of coaching mimic the skills of good teaching. These include asking questions that open the way for the other person to discuss and reveal his or her values, beliefs, creativity, and critical thinking. The coach is skilled at remaining congruent; paraphrasing back what was said to identify fact, feeling, attitude, or intention; and, of course, the valuable tool of active listening.

Practicing these verbal skills will make them natural and powerful. They are essential to an effective coaching program. In fact, they are essential for life.

SUMMARY

These last few chapters have laid the foundation for coaching—what it is, what it isn't, what roles people play, and what skills move the coaching relationship along. Coaching makes a profound and powerful difference in the way people feel about themselves, whether in teaching or in other professions. A coach can uncover a person's latent desires and abilities, allowing him or her to maximize life experiences.

A coach's success is tied to the success of the person being coached. What could be more empowering than having someone there for you with a strong desire and commitment to make you a better human being, a better teacher, or a better leader? Coaching helps people improve their lives in a context much larger than next month, next week, or next year. Coaching can help a teacher envision and create a legacy that will be carried forward by generations of students.

Pretty heady stuff.

And now we'll move into the three-pronged process of coaching that gives it a structure within which these powerful ideas can occur.

RESEARCH SHOWS

Agenda Skills and Communication

Research shows the ability to "read" others' nonverbal communication is one of the most important skills of effective peer coaching (Knight, 2007).

While little research has been conducted on the use of questions in a coaching/mentoring relationship, a substantial body of knowledge concerning the use of questions in the educational process does exist (Schroeder et al., 2007). Much of this information can be extended to peer coaching situations. Browne and Keeley (2009) suggest the ability to ask the right questions is essential in creating effective dialogue.

Research shows learning does not come merely from experiences, but from reflecting on those experiences (Haskell, 2001). Supportive yet challenging questions can encourage such reflection.

POSSIBLE ANSWERS FOR REPHRASING CLOSED-ENDED QUESTIONS TO OPEN-ENDED QUESTIONS

1. "Do you think your lesson will turn out well?"
   "How do you think your lesson will turn out?"
2. "Did you think the students were interested?"
   "What showed you the students were interested?"
3. "Give me another reason."
   "For instance . . . ?"
4. "What are you going to try now?"
   "What is important about the next strategy you use?"
5. "What part would you change?"
   "What changes do you think might work here?"
6. "When does it end?"
   "Where does this lead?"

II

THE COACHING PROCESS

5

The Preobservation Conference

The purpose of a preobservation conference is for a coach to use the coaching skills outlined in chapter 4 to engage in a one-on-one conversation with the person being coached. If, as poet and author David Whyte contends, "the conversation is the relationship," the preobservation conference will be profound, meaningful, useful, and memorable.

Why do I use the word "conference" instead of "session" or "meeting"? I use "conference" because the coach and the coachee are coming together to confer on whatever the coachee wants the coach to observe. *Webster's New World College Dictionary* (Neufeldt and Guralnik, 1997) says *to confer* means "to bring together, give, grant, bestow, compare" (p. 291). Two people confer about real issues, real goals, and generate an in-depth look at the coachee's behaviors, attitudes, mission, and vision. This conference may also lead to innovation and exciting changes.

Real and meaningful conversations with a purpose and a focus take more time than the usual "Hi-how-are-ya?" exchanges we hold every day. Suspended and shallow conversations take time and are a waste of breath. In a preobservation conference, the purpose is established and the focus is clear. Real conversation can swiftly cut to the chase, get down to the important issues, and move along quickly and efficiently with quality.

Often, staff development training in peer coaching precedes the implementation of the coaching program. I typically go to a school or district for three to five days to train on the basics of coaching, some of which I've covered in this book. The training includes techniques for developing the trusting relationship that needs to exist between a coach and coachee. This relationship becomes solidified at the preobservation conference stage.

Certainly two heads are better than one when strategizing or working on a skill or issue. Beyond that, however, the coach and the coachee build a solid agreement that the coach has the coachee's best interests at heart—the coach succeeds only when the coachee succeeds.

Honing the coachee's skills, behaviors, movements, techniques, curriculum, or other aspects of teaching becomes the focus of the relationship. The relationship creates opportunities for the coachee to share and expand the powerful success strategies at his or her disposal, whether they are apparent or latent.

The desired situation is that the coach be simply a coach. The coach does not double as an evaluator or "boss." Neither is the coach strictly a friend. The coaching relationship allows the coachee to step beyond his or her role in a job, family, or collegial relationship into the realm of improved performance and growth as a human being. This occurs because the coach receives permission, and has at his or her disposal the skills, to guide the coachee to achieve desired goals.

Cultivating the relationship occurs over the long term, so the process should begin as it is intended to continue—conferring openly, honestly, and truthfully in a safe and supportive collaborative environment. The timing and nature of the coaching sessions can vary. The preobservation conference, for example, can be via telephone, meeting place, e-mail, or in a casual at-home setting or coffee shop.

A large part of the training I conduct on coaching deals with how the coach and teacher can establish, and work together effectively in, a safe environment. But whether the coach and coachee have undergone training in coaching or not, the initial meeting of the two is best accomplished in a "getting-to-know-you" session. Thereafter, preobservation sessions focus on specific methods or behaviors the coachee wants to improve. In subsequent postobservation conferences, the coachee receives specific feedback and support on how well he or she has succeeded based on what the coach observed.

NORMS AND AGREEMENTS

Ideally, the initial meeting of coach and coachee will take place away from school in a comfortable setting where they can spend an hour or two simply getting to know one another. Whether or not such an initial meeting is possible, each pre- and postobservation conference is an opportunity to build rapport and understanding. To do this, I recommend the coach and coachee develop norms, agreements, or guidelines for how they will work together. These norms constitute a blueprint of the relationship—subject to upgrading or discarding, as mutually agreed—and can be referred to at various times should the coaching relationship ever go off course.

Some suggestions for norms or agreements that might be included in your coaching relationship are shown here. Some may seem redundant; different phrasing is designed for clarity and to trigger your own options.

- The coachee is not broken or in need of fixing.
- The coach asks the questions; the coachee has the answers.
- The power is granted to the relationship, not to the coach.
- The relationship is custom tailored to the coachee.
- The coachee is in charge; the relationship is focused on the coachee getting the results he or she wants.
- Except when expressly stated otherwise, all conversations in the coaching sessions remain private and confidential.
- The coach ensures that the coachee is always steering toward improvement, fulfillment, and success.
- The focus of the conferences is on the one being coached—the agenda comes from the coachee.
- The coach and the coachee agree to show up on time at scheduled conferences.
- Communication is open, honest, and truthful at all times.
- The coach and the coachee agree to identify a problem before trying to solve it.
- If something is not working in the coaching relationship, the coachee has the responsibility to speak about it as soon as he or she is aware of it, to keep the trust level high.
- The coachee has a responsibility to share with the coach what seems to be working well for him or her.
- The coach remains neutral, objective, and supportive.
- The coachee remains open to suggestions, changes, or improvements.
- The coach refrains from judging, evaluating, critiquing, or sharing advice or opinions unless requested by the coachee.
- The coachee agrees to do the work necessary to make changes, yield improvements, or learn skills or behaviors.
- The learning and working styles of both coach and coachee are known to each and taken into account in the coaching relationship.

There are many other agreements the coach and coachee may develop together. The point is the relationship can be defined; it should not be loose or open-ended. Too often, we enter into relationships or join teams or groups with no upfront roadmaps of how participants will work together. Countless unnecessary communication problems can be avoided by simply outlining the purpose, intention, and "rules of engagement" before the topics—whatever they may be—are raised. Two of the norms mentioned in the preceding list deserve further discussion.

Problems, Options, or Opportunities?

Just as people often gather together in groups or meetings without any articulated purpose, so too do people come together to solve a problem before it has been accurately identified. When a teacher feels he or she needs coaching on a certain behavior or skill, there seems to be a tendency to refer to it as a "problem." The coach and the coachee need to agree that a problem exists and what its nature might be before moving to solve it.

Often, the perception of a problem means the coachee simply does not see options that are available. Gathering the facts, stepping back and looking at the big picture, or brainstorming the genesis of the problem or issue are all good methods to discover if there is truly a problem or if the situation is more like an opening to explore together the options and opportunities for improvement.

Learning and Working Styles

The last norm or agreement noted in the previous list states, *The learning and working styles of both the coach and coachee are known to each and taken into account in the coaching relationship.* Just as learning styles are important to understand in students, they are equally important to relationships and communication among educators and other working adults. As you coach another, you want to pay attention to your coachee's preferred learning style so you can respond appropriately. A teacher's preferred learning style has an impact on how he or she teaches, and these preferred learning styles remain in play in a coaching relationship. Once you know your coachee's learning and working style, you can provide information in ways the coachee learns best.

Sensory Preferences

Every person has his or her own way of communicating knowledge that is part of a successful coaching relationship. The communication style of those with a particular sensory preference often shows up in verbal and nonverbal communication techniques and in the use of certain vocabulary. Recognizing the sensory preference of the person being coached allows the coach to mirror back similar language to help bond the relationship. It also assists the coach in saying things in a way the coachee can hear them best.

As an example, a teacher whose preferred sensory style is auditory might use such words as "Do you *hear* what I'm saying?" or "As I *listen* . . . ," or "There's a real *buzz* about . . ." A visual adult learner may say, "I *see*" or "I can't *picture* that." Tactual learners, who value relationship, touch, and inner feelings might refer to "getting a *feel* for it" or "it really *touched* me." A kinesthetic adult learner may use action terms, such as "Let's *pop* that into the lesson" or "*Run* that by me." The coach then uses similar words to reflect the teacher's style.

Aside from language, a coachee might exhibit behaviors that suggest, for example, that he or she is a kinesthetic learner. If your coachee participates in sports, takes hikes, or tends to fidget or move around in meetings, he or she is probably kinesthetic and learns by doing and moving his or her body.. As the coach of such a person, you could hold some of your discussions while walking around the school site to bring some movement to your session. Whenever possible, match the other person's learning and working style. And, at the same time, recognize your own style as you apply it to the coaching relationship.

Perceptual Preferences

Each person also has ways of perceiving and organizing information—perceptual and organizational styles. An abstract thinker perceives the world in symbols, concepts, ideas, even acronyms. A more concrete thinker prefers the real thing: something to look at, touch, and work with in the real world. As a coach, you will want to cover both abstract and concrete communication until you are clear about the preferred style of your coachee.

Let's look at how learning styles might play out in a coaching session where communication is key. We'll use differences in perceptual styles—abstract versus concrete.

A teacher wants to implement new procedures with her students that will improve her classroom management. This teacher perceives the world in an abstract way—thoughts, symbols, concepts. The coach is more concrete. The coach looks at the world with a preference toward real objects, physical reality, specific actions. Let's listen in on a hypothetical scene between these two when neither is aware of the other's style.

Abstract: "My students need to be informed of these new procedures, as I can see they will make an overall difference in the feel of my classroom. In many cases these requirements benefit them." (The general, overall issues.)

Concrete: "All right. What would you like to tell them and when?" (The concrete coach is interested in "What's next?" questions and specific actions rather than in abstractions and possible benefits.)

Abstract: "Well, they need to know the reason for the procedures. They will probably want to know about any consequences. Really, there is quite a bit that could be included." (The abstract thinker receives and reviews the questions conceptually without framing a specific question, which may frustrate the concrete coach.)

Concrete: "You think there may be a lot to this. So how did you plan to tell them? Have you thought about placing the new procedures on the school's website? You said you wanted to do this by Monday." (The concrete colleague is poised with pencil and paper ready for the abstract colleague to get down to specifics.)

Abstract: "Yes, I know; but it should also be done right! It has to cover all the bases. So I guess I will outline the procedures and then maybe I can write up something for the Web." (The abstract communicator is becoming a bit annoyed, sensing the concrete colleague wants to move ahead without identifying all the issues and generating all the meaningful information that should be considered.)

Concrete: "You intend to write the procedures and then develop something for the Web by Monday. What additional work do you see here that must be done?" (The concrete coach is trying not to show frustration but senses that the development of procedures for the students is still very open-ended and that nothing definite is being accomplished.)

This conversation becomes frustrating for both parties because the abstract thinker lacks specifics while the concrete thinker insists on dealing with particular problems before the issue has been given scope and a goal.

Organizational Preferences

Learning styles also entail how one organizes information, whether in a sequential or global fashion, and, here again, paying attention to methods used by a coach or a coachee can reveal those preferred styles. One who tends to take the global perspective makes broad connections, prefers to see the big picture, and takes intuitive leaps. The global person wants to understand the why and the concept. A sequential communicator tends to be detailed. He or she needs the step-by-step process, the grounding of how to get from A to B, and so on.

Once again, a conversation between someone who is global and one who is sequential can lead to misunderstanding and even conflict. The global learner's eyes may glaze over as the sequential person ticks off a list of one hundred items, one by one. If someone with a global style lays out the big picture in broad terms without a clear plan, you might see the sequential communicator become frustrated at the lack of a concrete process.

Temperament Types

Those of you familiar with the typology of temperament types developed by Myers-Briggs will appreciate that temperament affects how one values learning and teaching. What someone values translates to how he or she values the coaching relationship. A shortened version of Myers-Briggs shows how the different types show up in teaching and coaching.

Intuitive Feeler (NF)—These teachers value personal integrity. They are relationship oriented, focusing on personal values—their own and those of others. A coach working with an NF teacher would do well to focus on the relationship aspect of the coaching process. In learning, personal significance and emotional content are important. They do not like being labeled because they value being unique individuals, not types. The NF may have difficulty viewing a learning experience or making a decision from any but a personal, subjective, or empathic position.

Intuitive Thinker (NT)—Coaches or coachees with this temperament tend to be rational in their approach to life. They need (and give) logical reasons for their decisions, being concerned about competence and "doing it well." When communicating they analyze information, seek knowledge, and work to solve problems. In the intellectual sphere, an NT coach or coachee may at first appear cold or unemotional and have difficulty limiting a learning task or question to the issue at hand, relating it instead to larger complexities of life or school. Understanding differences in temperament goes a long way in building the coach-coachee relationship.

Sensing Judger (SJ)—SJ teachers and coaches have a strong sense of order and correctness; they are literal in communication and understanding. They value organization, predictability, usefulness in the here and now, and precise language. SJs want to "Do it right!"—and do it right the first time. Having things go smoothly is important to them. When working with an SJ, a coach may focus on those aspects of order. Loyal and committed, SJs often take on more responsibility than they can handle—again, so the job is "done right!"

Sensing Perceiver (SP)—SP teachers value variety and excitement in learning and in life. They are after the thrill of learning value and competency over predictability. Practical, an SP coach or coachee wants immediate results and can often be competitive. SP coaches may want their coachees to take on more risk. They tend to appreciate style and performance. Responders more than planners, they are the "firefighters" of the school or organization.

In a coaching relationship, conflicts might arise if, for example, the NF educator wants a friendly relationship with his or her coach. If the coach's style is different, that desire may get missed and misunderstanding can occur.

If a coach is an NT, he or she may build more thinking and analyzing into the coaching session, and the SJ coachee may not relate to it. Or the SJ teacher may be taken back by an SP coach's encouragement to take risks. In turn, the SP teacher may be frustrated by an overly cautious SJ or NF coach.

But wait! Coaching is not meant to be frustrating—on the contrary. Because a coach fluent in the language of temperament soon learns how a coachee takes in, perceives, organizes, and communicates thoughts and beliefs, and how he or she processes feedback, being aware of style differences and discussing them can be the starting point to defuse potential conflicts or misunderstandings.

If you have not yet had the chance to discover your own learning and working styles or those of your coach or coachee, you've come to the right place! Performance Learning Systems, Inc. (PLS) has developed a unique and highly effective instrument called *The Kaleidoscope Profile*. This learning-styles survey has been used successfully by hundreds of thousands of students, educators, administrators, and other professionals in the workplace with amazingly accurate results.

Using the educator version of the profile (there are two versions for students, one for educators, and one for adults in the workplace), you can discover your own learning and working styles. Typically the survey is completed using a unique folder and colorful sticker format. The survey is also now available online, and you or your school can actually purchase "seats" to take it, either one at a time or as a group.

And this is your lucky day! Since you are reading this book, you have permission to take the educator version online *free* using a code tracked to this book. To take the profile, follow these easy steps:

1. Go online to www.plsweb.com/QTCC2
2. In the box provided, enter this code exactly as written (upper and lower case letters): X2udcW
3. Click "Submit."
4. Fill out the registration form and click "Submit Form."
5. You have reached the profile. Read the directions and begin!
6. The results will be automatically compiled, and you will be shown what the interpretation may mean to you as an educator or as a coach.

You are, of course, welcome to cruise the rest of the PLS site: www.plsweb.com.

One way to become acquainted with or to start the coaching process at the first session with your coach or coachee might be to share learning-style surveys. This goes a long way toward closing the gap to understanding each other and to kick-start the relationship. (Pop quiz: what type of learner says "kick-start the relationship"?)

DISCOVERING AGENDA AND FOCUS

In chapter 4 we looked at various verbal skills a coach can use to uncover what is on a coachee's mind, to bring to the surface issues, ideas, concerns, and feelings about specific teaching situations—in short, to find out his or her agenda. These are the skills needed in the preobservation conference. What specific behavior or technique or skills does the teacher want to focus on? What does he or she want to learn, improve, change, modify, or simply become aware of? What feedback is wanted?

Beyond information sought and shared, the preobservation conference serves as a forum for the coach to employ specific questioning and paraphrasing skills to delve deeper into the vision, mission, beliefs, or values of the coachee. Empowering questions that elicit the teacher's creativity, evaluation, or more personalized thoughts help both the coach and teacher discover the focus the teacher wants in his or her professional career, teaching, or development.

In the preobservation conference, the coach listens, questions, paraphrases, observes congruency, and otherwise uncovers the coachee's belief system or values that, taken together, drive his or her vision. Uncovering the coachee's vision is an awesome task, yet it is crucial to guiding the coachee successfully. Uncovering the vision becomes a large part of the preobservation conference session. A vision does not double as a goal or an objective; a vision is a larger perspective. As Peter Block (1990) declares in his book *The Empowered Manager*, a vision is the preferred future, a desirable state, an ideal situation. It is an expression of optimism beyond the needs of bureaucracy and despite immediate difficulties (pp. 102–103).

A vision comes out of a desire to be great—to move from good to great, both in teaching and in personal or professional development.

If this seems broad, it is because each coaching relationship evolves differently. What a coachee wants to know or change will be as varied as those relationships are. There will not be a sample list of questions. Each coaching session and each coaching relationship will be different. The questions are created out of what the coach hears—out of listening to the one being coached.

Look at figure 5.1. There are two goals of the preobservation conference. First, uncover the *agenda* of the teacher. Questions are designed to bring out the teacher's vision or belief, how that vision or belief fits with the curriculum (strategy), and how that vision or belief will be carried out in the instructional activity or lesson plan—in other words, what lesson planning and teaching skills will be used (tactics and operations).

Second, discover the *focus* of the upcoming instructional activity or lesson plan that the coach will be observing—the observation phase. The actual teaching skills (operations) that the coachee will be using constitute the focus of this stage, yet another skill set or focus could be developed, depending on the coaching relationship and situation. How the teacher operates, performs, or carries out the skill becomes the focus, and the coach observes its achievement.

In figure 5.1 the questions asked by the coach are designed to funnel down to the focus of the observation: what strategies the coachee wants to work on, the specific tactics he or she will use in a given lesson plan, and how he or she plans to use the teaching skills—how they will operate.

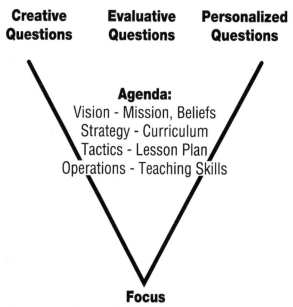

Creative   **Evaluative**   **Personalized**
Questions   **Questions**   **Questions**

Agenda:
Vision - Mission, Beliefs
Strategy - Curriculum
Tactics - Lesson Plan
Operations - Teaching Skills

Focus

Figure 5.1.   The Goals of Preconferencing

The focus of the observation will be driven by the first step: the coachee's agenda. As the coach discovers the teacher's driving vision or belief, he or she can better coach the teacher on the strategies and tactics based on that vision or belief. It all ties together when it dovetails with the coachee's value system.

A coaching program at Oakwood City School District in Ohio includes teachers, principals, administrators, and some staff. The superintendent, whom we will call Judy, was coached by Debbie, a computer science and journalism teacher. Debbie interviewed Judy at their preobservation session. She learned Judy was about to attend an important meeting of the Board of Trustees.

Judy wanted Debbie to observe her during the meeting and let her know if she was dominating the meeting. She was concerned she might be pushing her own agenda too hard, and she wanted Debbie's feedback on that particular aspect. In addition to the feedback she was able to give Judy on this topic, Debbie reported that by attending the session she gained tremendous insight into the superintendent's role and how she worked with the community to get what the district needed.

Information like this is an incidental but important offshoot of the coaching relationship. While the coach poses the questions and provides specific feedback, he or she also gains insight and knowledge about what the coachee does, feels, and envisions, even garnering some terrific strategies and lesson plans the coach can "borrow." In the example above, Debbie had a chance to experience the role of superintendent, something she never would have done outside a coaching relationship. More about the Oakwood coaching program appears in chapter 9.

Beginning teachers will want different coaching tips and guidance than tenured teachers. If the coach also serves as principal, the angle changes again. Coaches and coachees who work in the same building will have a different relationship than those who work in separate locations.

Here is an example of a preobservation conference I held with a teacher midway through her first year of teaching. I am coaching Shelly to learn about her beliefs; notice what questions I ask to elicit them. Also notice what specific jobs she assigns me to do as her coach.

Steve: "Hi, Shelly."

Shelly: "Hi, Steve. It's good to see you again."

Steve: "Thanks. How's it going?"

Shelly: "It's going well! It's been an exciting year."

Steve: "Tell me some of the exciting parts."

Shelly: "This year the third grade teachers—and teachers for other grades as well—started working together as a team. We have a conference planning time where we all sit down and share our ideas about what worked in our classrooms and what didn't work. We plan our lessons together so everybody can see what the other teachers are doing. That's been really effective."

Steve: "That's an ongoing, built-in coaching session you have! That's terrific. What would you say you've changed in your classroom because of the influence of working with other people on the team?"

Shelly: "One of the things I think I've changed is probably my approach to reading. Teaching reading. I've had some really good suggestions from other teachers about how to best teach the children how to read, which is one of the real problem areas in our school."

Steve: "And so you've put those suggestions to work."

Shelly: "I try to see which ones work for me and which ones don't."

Steve: "Great! One of the things that can happen with a first-year teacher is that as the year goes on, you're kind of revamping the vision that you brought into teaching. As you look back at this past year, how have you changed or modified your picture of teaching?"

Shelly: "Well, when I came in—and as an individual I'm very idealistic—I had very high goals and very high expectations. Although I didn't lower my expectations or my goals, I had to kind of adapt them to the group of people I was working with as well as the students I have. So in that way, I changed my vision a little bit. And that was kind of hard for me to adjust to that, because I did have such high expectations."

Steve: "I love your choice of words and that you are maintaining the expectation. It may just take us a little longer to get there."

Shelly: "And I have to go about it in a different way than I had originally intended."

Steve: "Sure. That happens in a lot of cases. Now, Shelly, regarding your upcoming lesson, how would you describe the teacher's role?"

Shelly: "Well, in the lesson you're going to see the primary role of the teacher is to see if her teaching over the year has been effective—if I have taught (well how to write) a friendly letter and if my students remembered."

Steve: "So in effect, you're checking on yourself?"

Shelly: "Exactly."

Steve: "Are you going to be doing that through questions?"

Shelly: "Through questions and through student participation. They are going to use some different hands-on types of materials to show the different parts of the letter."

Steve: "Shelly, while I'm seated in the classroom watching this lesson, I will certainly observe for you everything that's happening. And, I can also zoom in and watch something in detail that I can share with you afterward."

Shelly: "That would be great."

Steve: "What might I watch in detail that I can give you specific feedback on in our postobservation conference?"

Shelly: "I think one of the things I would like to know is how I'm doing in my interactions with students on a one-on-one basis. Am I getting across my point to each individual student? Are they responding to me?"

Steve: "And how would I tell that as an observer?"

Shelly: "Maybe you could watch to see their eye contact, whether they're focusing on me, watching me; if they're participating. Sometimes you can't see if all the students are participating. Sometimes some get lost in the shuffle and you just don't see them."

Steve: "Okay. I'll pay close attention to their reactions and participation. Sounds like a good lesson."

My task is to look specifically at the students and how they focus on Shelly. When are they focused on her? What does she do to maintain that focus? I also know Shelly has a belief system built around high expectations. So I know that when I'm observing in her classroom, I want to have that mind-set, and if I want to offer a suggestion to her in the postobservation conference, it would be as to how she might maintain those high expectations. Perhaps I might give her some options for working with students.

Topics in a preobservation conference may be related to internal feelings or behavior, such as "I want to know if my underlying feelings about Erica are coming through when I call on her." Or "I'm into total burnout, and I want some feedback on ways I can rejuvenate myself and my teaching practices."

Topics may be more student or classroom specific, such as designing coherent instruction, creating effective learning activities, improving pause time and pacing of instruction, or refining classroom management.

Once a coaching relationship has developed to the point where there is mutual trust and assurance that each is being as open and authentic as possible, the coach can ask questions that go deeper and uncover more of the coachee's thoughts, feelings, and behaviors. I have adapted questions to education, known as probing questions, from examples used by Susan Scott (2002) in her powerful book *Fierce Conversations*:

- "What has become clear since last we met?"
- "What is the area that, if you made an improvement, would give you and others the greatest benefit?"
- "What is currently impossible to do, which if it were possible, would change everything?"
- "What are you trying to make happen in the next three months?"
- "What is the most important decision you are facing?"
- "What's keeping you from making it?"
- "What topic are you hoping I won't bring up?"
- "What area under your responsibility are you most satisfied with? Least satisfied with?"
- "What part of your responsibilities are you avoiding right now?"
- "Who are your strongest students?"
- "What are you doing to ensure these students continue to be motivated?"
- "Who are your weakest students?"
- "What is your plan for these students?"
- "What conversations are you avoiding right now?"
- "What do you wish you had more time to do?"
- "What things are you doing that you would like to stop doing or delegate to someone else?"
- "If you were chosen to give input to your district, what advice would you give?"
- "What threatens you?"

CONSISTENT AND UNPREDICTABLE

It is important in a coaching relationship for the coach to be both consistent and unpredictable. Say, what? Being consistent means maintaining a safe environment based on always following the norms established between the coach and the coachee at the initial session. To the coach, there are no wrong answers. Support remains consistent within the relationship and throughout the process.

The unpredictable part comes from the questions themselves. The coachee never knows in advance what the questions will be or where they will lead. This keeps the coachee fresh, alert, and poised to think and feel honestly. Unpredictable questions set the foundation for coachees to reflect and to probe their thinking—ditto for students, by the way.

In an evaluation there is predictability; the teacher basically follows the map, does the expected, and can probably predict what the evaluation will say. In a coaching session, the goal is to achieve a higher order of thinking. The coach wants the coachee to stretch, to be creative, to dig for thoughts and ideas, and to share values and beliefs. Consistent support and mutual trust are the framework within which unpredictable questions evoke unpredictable answers to form new learning and fresh ideas.

LISTENING SKILLS REVISITED

In chapter 4 we looked at the importance of the coach having good listening skills. In a preobservation conference in particular, the coach should listen well enough to be able to complete three phrases:

"You believe that . . ."
"My *focus* when I observe you should be . . ."
"I should notice . . ."

At a minimum, the coach needs to ask and get answers to the first two phrases. Uncovering the coachee's beliefs remains a crucial part of coaching. Likewise, maintaining focus on what the teacher wants to be coached on is a key element in the coaching process.

If a coach can answer those two questions, he or she has permission to go into the classroom to observe the teacher. The two statements speak to the coachee's agenda, vision, and focus. If neither can be completed, the process of observation reverts to evaluating, not coaching.

The third phrase, "I should notice . . . ," is aimed at aspects of the coachee's behaviors or performance that are important to him or her and perhaps wouldn't get mentioned without the prompt. The teacher may want the coach to notice, for example, how he or she laughs with the students. A careful observation based on the teachers' concerns results in appreciation and gratitude on the part of the teacher.

The third phrase falls within the realm of "Well, since you asked, you might notice . . ." That can be anything from how the bulletin boards appear to looks on children's faces, to whether or not the coachee appears professional in front of the classroom or in a meeting. It may also be useful to notice the way the teacher uses his or her preferred learning style or how he or she rotates among learning styles to better reach all students in the class.

I call this last phrase the "extra credit" statement. If the coach points out something he or she noticed that is important to the coachee, good feedback results, and rapport, relationship, and trust improve. To be able to give this feedback, of course, the coach needs an understanding of the coachee's agenda and vision as established by the types of questions we have learned about already. Also, noticing shows the coach was listening.

Taking Notes

Taking notes during a preobservation conference also indicates the coach is listening, and it helps the coach remember the vocabulary or terminology the coachee uses. While evaluators use words of the system, coaches use the words of the people they are coaching. The same goes for learning and working styles.

Here's an example.

Evaluator: "Your materials were developmentally appropriate." (This terminology mirrors the words of the system.)

Coach: "You lit a flame! The kids loved it." (This mirrors words that the teacher had used in the preobservation conference as noted by the coach.)

I often suggest that the coach and coachee sit side by side in the preobservation conference as the coach takes notes about what the coachee wants observed. Once again, it builds trust as the teacher can see exactly what the coach is planning on recording during the observation. There is no mystery.

Sometimes the coach draws a diagram if the teacher wants a record of her movements around the room or the pattern of calling on students. The coach may also use a flow chart, indicating what the coachee says he or she wants to cover at various points in a lesson. Or the coach may simply take notes during the preobservation conference reflecting what the teacher is saying so the coach knows the focus of the upcoming observation.

Another coaching model that improves the preobservation conference can be illustrated by an equilateral triangle with the word "content" on one line, "theory" on another, and "skills/practice" on the third (see chapter 6, figure 6.2). The sides of the triangle represent three general teaching areas that are not necessarily as equal in reality as the triangle suggests. Sometimes they differ greatly. The coach and coachee can look at the triangle and together decide which of the three areas best represents the teacher's strengths. For instance, the teacher may know the content perfectly without being totally confident in teaching theories; or the teacher may have a great deal of classroom skills practice but not be confident in subject and content.

The coach and coachee identify together the "long" and "short" sides of the triangle for the coachee before the conference. As we shall see in chapter 7, this triangle gives coaches a model from which they can work in the postobservation conference after having observed the teacher in action.

PREOBSERVATION CONFERENCE: REAL-LIFE EXAMPLE

To gain a picture of what a preobservation conference looks and sounds like, I'd like to walk you through a coaching situation that occurred in Cranford High School in Cranford, New Jersey. This example is interesting because the coach and the coachee switched roles back and forth, each serving as each other's coach. This is not uncommon, and the relationship evolved naturally, partly due to shared interests.

While this example involves high school teachers, the same process would apply to elementary school teachers, principals, administrators, or others in a coaching program. Questions elicit information on which action is taken. Only the types of questions and the answers that drive the action vary from one coaching relationship to another.

Barbara Carroll is a language arts supervisor and an English teacher at Cranford High School, a suburban school with approximately a thousand students. She has taught for twenty-six years and has been a supervisor for seven. Barbara is coaching Karen Bailin, also an English teacher, who has taught for twenty-eight years. Karen came to see Barbara at their designated time, and the conference went something like this:

Barbara: "Hi Karen. How are you today?"

Karen: "I'm great. I had a full week with lots of projects both at school and at home. That's been great, except I am completely bogged down with paperwork, Barbara."

Barbara: "You're feeling a little overwhelmed with the administrative side of teaching."

Karen: "It's not so much the administrative paperwork required by the principal or district. That's actually doable. It's the inordinate amount of paperwork generated for and from the students. I have essays to grade, questions to write. I also write up study or focus questions as I read the books they're required to read. I just feel swamped in paper."

Barbara: "Yes, that's a departmentwide issue. I completely understand your feelings. I have twenty-seven students of my own, and I think I'm pushing papers more than teaching."

Karen: "That's exactly how I feel. I know the test questions and grading have to go on, and I just find that too much of my time is taken up in that."

Barbara: "What options do you have?"

Karen: "I actually wondered if the students couldn't do some of this themselves!"

Barbara: "You want the students to take over some of the paperwork."

Karen: "Well, either that, or have fewer essays or fewer questions or tests."

Barbara: "The essays you put together are valuable, Karen, and I know you believe they are terrific teaching tools that elicit quality answers."

Karen: "Yes, that's true. So what about having the students do some of the grading or questions—not their own papers, but others in the class."

Barbara: "In what ways would that impact your teaching?"

Karen: "It would free me up."

Barbara: "You'd have more free time to . . ."

Karen: "I'd have time to be innovative, Barbara. I don't feel like I have the time to be creative, innovative, come up with new and important work for the students because I'm too busy with paperwork."

Barbara: "From what I'm hearing, your issue is not so much that you feel there is too much paperwork, but that the paperwork has taken precedence over your ability to innovate—to be the creative teacher I know you want to be."

Karen: "Exactly!"

Barbara: "How do you see this evolving then?"

Karen: "Well, we have to read a book or two in class. I wondered if I could group the students and have one or two be responsible for coming up with a quiz for the others—maybe one student does it for one chapter, and one for another, and so forth."

Barbara: "You'd delegate some of the questions and quizzes to your students."

Karen: "Yes, and they could also grade each other's quizzes. That would take a lot off me."

Barbara: "My students are seniors in Advanced Placement, as you know, and I could readily see the possibilities in my class. Your students are juniors in an enriched class, and I wonder if you can predict how this might go over with your class."

Karen: "I haven't ironed out all the details, obviously, since we just came up with this. Yet I think it has merit, don't you?"

Barbara: "What's your feeling about it?"

Karen: "I'm excited. I think it has merit. They might learn a tremendous amount from one another, and in the process allow me to probe deeper, provide more insights as they move along. We just need to come up with a clear-cut plan."

Barbara: "You want me to design this with you?"

Karen: "Yes. And maybe we could do it with your class first, Barbara. You have a point about your students being more advanced. If it flubs in your class, there would not be as much damage as there would be in mine."

Barbara: "What makes you feel that way?"

Karen: "Your students would work with this as an interesting experiment in how to cover the trends or points in a book. They might lend some excellent ideas to our design once we come up with it."

Barbara: "You're afraid your students won't be ready."

Karen: "I think they would go for it. I just want you to try it out first!"

Barbara: "The idea is an excellent one, Karen. I'm willing to have my class try it out first. Would that make you feel more confident trying it out in your class?"

Karen: "Definitely. I would like your help and your ideas in developing the lesson design. Then we'll see how it works with your class, tweak the design a little, and try it in mine."

Barbara: "How will we know it is working?"

Karen: "How about I coach you while you deliver it. I'll observe your class, serve as your coach on this lesson. What do you think of that?"

Barbara: "It's fine with me!"

Karen: "Great! Let's do this: I'll map out what I have in conceptual form about breaking the students into groups, how they will develop questions for quizzes and some method of grading. Then let's get together and work out the details so we can begin with your class by the end of the month. How does that sound?"

Barbara: "Sounds great. I'll be thinking of ideas as well. I know your class will be reading *Brave New World*. I'm ambitious this year and hope to cover three books, so this may be a way to do that. And you'll have to take three books into account when you come up with your ideas. Me too."

Karen: "Okay. And I think the system works either way. When shall we meet for our preobservation conference?"

Barbara intended to have her Advanced Placement students read and discuss Joseph Heller's *Catch-22*, Ken Kesey's *One Flew over the Cuckoo's Nest*, and Margaret Atwood's *The Handmaid's Tale*. Barbara and Karen came up with a plan whereby students in Barbara's class were divided into three groups. The books were read and studied by each group, one at a time—that is, each group studied the same book at the same time before moving on.

Within each group, two or three students were responsible for covering a specific section of the book—say, three chapters. Before the assignment to read these chapters was given to the whole class, these students developed a quiz for the others based on the first three chapters. Barbara reviewed the quizzes they developed a day or two before the class. She discussed them with the smaller groups of students who later administered the quiz to the others in the class to ensure they had finished the three chapters that were assigned by the due date.

One group was assigned the task of modeling how and what they were going to discuss in their group. They made their presentation to the rest of the class before the discussions began. The core group of students—two or three per group—introduced the topic that they intended to cover that day, and the rest of the class could hear what they were going to be doing.

Barbara would give these students some ideas to model the kinds of questions that would generate discussion, but otherwise the students came up with the topics. Some included discussing a character or characters; others used the theme of reality versus illusion in their section of the book; still others asked their group to identify three main ideas of the book to discuss as a group.

The same two or three students who developed the quizzes would lead the discussion, facilitating it so that all participated. These students would be graded on the quality of the quizzes they developed, the discussion questions they generated, how well they led the group discussion, and how they graded the quizzes, which they took home with them.

Every student in the class would have a chance to perform the role of facilitating the group discussion, including development of quizzes, discussion questions, and grading papers. The groups rotated the presentation of what they would be discussing to the rest of the class.

Barbara and Karen agreed it would be important to model this lesson to the class before they formed the groups and began the process. Because the students were divided into groups with a core team of students taking over several chapters at a time, the students should be able to cover three books in the same amount of time as one. Barbara would monitor the quizzes, questions, and graded papers, but otherwise the students were on their own.

It occurred to Karen and Barbara as they worked on this design that the students who were not "working" on preparing lessons, quizzes, or discussion questions, could read for pleasure. While students developing the discussion questions and quizzes would be making notes, identifying themes, and otherwise reading their sections of the book as the teacher might, the others could simply enjoy the book and await the discussion questions and quizzes developed by their fellow students.

As an added bonus, Barbara avoided having to do the prep work and paperwork involved in teaching all three books.

Barbara and Karen are experienced teachers and coaches. That is what made them readily able to collaborate on problem solving in their preobservation conference—they've done this before. More often, when coaches start out, the preobservation conference serves to uncover the agenda and focus of the person being coached—and that's it. This is perfectly acceptable. The coachee may have as a focus reaching all learning styles, and the agenda may be to have the coach count the times the teacher rotated the style. Working out a problem about that issue would not typically be part of this type of discussion, as the focus is specific and can be readily noticed in the observation. From that, any "problems" can be defined and discussed.

Problem solving often occurs in a postobservation conference, which in turn evolves into a new *pre*observation conference. In other words, once a problem is identified in the observation and discussed in the postobservation conference, the coachee may ask the coach to observe a specific teaching skill in the *next* observation to address the initial problem. This has now become a new preobservation conference. Another observation occurs, and in the postobservation, they see how everything is moving along, improving, being resolved, or needing more work. Coaching, in short, evolves into an ongoing process of discovery, discussion, and improvement. The bottom line—it's a far cry from straight supervision.

In chapter 6, we'll see how Barbara and Karen's lesson played out during the observation of the lesson. For now, know that the preobservation conference is where coach and teacher can home in on exactly what the teacher wants to accomplish and what he or she wants the coach to observe.

SUMMARY

Questioning skills used in the preobservation conference elicit the value, focus, beliefs, and mission of the teacher as well as the specific agenda for a lesson plan, behavior, discipline issue, or any other facet of teaching. The preobservation conference can also serve to problem solve, develop creative ideas, synthesize thoughts that result in innovation to motivate, share, grow, and raise the bar in professional teaching.

Setting norms at the outset helps solidify the relationship, particularly the trust level. Working to identify a problem before trying to solve it goes a long way toward bringing the real issue to the surface. In Barbara and Karen's case the problem was "too much paperwork." Yet as Barbara probed further in her role as coach, it turned out the real problem was Karen's frustration at not being able to use her creativity and innovation.

A coach who remains supportive, consistent with the norms established, and consistent in the approach taken to uncover the teacher's agenda becomes free to be unpredictable in questioning. As we have seen in the examples, this unpredictability leads to refreshing ideas, new thought processes—what Oprah Winfrey calls "hallelujah moments."

Let's move to the "performance" now, the actual observation of a teacher teaching, an administrator facilitating a meeting, a coachee building confidence, or any of the myriad events that coaches can observe and on which they can provide feedback.

RESEARCH SHOWS

Learning Styles

- Research shows varying teaching strategies to address all sensory preferences increases learning, regardless of the individual student's primary preference (Eiszler, 1983; Thomas, Cox, & Kojima, 2000). Using varied multisensory techniques has been shown to increase achievement among slow learners who had not progressed with conventional strategies (Eiszler, 1983).
- "The work of Rita Dunn and Kenneth Dunn over an extended period, as well as an extensive study on the Dunn and Dunn studies by M. H. Sullivan, find both attitude and achievement gains when teachers address students' learning styles through flexible teaching. Likewise, numerous researchers report achievement gains when culture-based and gender-based learning preferences are attended to in the classroom" (Tomlinson, 2009, p. 30).
- Younger generations tend to prefer interactive media and interaction in collaborative groups. The prime learning time for Generation X is in the evening (Coates, 2007).
- "Gen Y is tech savvy and their love of technology allows them to adapt to technological advances of training design. Gen Y is responsible for the surge in online training. Discussion forums, instant messaging, blogging and emailing are not only expected in training design, [they are] becoming an integral part of the design. These communication tools allow for collaboration" (Rose, 2007).

6

The Observation

OBSERVATION: A REAL-LIFE EXAMPLE

Room 672 houses an Advanced Placement English class on the second floor of Cranford High School. The room is cheerful and brightly decorated with colorful posters. One poster shows actor Jack Nicholson in an advertisement for the 1975 film *One Flew over the Cuckoo's Nest*. Pictures of military equipment posted on the bulletin board reflect the atmosphere of Joseph Heller's novel *Catch-22*. Hand-drawn posters on the wall depict scenes from Margaret Atwood's novel *The Handmaid's Tale*.

These decorations display the work students accomplished as they studied the three novels during the school year. On this particular day, they are prepped to complete their work on the third novel, *One Flew over the Cuckoo's Nest*.

A group of students—group A—is seated in a circle at the front of the room, facing the class. The teacher, Barbara Carroll, stands at the blackboard behind group A. Her coach, Karen Bailin, has located herself in a straight chair at the back of the room. She's holding a small clipboard and pen.

Michelle, a student in group A, hands out printed quizzes to each student in the class. The students take five minutes to complete the quiz, which demonstrates they have read the assigned chapters of *One Flew over the Cuckoo's Nest*. Michelle collects the quizzes and puts them in her notebook.

Manuel, another member of group A, stands and asks the students to count off by threes. Amid a clattering and scraping of desks and chairs the students group themselves into three circles, forming groups B, C, and D.

Michelle and Manuel then explain to each group the three topics they are to cover in their discussion of the chapters they have been assigned. Michelle and Manuel, as part of group A, previously developed the quizzes and read all three sections of the book they were asking the others to read. Michelle and Manuel collaborated and developed three discussion questions to pose to the other groups: reality versus illusion, a specific character, and three main ideas in the section. To begin the process Michelle asks the students in groups B, C, and D to discuss the question of reality versus illusion as it arises in the section they have read. Manuel asks one person in each group to volunteer to be recorder and note the ideas his or her group develops and to report to the rest of the class when the discussion is completed.

Michelle hands out the question about reality and illusion to all four groups, and the discussions within each group begin.

The teacher, Barbara, had previously approved the quiz and the discussion questions developed by Michelle and Manuel. She moves around the room listening to the discussions, making herself available should questions or confusion arise.

Her coach, Karen Bailin, also moves around the room, trying to discern whether or not the students are delving into the topic sufficiently, whether the question posed elicits commentary that shows reading comprehension, and how much the students seem to be learning. She notes which students are actively participating and which remain quiet. Karen notices crossover discussions: A student from group B overhears comments from group C and introduces them in group B's discussion.

At one point, Karen and Barbara look at one another and smile. The room brims with lively discussion, excitement, and enthusiasm. Students are engaged and motivated.

After engaging in their group discussion, members of group A stand to bring the class back to order. They call on each of the recorders from groups B, C, and D to hear what they discussed regarding reality and illusion. Following these reports, Michelle and Manuel move to the next topic to be discussed (a specific character) and the process begins again.

By all accounts, the reading project Barbara and her coach Karen discussed in many preobservation conferences (and that we "heard" in chapter 5) appears to have paid off. Paperwork was reduced; that goal was met. When Karen observed Barbara in the classroom, she was able to validate that the goals of reducing paperwork while improving student involvement, excitement, and learning had been met.

How well had the students learned? Karen's observations and Barbara's feedback as well as written reflections by students will be discussed in chapter 7, where we will look at the postobservation conference. The preceding scene, however, illustrates what the observation process might look and sound like, based on Barbara and Karen's initial coaching session and the ideas generated by it.

EXPERTISE OF COACHES

We looked previously at the important differences among evaluators, supervisors, and peer coaches. Central to those differences are the trust and knowledge a coach has about when, how, where, and why to observe a coachee, whether in a classroom, meeting, or client presentation. As we have said before, in a school setting if a "coach" walks in to observe a classroom unannounced and uninvited, it's not coaching. It's evaluation or supervision.

Considering the level of expertise on a continuum (see figure 6.1), a coach who serves as an observer only—what I call "eyes, ears, and skin"—is at one end; a coach with expertise on the content on which the teacher has requested coaching is at the opposite end. Both are experts.

The observer is an expert at observing and collecting the data the teacher requested. The coach with content expertise may offer information beyond what was observed, such as classroom management skills or cooperative learning techniques. As an example, a twenty-year veteran teacher may serve as coach to a beginning teacher with specific areas of expertise.

I once served as an eyes, ears, and skin observation-only coach. I was asked to coach a teacher delivering her lesson entirely in French. She asked that I note which of the students responded to her queries and how often. I sat at the back of the class with a layout of the classroom and ticked off which students responded and how often they did so. Not knowing a word of French, I had no idea what the students said or whether the technique was effective. I was simply eyes, ears, and skin (in the sense of being present), collecting data.

In our Cranford, New Jersey, example both teachers were English teachers. Karen was able to serve as an expert coach of Barbara's content, and vice versa. In addition to commenting on content, Karen could coach on strategies or student behaviors. If, however, Karen had been a math teacher, it's possible Barbara would have asked her to recommend someone else to coach that particular lesson. In fact, one's "regular" coach can, if need be, recommend another coach if the content is not within his or her realm of expertise and the coachee has questions about delivery of content.

Observes Only
"eyes, ears, and skin"

**Content
Expertise**

Figure 6.1. Levels of Expertise

CONTENT, THEORY, AND SKILLS/PRACTICE

In the preobservation conference it's important to uncover and focus on areas in which a teacher wants to be coached. The equilateral triangle in figure 6.2 shows content on one side, theory on the other, and skills/practice on the bottom.

The sides of the equilateral triangle represent three general areas of teaching. A teacher might be a whiz at classroom management and group dynamic skills (skills/practice) but lack significant knowledge in the areas of content and theory (triangle 1). Another teacher may know more about content and theory and less about skillfully managing a classroom (triangle 2). Still others may fall short in skills and practice and even shorter in knowledge of teaching theory, yet know their content (triangle 3).

To build up the short side of a teacher's triangle, the coach can question the teacher in the preobservation conference, identify strengths in the observation, and then work with the teacher to improve during postobservation, according to a plan agreed upon between coach and teacher.

Skills / Practice

Source: B. Othanel Smith

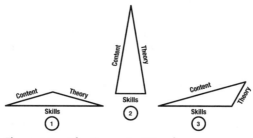

Figure 6.2.   The Competent Teacher

In the preobservation conference, coach and teacher identify the agenda, the focus, the how, when, and where of the coaching agreement. This can be as specific as where the teacher wants the coach to sit or stand in the room, or as broad as observing the teacher's level of professionalism.

Often coaches and teachers develop forms or rubrics in the preobservation conference that coaches will use while observing. As they sit side by side in the preobservation conference, coach and coachee can together work up a plan as shown on a worksheet that will serve them both in the observation process.

LENGTH OF AN OBSERVATION

An important point about the observation process: frequent observations are often more important than long observations. I find it more effective to have a coach observe for as little as ten minutes if the teacher is working on a specific skill. Visits should be short but more frequent if they are to reinforce a skill. Often coaching programs get bogged down because coaches do not feel they can afford to spend an entire class period with their coachee. They don't need to. A short visit with immediate postobservation feedback has proven more effective than long, infrequently held visits.

OBSERVING TEACHERS USING QUESTIONING SKILLS

In chapter 4, we looked at various questioning skills used by coaches. Teachers also strive to employ good questioning skills in the classroom. Since a primary coaching skill involves asking good questions, these skills are an excellent focus for an observation.

A Consciously Skilled coach (as illustrated on Gordon's Ladder) is able to break down one of his or her own complex skills into teachable steps. This mirrors what a skilled teacher does when explaining concepts or breaking down information for students. The same question-and-answer process applies to both teaching and coaching.

One of the proficiencies used most in schools is asking students questions rather than feeding them answers. We want to know what they recall from what they have studied. We want their opinions, their predictions, and their ideas. We want to hear how they analyze and evaluate. We ask them to summarize. Asking questions is an art—an elegant art. When looking at the art of asking questions, we can break that proficiency into learnable skills. Just as the coach is proficient in asking questions that elicit a coachee's creativity, values, or personal information, a teacher can be proficient in questioning students by asking questions in four different modes: memory, comprehension, creative, and evaluation.

Figure 6.3 indicates how this skill can be broken down from the complex to the simple through these four questioning modes. A teacher then may ask the coach to observe the questioning modes he or she used, and track how students responded.

Using table 6.1 the coach can identify when and how often the questions asked by the teacher were memory, comprehension, creative, or evaluation questions. The coach produces a map or record of the use of these questions and the responses of students while he or she is observing the teacher.

Student Answers, Teacher Responses

A teacher might also want to improve how he or she responds to student answers. There are four basic methods of responding to a student's answer. A teacher can praise, accept, remediate, or criticize.

Here again, the coach can chart during an observation how often the teacher responds in each way and what reactions are received from the students. Recording student reactions is an important part of the observation process. While coachees teaching alone may be aware of how often they respond with praise or criticism or a combination of both, coaches can observe students' reactions. Often the teacher moves on to the next task, question, or response without appearing to notice the student's response.

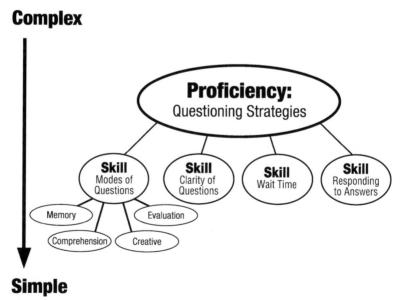

Figure 6.3.   The Proficiency of Questioning

Table 6.1. Identifying Modes of Questioning

Questioning Mode	Thinking or Information Sought	When Students Answer They . . .
Memory	Recognition, recall	Recall
Comprehension	Interpret, apply, analyze	Recall, use
Creative	New ideas, solutions	Recall, use, create
Evaluation	Opinions, judgments	Recall, use, decide why

The coach's eye can linger longer and pick up nonverbal feedback from the student, make a note of it, and share that data with the teacher. Here is an example:

> A teacher poses a question in a math lesson. The question posed is a memory question: "Students, how many quarts are in a gallon?"
>
> Hands are raised; the teacher pauses appropriately and calls on Frances, who eagerly says, "Six!"
>
> The teacher pauses another second and then responds to Frances by saying, "Now, Frances. Remember when we talked about this yesterday? Think again and see if you can come up with the correct answer."
>
> Frances is silent, staring straight ahead. "Anyone else?" asks the teacher. "George?" George responds correctly with "Four." "Very good, George!"
>
> The coach is observing the teacher's body language, the way she questions, and the facial expressions and body language of Frances and George. The coach notices that Frances appears embarrassed and George looks smug. The coach notes these for later feedback.

A summary of the interaction between students and teacher, while valuable to the teacher being coached, remains nonetheless subjective, as the coach might interpret body language and gestures of students that the teacher did not—or could not—even see. Beyond this subjective observation, which provides the teacher with good feedback, the coach might also chart clear and more obvious responses to questions posed in one class session, like the examples shown in tables 6.2 and 6.3.

Table 6.2. Sample Response Chart

Teacher Response to Student Answer	Frequency
Praise	4
Acceptance	15
Remediation	10
Criticism	6

Table 6.3.   Expanded Sample Response Chart

Praise	Accept	Remediate	Criticize	Unsure
Awesome!	Okay.	Not quite.	No.	Like we did yesterday.
You've got it.	Yes.	That's close.	That's incorrect.	
Exactly.	Go on. Hmmm . . .	Not exactly.	Wrong answer.	

Collecting data in this way provides an objective look at what happened and eliminates any subjectivity. Note that one column is marked "Unsure." This means the coach was unsure about how to categorize the response; these entries merit further discussion by coach and coachee.

John Goodlad (1984) says in *A Placed Called School* that acknowledging students empowers them and builds their self-esteem. The more praise, approval, and acceptance students receive, the more likely they are to be motivated to learn (p. 108). "Learning appears to be enhanced when students understand what is expected of them, get recognition for their work, learn quickly about their errors, and receive guidance in improving their performances" (p. 112).

Certainly the student gets it wrong sometimes, and yet isn't the effort worth a modicum of praise? Here's another way the teacher in our example might have responded to Frances' answer about the number of quarts in a gallon:

"Students, how many quarts are in a gallon?"

Hands are raised; the teacher pauses appropriately and calls on Frances, who eagerly says, "Six!"

The teacher pauses another second and then responds to Frances by saying, "That's a good try, Frances. You're close. Can you think back to when we talked about this yesterday? There were a lot of different numbers among pints, quarters, and gallons. Can you remember how many quarts went into a gallon?"

Frances is silent, staring straight ahead.

The teacher then says, "Okay. It will come to you. Thanks for responding. Can anyone help Frances out and remember how many quarts are in a gallon? George?"

George responds correctly with "Four."

"Very good, George! Do you remember now, Frances?"

Frances smiles and slaps her forehead with her hand, as if to say, "Of course, I knew that!" The teacher laughs gently and moves on.

With practice, responding with praise and approval becomes innate. The teacher immediately looks for something to commend the student on before making a correction or moving on to another student.

If the teacher being coached wants to improve his or her response mode, he or she works with the coach in the next preobservation conference to cite a goal. The teaching is then observed, and the coach notes the frequency of responses as before. In the postobservation conference, they go over the data and the coach can help the teacher practice reframing responses to include some form of praise or approval for the student.

Charting Answers and Responses

Another method the coach can use to chart a teacher's responses to student answers is to re-create the layout of the classroom with student names and indicate with initials the kinds of responses the teacher gave, as shown in figure 6.4.

The chart in figure 6.4 is an easy way to record the response (acceptance, remediation, criticism, or praise) to each child by the teacher.

Having objective data to work with, the coachee can become more consciously aware of "the numbers" as he or she responds to student answers. Reviewing this feedback with the coach, the teacher begins to see how praise works to increase participation and motivation on the part of the students. This could also be readily apparent in a videotaped lesson. Having the coach collect data on the responses given only augments the empirical data.

The number of techniques, strategies, skills, designs, lessons, and professional behaviors to be coached through observation and feedback are endless. Here are a few examples of teacher behaviors that could be the topic of observation:

Gender bias
Pause periods
Modes of questions
Other biases
Use of humor
Responses to students
Nonverbal communication
Handling student behavior
Behavior in cooperative learning activities
Learning styles being reached
Multiple intelligences being reached
Strongest (and weakest) teaching styles
Congruency
Effective questioning skills
Classroom management
Experiential learning experiences
Effective lesson planning

Student behaviors and lesson characteristics are also important areas to observe. At times it is important to simply observe other teachers teaching

Codes: P = Praise
A = Acceptance
R = Remediation
C = Criticism

Alexia

A

Michelle

P, A

Cameron

P, A

Yolanda

P, A

Ryan

A

Adam

A, A
A

Olivia

C, A

Michael

A

Jose

Angel

C, R

Jill

A, A

Kendall

Vashti

Maria

Rosa

R

Chan

A, A
P, A

Figure 6.4. Teacher's Responses to Students

(with no coaching involved), just to get ideas for one's own teaching, such as an observation of another special needs classroom or another English or history class. For a thorough list, see figure 6.5, Options for Observation and Coaching.

OPTIONS FOR OBSERVATION AND COACHING

A successful postobservation conference relies on collecting the data requested in the preobservation conference. Certainly everyone wants approval, and kudos such as "Good job!" or "You did fine!" are always welcome. Yet they are not much help to a teacher wanting specifics on how to improve a specific skill. A combination of empirical data—observing firsthand what teachers did and said and the responses they received—as well as charts or graphs (statistics) that log instances of particular skills being used that can provide substantial assistance in changing a coachee's behavior. (See a thorough list of options for observations and coaching on pages 112 through 116, figure 6.5.)

TRACKING TEACHER AND STUDENT MOVEMENTS

Figure 6.6, on page 117, shows yet another method for tracking teacher behavior. Here the coach developed a replication of the classroom and charted the teacher's physical movements, the students' movements, and the order in which each occurred. Much like a football coach's outline of the team's "plays," this chart reflects each movement, and the teacher can see graphically just what occurred and when.

Both subjective and objective feedback are reviewed in the postobservation conference. The coach reveals what he or she observed and felt, and also exactly what happened, how often, or in what order. Feedback and coaching in the postobservation conference carries over to the next preobservation conference (discussed in chapter 7).

The observation phase occurs between the pre- and postobservation conferences. The coachee's real performance, practice, self-accounting, and coaching is observed as the teacher goes through the paces of whatever skill, technique, strategy, or behavior he or she wants to improve. See figure 7.3 in chapter 7, a feedback form completed in the observation phase, but used in postobservation to provide the coachee with feedback.

PROFESSIONAL BEHAVIOR: CONFIDENT DEMEANOR

Having made the point that objective data is important for defining discrete skills, there is also a place in coaching for the coachee to improve his or

The following is a partial list of options for observations and coaching. There are many more possibilities.

Teacher Behaviors

1. Gender Bias
   a. How many times do I call on males versus females?
   b. What types of questions do I ask males versus females?
   c. How many times do I offer help to males versus females?

2. Pause Periods
   a. How long do I pause before calling on a student?
   b. How long do I pause after calling on a student?
   c. How long do I pause after a student answers?

3. Modes of Questions
   a. How many times do I use memory questions versus higher-level questions?
   b. In what order do I ask various types of questions?
   c. Do I ask certain types of questions of some students and not of others?

4. Other Biases
   a. Do I show favoritism to loud versus quiet students, funny versus serious students, highly-verbal versus less-verbal students, high-achieving versus low-achieving students, etc.?
   b. Is there a difference between the way I treat students in one class period or activity and another period or activity?

5. Use of Humor
   a. Does my use of humor add or detract from my lesson? If it detracts in any way, how can I change how I use it?
   b. Is my humor tinged with sarcasm?
   c. Where in the period or lesson could I use more humor?

6. Responses to Students
   a. Which do I use the most when responding to students: praise, approval, acceptance, remediation, or criticism?
   b. Positive reinforcement: Do I give enough? Is it varied? Do I give it to all students? Does it sound sincere?

(continued)

Figure 6.5. Options for Observation and Coaching

7. Nonverbal Communication
   a. When gesturing, how often do I use a pointing finger or an open palm?
   b. What do I do with my hands when I teach?
   c. Do I use a sarcastic tone of voice when responding to any students?
   d. To what students and areas of the room do I give eye contact?
   e. Do I move to all areas of the classroom during one class period?

8. Handling Student Behavior
   a. What could I do to better respond to _____ [student's name]?
   b. Are there things going on with students that I am not aware of?

9. Teacher Behavior During Cooperative Learning Activities
   a. Am I using appropriately sized configurations for the types of activities I assign?
   b. When I assign groups an interpersonal skill to work on, do the students understand how the skill will look and sound in their groups?
   c. Am I entering groups only when necessary?
   d. Am I allowing groups to solve their own problems?

10. Learning Styles/Intelligences
    a. What learning styles am I reaching with my presentations?
    b. What intelligences am I reaching with my presentations?
    c. What are my strongest (and weakest) teaching styles?
    d. Are there students with certain styles whom I am not reaching?

Student Behaviors

1. Focus of Attention
   a. Are students engaged in lessons? When? Which students?
   b. Are students showing signs of boredom? When? Which students?
   c. Are there things in the classroom or in my presentations which cause students to be distracted or bored?

2. Student Reactions
   a. How do students respond to my use of humor?
   b. Are there negative student responses which I am missing?
   c. Do most students seem engaged when I am making presentations?

3. Problem Students
   a. How can I respond more positively to _____ [student name]?
   b. What is a better way for me to handle the group of students in the back of the room who get off-task?

(continued)

Figure 6.5.   (*continued*)

4. Student Performance
   a. Is there something I can do to get _____ [student name] more engaged in learning?
   b. Do you see ways in which I can engage more students in this lesson?
   c. Am I doing anything which might intimidate students and keep them from responding verbally during class?
   d. Are there any students who are intimidated by other students, causing them to do less than their best?

Lesson Characteristics

1. Format
   a. What changes can I make in the order in which I present the elements of this lesson to engage more students?
   b. How is the way in which I present this lesson "turning off" students?
   c. Am I reaching my objectives with this lesson?
   d. Would it be better to demonstrate how to do_____ at the beginning or in the middle of the period?

2. Materials
   a. What visual aids could I use to enhance this lesson?
   b. What could I use that would make this lesson more real life for my students?
   c. What could I use to make this lesson more active?

3 Activities
   a. How could I turn this lesson into a simulation?
   b. How could I use role-plays to teach this material?
   c. What types of activities would get the point of this lesson across better than those I am using?
   d. I am going to try _____, which I have never done before. Please give me feedback on how well students seem to comprehend the information when I do this.

4. Sequence of Activities
   a. I want you to observe me teaching for two different class periods. I will be doing this lesson in two different ways. Give me feedback on the strengths and weaknesses of each approach.
   b. I want to reorder the activities in this lesson so students will internalize the information more quickly. What would be a better sequence for this purpose?

(continued)

Figure 6.5. (*continued*)

5. Content
   a. I have taught this lesson a number of times, and students still don't seem to understand it. What could I say or do that would improve comprehension?
   b. What information could I present to students about this topic which would interest them more than what I am presenting now?
   c. What real-life activities could I use to cover the curriculum and teach life skills?

6. Pace
   a. For which students do I present my lesson too quickly? Too slowly?
   b. Where in the lesson do I need to slow down and elaborate more? Where should I speed up?

7. Assessment
   a. What could I be adding to student portfolios that would give me more information for assessing this unit?
   b. What type of rubric could I create that would help students use self assessment during this unit?

Observations for Special Needs

1. Observe classes at your same grade level to get ideas for classroom management, how materials are presented, new activities, etc.

2. Observe classes at grade levels lower than yours to understand what content is being covered and how, before students come to you.

3. Observe someone in your same content area to get new ideas for how to present information, new activities, and new ways to review, test, assess, etc.

4. Observe teachers who are especially good at:
   a. Teaching to different learning styles/intelligences.
   b. Using visual aids.
   c. Doing live-event learning.
   d. Creating simulations.
   e. Using creative drama.
   f. Assigning portfolios.
   g. Using positive discipline.
   h. Orchestrating cooperative learning.
   i. Leading visualizations.
   j. Giving spell binding lectures.

(continued)

Figure 6.5.   (*continued*)

k. Using multimedia/computers/video/the Internet.
l. Questioning techniques and Questions for Life.
m. Using specific types of activities.
n. Storytelling.
o. Employing peer-helping tools (tutoring, study buddies, etc.).
p. Group testing.
q. Conducting reviews.
r. Playing learning games.
s. Teaching life skills throughout the curriculum.
t. Teaching note taking.
u. Employing strategies for ADD/ADHD.
v. Developing self-esteem.
w. Planning fund-raisers.
x. Teaching self-discipline and responsibility.
y. Modifying lessons for inclusion.
z. Doing creative activities.

5. Cross Curriculum/Grade Level Observations
   a. Observe a history teacher teaching about the time period in which one of your reading stories takes place.
   b. Hear what an English teacher has to say about plagiarism before assigning a term paper.
   c. Listen to a social studies teacher talk in-depth about certain current events before discussing them with your students.
   d. Have high school teachers observe elementary teachers to gain ideas for activities that add interest to lessons.
   e. Have elementary teachers observe high school teachers to see where their students are headed and what skills they are expected to have.

Figure 6.5. (*continued*)

Codes:
— ▪ — ▪ —➤ Students told to move

▪▪▪▪▪▪▪▪▪▪▪▶ Students move on-task

▪ ▪ ▪ ▪ ▪ ▪▶ Students move off-task

——————➤ Teacher movement

(1) Teacher / student exchanges

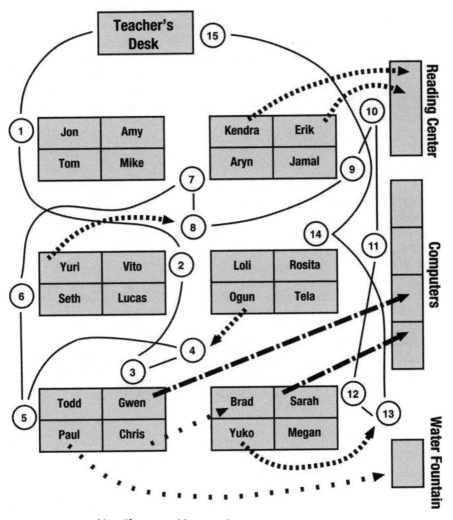

Figure 6.6. Tracking Classroom Movements

her confidence and self-esteem. Often a teacher wonders how his or her demeanor, assurance, attitude, trust, and image come across. Certainly these are all subjective observations on the part of the coach, yet the one being coached can ask for specific feedback on the impact his or her behavior, attitude, or demeanor has on others—how his or her professional image is projected and received.

Learning styles play a part in how a coach might observe a teacher. If the coach, for example, has a sensory preference as a visual learner, he or she might *see* things the teacher would not notice, such as students interacting or texting during class. Even when viewing a video recording of the session, teacher and coach might not see the same thing.

Likewise, an auditory coach would *hear* what a teacher misses. The teacher/coachee might have a tactual preference and *sense* the students' emotions during a lesson and, when discussing them with the coach in the postobservation conference, learn that the coach did not sense anything at all. The coach may be kinesthetic and note that the students with kinesthetic tendencies are not getting their learning needs met through movement, which might be lost on a teacher who does not have a kinesthetic preference.

The different temperaments—Intuitive Feeling, Intuitive Thinking, Sensing Judging, or Sensing Perceiving—play out in how the teacher or the coach perceives his or her world, abstractly or concretely, as described in chapter 5, as well as how he or she values learning. Communication before observation goes a long way toward turning differences into a synergy of strengths between coaching and coachee.

A coach can be a tremendous help in transforming otherwise uncomfortable, negative, or just plain tired behaviors or attitudes into shining examples of those held by true professionals. In other professions, life coaches use a variety of techniques to assist people to achieve goals in ways that enhance their performance in the world, attracting both people and prosperity to them naturally and with excitement and fun.

There is no reason why a teacher cannot benefit from improving his or her level of professionalism. Teachers need to feel assured they are getting the job done, that they are succeeding as professionals, that students are learning, that their ideas are well received, and that they are respected. Teachers, like all human beings, operate at their best when they feel confident; with high self-esteem and assurance, they can get the job done when they know they are trusted.

To find ways a coach can instill this sense of confidence and well-being in another professional, we need only to look to our brains! As noted in chapter 4, John Grinder and Richard Bandler developed neurolinguistic programming in the 1970s. This technology focuses on the art and science of personal excellence, developed by applying a method of coding and understanding successful behavior that can be replicated. Without delving into all the aspects of this theory, some basic elements can be used to coach coachees through a process to ramp up their success.

The first element addresses physiology. Physiology means body language. It encompasses the body's stance, its structure, how we hold ourselves. In the Triune Brain Theory, developed by pioneer brain researcher Dr. Paul MacLean (1978) and reported in his article "A Mind of Three Minds: Educating the Triune Brain," there are three areas of the brain: the reptilian area, or brain stem and cerebellum; the limbic or midbrain section, containing the amygdala, hippocampus, hypothalamus, pineal gland, and thalamus; and the neomammalian section, consisting of the cerebrum and neocortex—the frontal lobe.

Problem solving, planning, and critical thinking occur in the frontal lobe; the limbic brain primarily governs emotions. Several bodies of research on the limbic system show it as a primitive brain that, while it does not cognate, read, or write, nonetheless serves as an emotional compass indicating to us what is real, true, and important. Studies by Daniel Goleman in emotional intelligence indicate that emotions may be more important to success than higher-order thinking skills.

So what does all this mean for coaching? Put simply, our physiology mirrors our emotions. As such, our physiology can be altered to impact emotions. As an example, if your body is slumped over, head in hand, brow creased in worry, that stance both reflects and generates a certain internal emotion. In contrast, you can stand straight, shoulders broad, feet planted on floor, head up, a smile on your face, a laugh emanating from your mouth. That behavior reflects and also generates a different emotion. The words we choose and our voice intonation adds more information about our emotions and attitudes.

Our emotions influence our actions—we act one way in the slumped mode and another in the standing, smiling mode. Of course, whatever actions we take lead to results or achievement of the goals we established in our intellectual, frontal lobe of the brain.

The coach assists a coachee who wants a certain result by monitoring the coachee's body language, the emotion it reflects and generates, and therefore the action taken. This can certainly happen if the coach has brought to the surface the coachee's vision and focus. If a coachee wants to achieve a certain outcome or result in his or her presentation, the coach can assist by walking through the steps that rely on body movement, choice of words, and feeding back what the teacher believes about his or her abilities.

The Story of Ned

Let's look at an example to see how this brainy stuff can work. Ned Baxter taught middle school for nine years in a semirural community. He was a good teacher and enjoyed his work. His wife, Sally, was offered a wonderful opportunity to advance her career; it would mean they would have to move to a new location, a city. Ned learned that the only teaching job available to him was in an inner-city high school. They talked over their options and decided it would be worthwhile for both of them to move. Ned felt that while he had never taught high school, his skills as a teacher could easily translate.

He applied for and received the teaching job. He was unprepared for the huge differences he found between his semirural middle school children and the tough, inner-city high school students. They taunted him, laughed at him, were disrespectful, and barely obeyed his directions. He was at a loss as to how he could gain their respect.

Ned became intimidated, fearful. His self-esteem and confidence as a teacher was nearly shattered. He asked for and received permission to enter a coaching program at the school. His coach was Stan Johnson, a seasoned teacher and twenty-six-year veteran of the high school.

Ned and Stan spent several initial sessions getting to know one another and developing a trusting relationship. Stan then used the neurolinguistic programming theory to help Ned overcome the feelings he was having about teaching and his students, feelings that were clearly getting in the way of performing at his best.

In one session, Stan sat facing Ned, who was hunched forward with his hands clasped between his knees. His brow was furrowed and his body tense as he described a specific incident that had happened in his classroom earlier that day. His voice was weak, a little shaky, and he exuded exactly zero confidence.

Stan asked Ned to stand up. He told him to straighten his back, place his feet firmly on the floor about shoulder-distance apart. He told him to take some deep breaths and then smile, whether he felt like smiling or not. Ned did as he was told.

Then Stan asked Ned to talk about his teaching days back in the middle school. He asked him to describe the classroom, what he typically did on any given day, a lesson he conducted that was particularly powerful, or anything else he wanted to say, so long as it was a positive memory. Ned began to talk and shared—almost boasted—about what a good teacher he had been back then. He became animated, his stature grew, and he actually started feeling better.

Stan then asked him to share a successful story about his high school class, whether the situation had actually occurred or not. He told Ned to make it up if he had to, say how he might want it to be, all the while continuing to stand, relaxed, and solid. Ned again complied and found himself laughing as he made up a really preposterous story about how all the students in his class suddenly began applauding him, giving him a standing ovation.

By the end of the story, Ned actually felt happy, confident, relaxed. Stan suggested that he practice his body stance; start thinking about how he would like his class to react. He even suggested that Ned talk aloud, saying what he believed he could achieve—"My students have had a change of heart about me." "My class has come around so nicely. Everyone is now cooperating. We're actually having fun." "I'm a good teacher and they know it." "I've finally got the hang of teaching these high school kids!"

Stan's point was not that Ned needed to brainwash himself but rather to re-create in his body and his language and his emotions what it looked like, sounded like, and felt like to be confident, assured, and successful in his classroom and his teaching.

The theory is that as Ned practices the physiology and language along with a focus on the desired outcome—in short, once the brain and physiology have that performance pattern down pat—the resulting emotions will cause him to take actions to achieve his outcome. He will begin to talk to his students differently, use powerful and confident body language, say things in a different way to reflect his conviction that he is a good teacher and that he can teach these students as well.

With Stan supporting and coaching him, Ned practiced language and movement; he spoke aloud his beliefs about his abilities as a teacher, moving around the room with confidence and self-assurance. Sure, he felt silly at first. Yet he began to see it was paying off, if in no other way than in his emotional state. As his emotions improved, so too did his approach to his teaching, his students, his colleagues, and his wife. He was, as we mentioned in chapter 4, "faking it 'til he made it."

Stan observed Ned in his classroom frequently, for ten minutes or for thirty, depending on what Ned requested. As Stan watched Ned, he made notes about what he saw in Ned's body and the words Ned selected to use when teaching or giving directions. He made observations about the visual reaction his students had to Ned's confident approach. Not surprisingly, the student reaction was positive and reflective of Ned's "new" confidence as a teacher.

While this example does not speak to a specific skill or technique, what Ned really needed was some psychological coaching—someone to help him over a rough spot in his career. This kind of assistance not only helped Ned in his first year teaching in an inner-city high school but helped in the following years of his career. Whenever he found himself in an uncomfortable, unhappy state, he immediately noted his body stance. What was he doing? What could he do that would redirect the energy in his body? What emotion would serve him best? When he adjusted his body language, began using more effective language and vocabulary, the emotion would inevitably arrive to help him into action.

Observation of another's action and behavior, especially by someone whose whole purpose is to help that person succeed, is a valuable gift. It not only helps the teacher and coach but impacts students. They can see an improved teacher and thus improve their learning. So, as you can see, a coachee can ask to be observed on any number of techniques, skills, behaviors, or attitudes.

SUMMARY

The coach is invited into the classroom or boardroom to provide feedback and support on the exact things the coachee requested. Observations need not last long. Frequency often becomes preferable to duration, as it provides more feedback and thus reinforces the practice that helps the teacher or coachee to internalize the enhanced skill or behavior. The coach may accomplish more with the coachee with less time and stress on the coach's schedule.

Observation can be subjective or it can include a format that cites measurable, specific, behaviors or skills. Both are of value to the person being coached, particularly since he or she articulated them to the coach in the preobservation conference. Learning style preferences also play a role in the way a teacher is observed by a coach, again pointing to the value of coach and coachee learning each other's styles and turning their differences into strengths. Once the coach has completed his or her observation, teacher and coach debrief what occurred, and the cycle begins again with continued practice or with the next skill, behavior, or attitude the teacher wants to work on.

The postobservation conference, as we shall see in the next chapter, provides a forum for debriefing what was observed, and that in turn provides the stepping-stone for the next preobservation conference.

7

The Postobservation Conference

The postobservation conference brings everything together. Here the coach and the coachee debrief what occurred during the observation, based on what was discussed and agreed upon in the preobservation conference.

In the postobservation conference, the coach shares observations with the teacher and provides feedback. The postobservation conference is an opportunity for the coach to offer encouragement and reinforcement for the teacher as well as make suggestions for improvement.

A postobservation conference is quite different from an evaluation. An evaluator reporting what he or she has found does most of the talking. In a coaching conference, questions are designed to draw the teacher into the conversation, to encourage the teacher to do some hard thinking about what occurred and what might be improved.

In the postobservation stage the focus covers the skills and behavior agreed upon between coach and coachee, and perceptions as to students' responses.

The primary reason for including a coaching program in a school is to improve teaching and thus improve student learning (see figure 7.1). At times teachers focus on the skills and techniques of teaching to the extent that they lose sight of student learning. Teaching can be

- neat;
- orderly;
- sequential;
- managed;
- documented.

Teaching	**Learning**
(Can be)	(Often is)
• Neat	• Messy
• Orderly	• Spontaneous
• Sequential	• Nonlinear
• Managed	• Irregular
• Documented	• Complex

Figure 7.1.   Differences in Focus: Teaching and Learning

A well-planned lesson delivered in a sequential and orderly manner with students tested immediately afterward may indicate that the lesson was taught well; but without student feedback or follow-up with next year's teacher, who can say whether or not the student really learned the lesson. Learning is often

- messy;
- spontaneous;
- nonlinear;
- irregular;
- complex.

The tension between a focus on teaching and a focus on learning creates an opportunity for coaching. Coaches can collect indicators that students were learning. They can pick up the data about how a lesson or teacher behavior was received. While the coachee is busy teaching, the coach is busy observing what the students are saying, doing, and feeling, and how they are acting—and all this is revealed to the coachee in the postobservation conference.

But revealed how? Using which skills? What if the lesson bombed? How does the coach give the appropriate feedback? Well, you've come to the right place to find out.

THE COACHING ENVIRONMENT

The postobservation conference provides a safe environment within which the coach and the coachee can relax, look at what just occurred in the "performance" of teaching and learning—the observation—and together work toward improving, enhancing, or celebrating what has occurred and will likely occur in the future.

Figure 7.2 illustrates how a teacher goes through a continual process to deliver sound teaching. The coach asks questions and provides input that increases what a teacher *Observes*. So often the coach sees, hears, and feels things that are not always obvious to the teacher. Questions and feedback prompt the teacher to reflect on how students were learning, thereby gaining precious information through the gift of hindsight.

These coaching questions and conversations increase the teacher's ability to *Think* about what occurred and where it did or did not meet standards, whether the teacher's own standard or those that are state or district mandated. From this exchange comes a desire to produce or *Create* new ideas or plans or activities. The teacher who engages students in a newly created learning activity is really conducting an *Experiment* to see if the idea has met the mark.

Identifying whether not learning occurred as a result of the new activity brings the teacher back up the cycle to *Observation*, then *Thinking*, which leads to the teacher's next decision and *Creation*. Meanwhile, the coach remains in the center of the circle, continuing to ask the questions and provide feedback to guide the teacher in the pattern.

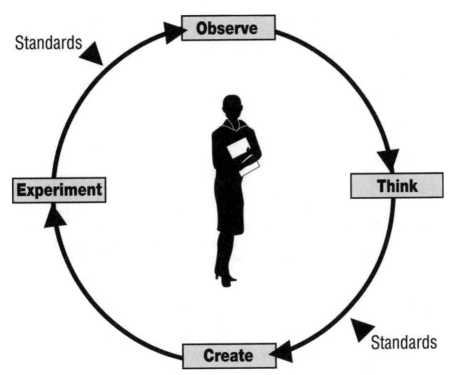

Figure 7.2. The Teaching and Coaching Process

In the postobservation conference, the person being coached receives feedback based on what was discussed or created in the preobservation conference. The coach guides, advances, and supports the positive aspects of what the coachee has accomplished. Options and ideas will arise and can be reinforced based on the positive aspects of what just occurred in the observation.

The timing of the postobservation conference depends somewhat on the agenda and vision of the person being coached. An observation could continue for a month or so after the preobservation conference, or it could take only one day or cover only one section of a lesson, depending on the coachee's specific agenda. Regardless of the length of the actual observation, the postobservation conference should occur as soon as possible after the last observation so the information is fresh to both the coach and coachee.

Timing is important because the teacher will appreciate the prompt attention, which reinforces the trust and rapport developed in the preobservation stage. If you wait too long to hold the postobservation conference, this trust and rapport can easily be compromised.

Coaching, unlike an evaluation, provides more than feedback: "This is what you did and this is how well you pulled it off." I like to think observation and follow-up coaching at the postobservation conference *together* allow the coach to provide feedforward for the coachee as well. To move the relationship and the vision forward and to make the coaching situation safe requires a positive environment.

A Positive Environment

The most important component of a safe coaching relationship is the establishment of a positive environment within which coaches can share their observations without any hint of evaluation that might cause discomfort to coachees. While this seems obvious, hitting the right note can be easier said than done. A positive environment includes positive attitudes with a focus on success and support. This paves the way for a relaxed, enthusiastic discussion, without hectic talking and nervous energy. In fact, research shows more work with less conversation occurs in a positive supportive setting.

Somehow we humans gravitate toward the negative. I use the word "gravitate" almost literally—it's as if negative energy mimics gravity, and we need to make an effort to create a positive climate, to get buoyant, to stay erect, and keep moving forward. We are accustomed to a negative mental set. We see it in the news, in weaknesses in our institutions, in mismanagement, and when we receive bad service. Negativity generates an unproductive and even counterproductive spiral. A positive mental set, on the other hand, produces a positive, upward spiral.

When I train professionals or students, I often use a simple exercise on the board, writing "Enjoy" at the top of one column and "Avoid" at the top of the other. I use a green marker to write Enjoy and a red one to write Avoid, reminiscent of a stoplight. People list some of the things they enjoy on one side (usually not work- or school-related activities), such as walking, traveling, cooking, golf. On the Avoid side, they often list tasks or situations that feel like punishment, things that have no reward or seem never ending, such as house-cleaning, doing the laundry, paying bills, or preparing income tax forms.

The reason I strongly support and promote a coaching program in schools is that it removes some of the tasks and situations we wish to avoid in the teaching profession by providing teachers with more options so their daily experiences at school appear more often on their Enjoy lists. The more enjoyment teachers have as they teach, the better they will be at reaching students, and the easier it will be to cope with the "un-Avoidable."

Positive Phrasing

In addition to a positive environment, certain skills must be used while coaching to ensure that the give-and-take between coach and coachee not only remains positive but also provides feedforward and underscores the trust in the relationship. An example is the use of Positive Phrasing.

Positive Phrasing involves making statements of what you *do* want, not what you *don't* want. You focus on what you want the other person to know or do.

Here's an experiment. Don't think about the Golden Gate Bridge. Ha! Gotcha! You had that orange-painted bridge firmly suspended in your mind, didn't you? Yet I told you *not* to think of the Golden Gate Bridge. What gives?

Research reported in *Behavioral Kinesiology* by John Diamond (1979) that when you give instructions, the information will sink in 47 percent faster if you explain what needs to be done rather than what not to do. There are two theories for why this works. They come from related theories that the right and left hemispheres of the brain have separate functions.

Some scientists believe the right brain does not interpret or process negative messages. The right brain simply drops the "don't" part in a command. The direction "Don't squeeze the lemon" to the right brain means, forget that "don't" part, and squeeeeeeeze! That is why, when you were told "don't think about the Golden Gate Bridge" above, your mind dropped out the "don't" and fixated on the image of the bridge itself—something it could see, not something it could *not* see.

A similar theory is that when the left-brain hears the command "Don't squeeze the lemon," it has to translate that into a behavior the right brain can carry out. A time lapse occurs as the brain attempts to comprehend what "don't" means. As the brain makes the translation or moves on to other stimuli, the opposite behavioral response occurs, and, yep, you guessed it, squeeeeeeze!

When we rehearse events in our mind—when we visualize succeeding or performing, for example—we always focus on what we want to occur. Visualizing what we do *not* want to occur constitutes worry. While there may be some value in visualizing to prepare for a worst-case scenario, we visualize primarily to "practice" a successful behavior or to set our intention for achievement. It's difficult to visualize *not* doing something, to visualize a void.

Using Positive Phrasing in coaching serves to instill a desired behavior in the mind of the one being coached. You want coachees to remember what they want to do, what they should do, not what they don't want to do, or shouldn't do. You want them rehearsing the correct, positive behavior.

This is easier said than done, by the way. We are all familiar with negative phrasing, such as "Knock it off," "Don't worry," "Don't compare yourself to that veteran teacher," "Stop thinking about how you look and concentrate on doing it right."

To reprogram our thinking, try changing the following negative coaching phrases to positive ones. Suggested answers are at the end of this chapter.

1. "Stop using outdated, messy materials."
2. "Don't look only at one side of the room when you are teaching."
3. "Don't slouch when you sit at the conference table."
4. "Stop calling only on boys when you ask a question that involves math."
5. "Don't go so fast."

Positive Phrasing consists of two steps. The first is mental—think positively. The second is to focus on what you want the other person to know and do. Positive Phrasing is a skill that can be used by itself or with other verbal skills. It has a ripple effect when used with Open-Ended Questions, Supporting Statements, Empathetic Phrases. Positive Phrasing means, *look at the glass as half full and then concentrate on filling the rest of the glass.*

When a coach lends his or her ideas to a coachee about changes in behavior, the positively phrased suggestion or idea must

- be clear and specific;
- be congruent with the teacher's vision;
- offer some kind of payoff.

By being *clear and specific*, I mean the coach has to refer to exact behavior. Saying "you handled that well" does not tell the coachee what specific thing he or she did well that constituted "handled." A Positive Phrase is helpful when it includes details: "When you asked the student to stand up, you really defused his disruptive behavior."

Evaluations seldom change teacher performance because they usually do not refer to specific behaviors. An evaluator may say to a teacher, "You need to be more positive." This is a generality, and doesn't convey information a teacher can use. It could mean, open your body language, relax and unfold your arms, phrase directions in a positive way, make pleasant eye contact, smile—it's not clear what it means.

Second, in addition to being clear and specific, *the coach needs to be congruent with the coachee's values and vision*. Being congruent means the idea or option the coach offers fits with what the coachee values. Congruence implies that the coach has listened and learned the teacher's agenda in the preobservation conference.

Finally, the Positive Phrase needs to *offer some benefit*, some incentive for the coachee to make a change. As Dr. Phil McGraw (1999) points out in *Life Strategies: Doing What Works, Doing What Matters* and in his other related books, no one does anything without perceiving some purpose or value in doing it, or what he calls "a payoff." The payoff for making a change has to be at least as great as or greater than the cost of making the change.

As we will see in chapter 8, there are intangible costs beyond the financial costs to implementing coaching programs in schools or districts. People implementing the program must be convinced that the payoffs (the benefits) of coaching outweigh the costs (added time, commitment) or the program will not be implemented or successful.

Likewise, a teacher being coached to change a lesson plan that, for example, is fun and well received by students but where no substantive content is involved must be assured that the payoff of revising the delivery merits the cost of discarding a favorite lesson.

Needs/Benefit Statement

A Needs/Benefit Statement employs Positive Phrasing that tells someone what you want to be known or accomplished, and then attaches a benefit that will result if the person follows through on the suggestion. It offers a payoff in terms of improving effectiveness, replacing behaviors that no longer serve. Here's the key to using it effectively: *The benefit must match the other person's agenda.*

As an example, let's say you fully understand the beliefs, values, and vision of the person you are coaching. You know that he values strong communication skills and endeavors to improve them at all times. During the observation of his teaching, you note that he is clear and precise in his delivery; his communication with the students is good. Yet his eyes remain fixed on one side of the room. He only glances occasionally at a whole group of students residing on the other side of the room.

You want to alert the teacher to this habit in a way that is both positive and motivating. Since you know he values communication, there
is built-in motivation. A suggested Needs/Benefit Statement might be,
"To improve communication with all your students, Fred, you might try
sweeping your eyes across the entire room as you speak to them, making
eye contact with each student as you do so. That way you communicate
more directly."

As a coach, it is your job to tell those you are coaching how they will
benefit when they try new strategies. Let's try another one.

The person being coached wants to be promoted. She has been over-
looked in the past and now really wants to accelerate her career. As her
coach, you observe her in a meeting, noting that she brought in a messy
notebook, kept rustling through papers, was constantly fidgeting, and otherwise looked very unorganized and less than professional. At the same
time, this person prides herself on her organizational skills; she just gets
flustered when she attends a meeting where those who could advance her
career are present. She's not at her best; she becomes nervous, trying too
hard to make a good impression.

To improve her odds of getting a promotion, her "need" is to organize
her materials, center herself before the meeting, and remain calm during the
meeting. The "benefit" of doing so is that she will come across with more
confidence and appear organized and efficient. A Needs/Benefit Statement
by her coach might sound something like this: "You have a lot of expertise,
Maya. Organizing your papers ahead of the meeting will allow you to present a calm demeanor which your superiors would surely notice."

A coach provides a coachee reinforcement and feedforward through
clear, specific, congruent, and Positive Phrasing with a Needs/Benefit Statement indicating a positive payoff.

When dialogue flows, the coach will find opportunities to fit one or two
suggestions into the conversation. Remember that trust is built by keeping
the postobservation conference focused on the agenda established in the
preobservation conference.

You may recall that in chapter 3 we looked at creative, evaluative, and
personalized questions driven by what the coach had come to know of the
coachee's vision or agenda. In the same vein, a Needs/Benefit Statement can
be used to restate and reinforce the teacher's values and vision as revealed
by answers to questions posed in the preobservation conference.

The preobservation conference provides the opportunity for coach and
coachee to get to know one another, and to uncover the coachee's agenda
and focus. In the postobservation conference, the coach softly prods the
coachee to perform at his or her best with needs being met and benefits
realized based on what the coachee values.

Compliments and Praise

We all like approval, but sometimes we brush off a compliment because we're embarrassed or don't particularly like being flattered. We may not think we earned the praise, but who doesn't secretly relish being praised or complemented?

A compliment consists of positive feedback that focuses primarily on a personal attribute, appearance, or acquisition. Examples might include the following:

"I really like your house."
"You have a great car."
"I like your new haircut."
"Congratulations on winning the award; you deserved it."
"You always wear lovely clothes."

These statements focus on the outer aspects of a person and items connected to that person. Praise, on the other hand, offers positive feedback for something a person has accomplished, achieved, or completed. Examples might include the following:

"Your presentation got a standing ovation. Congratulations!"
"Awesome job of getting in shape for the Marathon—you completed it in less than seven hours!"
"You delivered that Needs/Benefit Statement perfectly—good job!"

Both compliments and praise come from someone else's standards or opinions rather than those of the recipient. They come from the other person's perspective rather than from our own. If we don't agree with their assessment—maybe we know we could have delivered a better presentation or perhaps we hate our haircut—we become uncomfortable. There's a fine line between sincere praise and flattery. No wonder compliments and praise are so hard to accept at times.

Approval Statements

Just as the Needs/Benefit Statement identifies something that rings true for the coachee, the Approval Statement also ties in to what a coachee finds significant and meaningful—what he or she values. Yet it goes beyond values to touch on a person's self-worth and self-esteem.

Feedback and encouragement are provided to the person being coached in the form of an Approval Statement. The Approval Statement reflects what the person did that was consistent with what he or she values: it worked, it clicked, bravo, keep going, do it again. It offers feedback and encouragement in a positive light.

An Approval Statement differs from praise or a compliment and is delivered in a way that the person does not become embarrassed or shy about receiving the approval. Here's why.

We all have certain qualities we are proud of. Some people pride themselves on their creativity; others on clear thinking. One person may take particular satisfaction in being loyal, while another may consider his or her leadership ability to be important. The positive attributes people esteem in themselves are a road map on which their self-concept is built. To encourage others and to keep the focus on what's working over what is not up to par, offer approval in ways that affirm the person's own perceived strengths. What the person holds in high regard can be seen in his or her actions and in the results of those actions. To offer an effective Approval Statement, apply positive adjectives to those actions a person holds dear.

"That was a well-organized and stimulating lesson" includes adjectives ("well-organized" and "stimulating") showing that the coach has retained and thought about what he or she learned in the preobservation conference. Each person receiving one of these messages from his or her coach hears an affirmation of what he or she values of what the coach determined from the preobservation conference or from simple observation, from listening, and from the coaching relationship itself.

"Your *concern for children* is evident in the way you speak to them."

"Your questioning strategy was *well thought out* and *kept your students on task*."

"Your response to the parent was *honest and authentic*."

"Your willingness to change based on ideas generated in our last coaching session shows your *commitment to your students*."

Table 7.1 offers a list of approval adjectives. Each connects back to qualities or behaviors a person might value.

When offering an Approval Statement, you must remember to check the reaction of the person receiving it to ensure the statement does, in fact, reflect what the other person esteems as valuable. This is not always easy to do in an e-mail, "tweet," or blog. Body language plays a big part, so being with the person when initially delivering Approval Statements would be preferable.

Compared to compliments and praise, Approval Statements present a more favorable environment for the other person to really hear and accept the approval because, if you've done your homework, they hear something of value to them, something that resonates.

There are certain guidelines to use when giving Approval Statements that tend to reach the mark more effectively.

Table 7.1. List of Approval Adjectives

Approval Adjectives

accurate	expressive	pleasant
achiever	flexible	polished
adaptable	fluent	polite
agreeable	forward	popular
appreciative	frank	positive
artistic	friendly	prompt
athletic	generous	realistic
attentive	gentle	relaxed
attractive	good-looking	reliable
calm	good sense of humor	responsible
capable	good mixer	responsive
careful	good-natured	self-starter
cheerful	helpful	smart
competitive	honest	soft-hearted
conscientious	humble	sophisticated
considerate	humorous	spirited
convincing	inspiring	steady
cooperative	intellectual	strong-willed
courageous	intelligent	supportive
creative	interesting	tenacious
daring	kind	thorough
dependable	leader	thoughtful
detail-oriented	likable	tolerant
direct	loyal	trailblazer
disciplined	modest	trusted
dramatic	motivated	trusting
dynamic	neat	trustworthy
eager	neighborly	understanding
easygoing	optimistic	unique
effective	organized	upbeat
efficient	outgoing	verbal
energetic	persistent	vigorous
enterprising	persuasive	vivacious

Source: *Coaching Skills for Successful Teaching* by Hasenstab, Barkley, & Flaherty (1996)

1. Offer approval in a sentence by itself. Oftentimes in postobservation conferences, novice coaches tend to deliver Approval Statements followed hurriedly by coaching, so it sounds like this:

> That was such a creative opening to the lesson! The way you engaged your students when setting up the activity was really impressive *and* . . .

On the word "and," you lose the coachee. At that point, the coach looks down at notes to see what to say next. Once eye contact is broken, the coachee receiving the approval remains hanging on the word "and" rather than enjoying the authentic approval.

Said differently, after you give an Approval Statement, "shut up!" After a pause, say, "That was such a creative opening to the lesson," and then pause again. Anything you add after the approval diminishes it. Let it sink in at the person's heart level. If you deliver the approval and move on too quickly, coachees go back into their brain or thinking functions, and the heartfelt approval gets washed out.

2. Maintain eye contact for several seconds after delivering an Approval Statement. Maintaining eye contact emphasizes the approval and gives the person delivering the Approval Statement an opportunity to read the response. Did it hit the mark? Did his or her eyes light up? Or did he or she look confused? If you let the Approval Statement hover in the air while making direct eye contact, you will know.

3. Read body language for reaction. Body language constitutes the lion's share of communication. You can tell by people's body language whether your approval met with their own. There will be a big smile, a laugh, a visible relaxation of the shoulders, or other evidence of satisfaction. A frown or no reaction means you need to try something else. You have not hit on something the person values.

4. If you get a negative reaction, give more approval. When the reaction suggests the coachee did not accept the approval, whether revealed in body language or by actual comments, give more approval, ask a question, or use a paraphrase to learn more. Keep checking to make sure the approval speaks to the coachee's values; that the approval is something he or she enjoys or appreciates. And, in the best of all possible worlds, the Approval Statement coincides with your own values, thus bonding the relationship further.

Approval feeds the ego. A compliment or praise is more evaluative—it's based on someone else's opinions, values, focus. Approval also requires that the person delivering the Approval Statement is known to the one receiving it. A compliment or praise can be delivered to a total stranger; not so with an Approval Statement.

POSTOBSERVATION CONFERENCE: A REAL-LIFE EXAMPLE

In chapter 5 we witnessed a preobservation conference between beginning teacher Shelly and me. Here is how our postobservation conference played out. Notice my use of questions and Approval Statements to engage Shelly, as well as the use of a suggestion she might take away from the postobservation conference experience.

Steve: "Shelly, you asked me to observe your students' attention or focus on you and your awareness of whether or not you engaged them."

Shelly: "Well, I hope I did. Most of them seemed to be watching me and focusing on what we were doing as well as listening to the other children. That's kind of how you gauge it—if they are listening to the person that spoke before they did. So in that regard, I think they were listening and paying attention."

Steve: "It sure looked to me like you had their attention the entire time. I focused on some of the things that I thought caused that. What would you guess caused the students to be focused on you?"

Shelly: "Well, I try to use a variety of teaching methods. Some teacher-directed things. Some student interaction, hands-on materials. Those types of things, I think, helped them stay involved."

Steve: "I noted that the students had to move from their focus on you when you labeled the parts of the letter on the board, to labeling the parts on their own paper, and then back to you again. That required each student to stay with what you were saying and doing."

Shelly: "Right. They would have to be with me to capture that."

Steve: "Do you have any other thoughts about what might cause them to be focused on you?"

Shelly: "Well, not any others, right at this moment. No."

Steve: "To what extent do you sense that you're on stage when you're teaching?"

Shelly: "Oh that's probably a large part of it. I just never think about it. You have to act out what you're doing. The more animated you are, the more focused they are."

Steve: "You have an interesting style of body language for nonverbal communication. At the beginning of the lesson when you stepped in to introduce the story, the use of your voice, your body posture, and your hand movements sent out a real stage presence. You also used body language to encourage and clue the students. If their answers were going down the wrong path, you held an exaggerated look in your eye, or when they were getting it correctly, you had exaggerated encouragement in your smile that said loud and clear, 'You're on the right track, keep it coming.' This animated body language has a lot of use for you when focusing on your students."

Shelly: "I talk a lot with my hands! If I didn't have them, I'd probably get into trouble."

Steve: "You make it easy for students to pay attention to you."

Shelly: "Good!"

Steve: "What role do you figure your relationships with students plays in terms of keeping their focused learning attention?"

Shelly: "I think it's so important to understand each child that's in your room, to know their backgrounds and what motivates them to want to learn. Because they don't all learn in the same way, and not everything motivates each student the same way. And sometimes it's hard to pick out what motivates each individual student. It's hard to always focus on that in each lesson. The more you can do that, the more likely they are to achieve."

Steve: "There was a sequence with Terrance when he gave you the wrong answer. Again, you used your body language to send a caring message out to him. Your actual response was, 'Real close. You got the Sword there.' Then you went on to another student who gave the correct answer. But it was clear to me you kept Terrance in mind, because when it was time for the answer that he gave to be the right answer, you slid back to him, and pulled him back in. That's a powerful strategy. If a student were going to lose interest in the lesson—to stop focusing on it—it would be right after giving a wrong answer. And when an answer he or she gave is the one for another question, that is the perfect chance to come around and bring him or her back in. You did that well."

Shelly: "I try to keep it in mind. It's hard to always remember, but I did remember that time, because that particular student needs reinforcement."

Steve: "Your use of names is good too. Not only using names when you call on students, but also when you come back to them. Or when you talk about their answers, there's more personalization there. One area you might want to look at for increasing student focus is on the length of time you allow after your question before you call on a student. There's a tendency on all our parts as teachers to speed on to the next student if the first one doesn't start to answer the question right away. That might be an area where you could cause more students to stay with you a little bit longer by increasing that time frame. Have you done any work with that—with pause time?"

Shelly: "No, but I've heard a lot about it. It's very hard to focus on timing. There is a tendency not to concentrate on anything except 'Okay, I've got to keep this moving, I've got to keep this going.'"

Steve: "A teacher's strengths can also get in the way. Teachers who have lots of energy and enthusiasm—and I would say you're that type of teacher—find that teaching has its own momentum that builds as the lesson is going on. To slow down, to pause requires a conscious shift that may feel wrong at first. It's a technique that all of us—even experienced teachers—need to come back and review from time to time."

Shelly: "That's good to know."

Steve: "As a matter of fact, I wouldn't mind doing some conscious practice on it myself. If you're willing, I'd like to find a time when you could observe me making a presentation. What I'd like you to do is record my pause time for me. I think that knowing you are in the room would help me become more conscious of slowing down, pausing, letting the question sit for awhile. Then if you like, I'd come back and do an observation for you again."

Shelly: "That would be wonderful."

REINFORCEMENT AND ENCOURAGEMENT

Let's look again at the notion of reinforcement and encouragement. Having viewed hundreds of videotapes showing teachers teaching, I have been struck by the fact that most teachers are unable to provide their own reinforcement; they aren't always conscious of what they are doing right. The videotape format makes their shortcomings seem larger than life, while their successful practices fly by unnoticed. If this phenomenon occurs in the videotape format, then surely even less self-reinforcement takes place in the classroom when a teacher's attention is focused on students and the delivery of a lesson.

Reinforcement of specific, effective teaching skills can make teachers conscious of their behavior in the classroom. This consciousness, in turn, increases their use of effective behaviors and adds to their level of professionalism. Teachers who do not have the benefit of coaching feedback—and are Unconsciously Talented—consider themselves just lucky, not skilled. A coach using Positive Phrasing that is clear and specific, congruent with the teacher's values, and cites a positive payoff for the teacher not only reinforces the teacher's behavior but also paves the way for further improvement.

Moving from reinforcement to encouragement brings us to the next step. Encouragement searches for and accentuates the positive. It is aimed at helping the coachee increase self-acceptance and self-worth. Teachers—or anyone, for that matter—need self-esteem before risking change or experimentation. Encouragement speaks to an individual's vision and beliefs. Coaches can provide encouragement when they understand how the teacher perceives his or her brand of teaching, both now and in the future. Recognizing, reinforcing, and encouraging a teacher increases the likelihood that new skills and behaviors will be internalized.

Sadly, encouragement in a standard evaluation process is rare, possibly because it involves a commitment to addressing the other person's needs as opposed to one's own needs or those of the system. When training administrators, mentors, department chairpersons, and coaches, I have uncovered two myths that decrease the use of reinforcement and encouragement.

Myth 1: Educators who have been trained to give approval to students will perceive reinforcement and encouragement from peers as being manipulative.

Many educators who hold this point of view are surprised at how satisfying they find approval to be in the context of a coaching relationship built upon trust. I have personally observed teachers "sitting tall" after several coaching colleagues created a list of reinforcing statements for them.

Myth 2: When professional friendships have developed over years of working together, Approval Statements are unnecessary.

I uncovered this myth after observing fifteen school administrators conducting coaching conferences with staff members with whom they had positive professional relationships. When I commented on the lack of reinforcement in the conferences, the teachers quickly defended the administrators, saying, "I don't need it," or "I know that he [or she] approves of what I do."

Administrators responded by identifying that they wanted to offer more approval and were not sure the teachers would value it (see myth 1). Continued discussion revealed that both teachers and administrators would enjoy genuine approval and signs of acceptance.

As in other relationships, we assume our unspoken messages are somehow communicated. Reinforcement and Approval Statements must be plainly stated. This purposeful focus rewards both the giver and the receiver.

Here are some guidelines to assist coaches in providing effective reinforcement and encouragement:

- Communicate your enthusiasm and sincerity through your statements. Make each one a minicelebration. Intonation and body language play an important role in communicating approval.
- Always think of your statements from a particular coachee's perspective. Are you reinforcing and encouraging behaviors that fit this individual's vision, beliefs, and values?
- Be specific. By citing the specific occurrence you are reinforcing, you not only add value to the reinforcement, you increase your own credibility as a knowledgeable coach.

Appreciative Inquiry

Throughout our discussions of coaching, we have emphasized the importance of using Positive Phrasing and discovering positive attributes and values. The focus has been on working with others to improve what they already have, not to evaluate or make wrong what they do as teachers and as human beings.

In coaching the assumption is that you are working with a fully functioning adult who is a skilled teacher. To broach the topic of one peer offering improvement to another can be tricky and, done wrong, can result in resistance to coaching. Framing the process in a positive, forward-moving light spells the difference between a successful coaching culture and one that remains suspect, wanes in enthusiasm, or disappears altogether.

We have all experienced times when our lives are working favorably, when things are going well, when we're working in high gear from a position of strength. Wouldn't it be wonderful if we could capture that essence at every opportunity? Wouldn't it be powerful if other individuals and organizations began to appreciate what they already have—and go from there?

The theory of Appreciative Inquiry, or AI (pronounced: a eye), was developed by Dr. David L. Cooperrider (1999) of Case Western Reserve University in Cleveland, Ohio (http://www.appreciativeinquiry.case.edu). The focus of this theory is finding the strengths within people and organizations, finding positive aspects of situations, and providing a refreshing and more creative approach to problem solving and decision making.

In other words, AI defines a theory and an approach to organizational change and staff development from a positive framework. Its premise is that what you focus on, you get. If you focus on problems, you get more problems; if you focus on the negative, you attract negativity.

Acquiring a negative mental set comes easy. It is contagious. When someone is negative, others join in. Somehow it's easy for negativity to become a habit; other's flaws and errors, the weakness of institutions and mismanagement, can blot out our view of what's working, and the goodness in people.

Negativity generates a negative spiral; it can be unproductive and even counterproductive. Remaining positive, looking for ways to respect ourselves and others, finding things we can approve of, and generally looking for a positive perspective creates a positive spiral that opens the imagination to positive solutions.

The term "appreciative" refers to something that increases in value, as money earns interest or an investment "appreciates" in value. "Inquiry" is the process of seeking to understand through carefully constructed provocative questions—questions designed to evoke positive images and enliven the individuals responding to them. AI acts on the theory that the type of inquiry shifts the discussion toward the direction of the inquiry, so that a positive question creates positive energy and productive answers.

Dr. Cooperrider (2003) asks us to pay special attention to "the best of the past and present" in order to "ignite the collective imagination of what might be." In short, AI, like coaching, does not rely on a deficit-based mentality. Rather, it elicits positive change in a positive environment. Throughout the process we stress positive relationships, and since questioning strategies are a large part of coaching, the concept of AI fits in nicely. It offers an experience of positive interaction through the use of constructively designed questions or statements that elicit positive images.

To conduct an initial AI session—whether with a coachee, other colleagues, your students, faculty, family members, or friends—you would first focus the discussion on what worked in the past. What was it like when things were going well?

Typically in such a session, people pair up and discuss what was presented in an inquiry or statement. One interviews the other as a reporter would and notes the themes and patterns that emerge as the other person shares with enthusiasm his or her story; then partners switch and repeat the process.

As an example, the coach might ask the teacher to reflect on the past semester and ask what highlights he or she could recall. The inquiry might go something like this: "What teaching moments do you recall that generated enthusiasm, learning, and success for yourself and your students?" The coach may probe further: "What conditions were present that caused that success?" Or "What were the qualities of excellence you experienced for yourself in those magical teaching moments?" If any of the lessons were documented on video, the coach and teacher could review them and decide which of those captured teaching moments best exemplified the rewards of teaching, those that thrilled the teacher when they were caught on video.

Recollection of success tends to breed success in other areas, opening possibilities and imagination about how those conditions of excellence or quality can be repeated elsewhere. The coach might ask, "What elements or practices on your part created those moments for your students?" and "What ideas can we generate to create more conditions that support excellence?"

AI brings out positive stories, enlivening the conversation, and creating the space for innovation—new ideas and solutions. Energy flows between the person sharing the story—in this case, the teacher—and the one inquiring into its details, the coach.

AI is also an excellent approach to seeking solutions to problems holding groups or teams back. An AI session might involve teachers and administrators identifying times when obstacles were overcome or successful changes were implemented. When a question is aimed at generating solutions, positive energy tickles the imagination and the focus of that energy moves toward the strengths of the individuals involved.

Once identified, strengths that worked in one area can be applied to creating solutions in other areas. AI helps in the discovery of solutions based on what's possible, not on problems to be solved. A positive approach such as AI tends to stimulate creativity, enthusiasm, and commitment to a vision, such as the vision of teachers being coached to become even better at what they already do well.

Beyond the theory of AI, research affirms that a focus on what is positive enhances productivity. Applying both AI and other positive approaches in coaching creates a constructive emotional climate that shores up trust, increases learning, and sparks the enthusiasm we all need to succeed.

PLANNING A POSTOBSERVATION PROCESS

Techniques that create a safe, positive environment while coaching are all focused on giving a teacher the framework he or she needs to continue to improve and grow.

Figure 7.3, the Postobservation Conference Planning Sheet, shows the form I referred to in chapter 6.

Figure 7.3. Postobservation Conference Planning Sheet

There are three symbols topping three columns on this form. The first is a heart, the second a question mark, and the third a blazing light bulb. These represent heartfelt approval, questions, and ideas or suggestions. When planning a postobservation conference, it is useful to plan it backward, starting with the last column. This will represent what the coach wants to convey by the end of the postobservation conference.

After observing the coachee, the coach starts at the right side of the sheet and notes first one suggestion or idea designed to help the teacher achieve his or her desired goal. In the preobservation conference, the teacher's agenda revealed what he or she wanted to work on; the coach and teacher together uncovered a suggestion or idea for improvement. Usually only one idea is sufficient; otherwise, the session begins to look like an evaluation. As teachers work on one change, it typically leads to other changes, so starting with one is not limiting in the long run.

Here is an example of how the form might be used: A coach observes that his or her coachee delivers a lesson from the front of the room at a rather fast pace. The coach notices that students are struggling to keep up. A suggestion might be that the teacher move around the room to slow down the pace. The coach makes a note in the Idea column (light bulb): "Add more movement."

Next, after the coach has jotted down the suggestion or idea, he or she poses questions about the lesson or the observation that might help in forming an Approval Statement. In an example I gave earlier, the teacher stationed himself in one spot in the room. The question the coach came up with focuses on his reason for doing that: "What is your thinking about the way you have the room arranged? In an ideal situation, what would you prefer?" So the coach jots questions down under the question mark on the form.

The coach knows this teacher values being as dynamic and interesting as possible. So the question then leads to what the coach might write in the first column, the Approval Statement (the heart): "When you walked over to the map and helped students locate the country, you were really engaging their interest." "Your use of space in the room was very powerful as you went around assigning each student a country to work on."

While the heart/question/light bulb form is filled in backward when planning a conference (right to left), the Approval Statement (from the left-hand column) is delivered first in the postobservation conference. The form is used the way it is sequenced.

In the example involving Ned Baxter in chapter 6, the teacher who moved to an inner-city high school, the coach delivers the Approval Statement stating the teacher really engaged the students and came off as very dynamic, powerful, and interesting when he moved around the room. The coach cites several examples of how moving around the room improved the delivery of the lesson. Using all the guidelines for an Approval Statement, the coach delivers it in such a way that the teacher is pleased. "Oh, good," Ned thinks to himself. "I wanted to come across that way in this lesson."

Next the coach notes that despite the fact he or she knows the teacher values the interest he can engage through movement, for a large portion of the lesson, the teacher remained at the front of the room in one spot. The coach asks about the teacher's thoughts on arrangement and use of space.

Since the teacher has already received approval for having moved and engaged the students, he knows that he did accomplish this task and is capable of doing so again. Because the coach expresses curiosity as to the teacher's thoughts about movement in this lesson, the teacher can respond honestly, and together they can explore what occurred and how the teacher might change his behavior in the future. This opens up discussion to move from approval to questions back to approval.

Somewhere within that discussion, the coach can make his or her suggestion. Unlike the extra candle that a child might receive at a birthday party, "one to grow on" ideas and suggestions are not a list of evaluative phrases. An Approval Statement works its way out of a conversation in a safe coaching environment; both coach and coachee have the same positive end result in mind. The coach's suggestion in this case outlines a way the teacher can make a note in his written lesson plan to move around the room to introduce a new point in the lesson in a nonverbal way. The teacher can put a symbol on his sheet that indicates "Time to move!" "Get interesting, here!" "Keep moving and energizing yourself and your students."

The tone of a postobservation conference changes depending on the teacher's level of experience. A new teacher might need a lot of support and approval with limited suggestions for behavioral changes. Someone with more confidence and experience might bring a lot of content information and skill into the room. That teacher would know when he or she was "off" and why, and the coaching would therefore be more in-depth and sophisticated.

THE NEXT PREOBSERVATION CONFERENCE: A REAL-LIFE EXAMPLE

A good postobservation conference triggers the next preobservation conference, and the two may occur at the same time. The teacher in our previous example asks the coach to observe his movements in class; to note whether or not the suggestion worked; and to watch how the students react and whether their level of engagement improved.

Remember our English teachers from Cranford High School? We looked at the preobservation conference between Barbara Carroll and Karen Bailin concerning Karen's complaint that there was too much paperwork and not enough time to be innovative. Karen came up with the idea of having the students create the actual quizzes and topics for discussions, and it was agreed that Barbara would "test-drive" that idea in her Advanced Placement English class.

In chapter 6, we "saw" what happened when Barbara tried out the idea. Karen observed Barbara's lesson plan and noted how the students reacted they made their presentations and worked in groups.

Karen then decided to try out the lesson plan in her class. Her students were in an "enriched" class, a couple of levels below Barbara's Advanced Placement class. They were reading only one book, *Brave New World*, by Aldous Huxley. She conducted the lesson in a similar format as Barbara, and Barbara observed her teaching. They switched roles!

Here's what happened in the postobservation conference immediately following one of the classes:

Barbara: "What thoughts are you having about how it's going?"

Karen: "I don't think it went as well as it did in your class, because I had to keep prompting them for perceptions and insights."

Barbara: "You are disappointed they weren't more insightful."

Karen: "Yes, but I did like that they all participated."

Barbara: "I thought the way you pulled Peter into the group was marvelous."

Karen: "He's always the reluctant one."

Barbara: "You must have inspired him, as he wasn't reluctant today!"

Karen: "Actually, on the days that the students present, no one has ever been absent. They all show up to do their part when it's their turn."

Barbara: "You asked me to observe whether or not you were letting the students run the show, stepping back and facilitating. I saw you standing up and leading the group three times; otherwise, they were in charge and you were facilitating their learning."

Karen: "When Rebecca said, 'Lenina's not happy,' that wasn't enough. I could see they weren't using good thinking skills, so I wanted to prompt her for more."

Barbara: "And you did. She thought about it and expressed herself a little more. Actually, the kinds of questions you asked Rebecca and others were similar to coaching questions. You kept them open-ended, allowing the students to delve a little deeper."

Karen: "Well, that's true."

Barbara: "I wondered why you did not give the students a choice of books. What made you decide to stick with one book and do the lesson every day?"

Karen: "I didn't know if they were advanced enough or fast enough readers to read three books as in your class."

Barbara: "What other options did you consider?"

Karen: "I thought about having a choice of books. I think if they chose the book, they would like it better and get into it more."

Barbara: "What ways could we structure the lesson so that this was possible?"

So they began restructuring the lesson in order that the students would have a choice of books to read. They agreed that having more choice, a brain-based tool, would empower the students and allow them to take more ownership. They also agreed that the students did very well, considering they were learning a whole new skill set that's called teaching!

Looking for new opportunities or options in the postobservation conference segued the same session into a preobservation conference where Karen asked Barbara to help her focus on how and what she wanted Barbara to observe when she again launched into this lesson plan.

Most of the learning in a coaching process occurs in the postobservation conference. This safe, positive environment allows for positive, clear, and specific feedback, and the benefits of changing behavior if necessary. Here the coachee can feel as if he or she is advancing as approval is received and feedforward established.

As the coach and teacher review what occurred during the observation, they can then collaborate on solving any problems they noticed or work on options that present themselves. This leads to the next preobservation conference and a new opportunity to experiment, take risks, improve skills, or otherwise advance the teacher's professionalism.

Sound good? Coaching is extremely effective and supportive of great teaching. It shores up a teacher's self-confidence, provides opportunities for creativity and innovation, enhances his or her career, and leads indirectly to a higher level of learning for students.

SUMMARY

There's an expression used in film and video production when a shot isn't right or someone forgets his or her lines: "That's okay, we'll fix it in post." This refers to postproduction, where film or video footage is edited, pasted up, new lines are inserted, or problems otherwise ironed out to perfect the finished product.

In a similar way in the postobservation conference everything the teacher and coach have worked on comes together to be reviewed, patched up, improved upon, and made as perfect as possible for the next "performance."

The postobservation conference requires a safe, positive environment, and it requires planning. The coach can use the form suggested or other format to observe the teacher in a way that leads to the postobservation discussion. Suggestions or ideas for the teacher, along with any questions and, in particular, comments focused on what the teacher values—the Approval Statement—are vital for a successful conference.

The Approval Statement requires some skill to deliver. It needs to be based on what the teacher values, what the coach knows has meaning for the coachee and, for that matter, him- or herself. Delivery comes with direct eye contact and a significant pause to determine if the coachee valued the statement and to allow the approval to sink in.

Invariably, a postobservation conference leads to the next preobservation conference as teacher and coach discover if the teacher wants to try out new skills or practice old ones under observation.

This cyclical process enhances teaching and student learning along the way. The coach and teacher, in a trusting relationship, carry that trust and that support to others. In that way, a coaching program within a school or district leads to the creation of an effective team with high morale and professionalism.

In chapter 8, we look at ways you can introduce coaching to your school or district.

RESEARCH SHOWS

Postobservation Conference

- "Momentum for change requires large amounts of both positive affect and social bonding things like hope, inspiration, and sheer joy" (Orem, Binkert, & Clancy, 2007, p. 177).
- "Questions that help them paint positive images of the future are most helpful" (Orem et al., 2007, p. 70).
- Research shows approachability and trust are important antecedents in the development of rapport (Granitz, Koernig, & Harich, 2009).
- "Help faculty through the stages of change by raising and exploring teaching assumptions and providing a supportive and knowledgeable community to provide suggestions, ideas, and encouragement" (Qualters, 2009, p. 5).
- "Effective coaching is rich in feedback. However, if the feedback from the coach is perceived by the client to be either a casual opinion or outside advice that fails to comprehend the nuances of the client's unique position, then even the most expert coach will be unlikely to help the client make the changes necessary for renewal. Renewal coaches provide a rich variety of feedback, including assessments, observations, and document reviews" (Reeve, 2009, p. 233).

ANSWERS FOR REPHRASING
NEGATIVE PHRASING TO POSITIVE PHRASING

1. "Stop using outdated, messy materials."
   Positive Phrasing: "Always use the latest and most professional materials available."
2. "Don't look only at one side of the room when you are teaching."
   Positive Phrasing: "Look at the whole class when you speak."
3. "Don't slouch when you sit at the conference table."
   Positive Phrasing: "Sit straight at the table, look and feel confident, show an interest."
4. "Stop calling only on boys when you ask a question that involves math."
   Positive Phrasing: "When you ask a question involving math, call on a mix of boys and girls for the answers."
5. "Don't go so fast."
   Positive Phrasing: "Slow down."

III

APPLICATIONS OF COACHING

8

I'm Ready! How Do I
Create a Coaching Culture?

"Every change begins with a conversation," says author, lecturer, and global activist Margaret Wheatley (2002, p. 32) in *Turning to One Another: Simple Conversations to Restore Hope to the Future.* Likewise, the implementation of every coaching program begins with a conversation.

I am convinced that coaching programs in schools improve teaching and student learning. They also enhance the professionalism of the staff. Yet I am also aware that each school, district, and organization differs from others in needs, culture, circumstances, demographics, finances, and personnel. While the coaching process outlined in this book remains the same or is similar in every program, the focus or purpose of each program will differ depending on the circumstances.

Some school districts are experiencing a large influx of beginning teachers who can use direction; others suffer from brain drain, needing new teachers badly. Some schools include vocational and academic tracks and want coaching programs that blend the two. Some schools, in resource-poor communities, suffer from lack of funding; others enjoy grants and funding sources that ensure extras.

The rationale for bringing a coaching program into schools to address a variety of circumstances is well rooted in research. Coaches provide ongoing support on instructional methods, curriculum components, and new formats and ideas for instructional delivery and effective professional development. As we have seen in this book, coaching can move a teacher from good to great. It can create quality in teaching and in learning. Through celebration of achievement and positive feedback, the coaching enriches and empowers schools and teachers.

A coachee may share a need with a coach, and the coach's support and feedback helps fill that need. Teaching can be a lonely profession; incorporating a coaching program brings in collaboration, which leads to increased resources and options.

Celebrating a teacher's perseverance in conquering a new skill or fine-tuning an already successful lesson plan creates energy for the coach and the coachee. This energy then transfers to students and learning. I encourage all schools that have coaching programs in place to develop celebrations on an ongoing basis for the work that is accomplished. Celebrations give a boost to the ego and make teaching fun. I tell people to keep champagne in the school at all times to celebrate coaching successes. The champagne need not be alcoholic; what people like, and what makes the celebration, is the "pop!"

Coaching reduces stress, an everyday condition in the life of a teacher. We are constantly faced with changes, new technology, new rules, and fast-paced schedules. When stress becomes chronic any support that alleviates its impact creates a more positive environment.

We all know a teacher's role continues to expand. A teacher wears the hats of social worker, guardian, disciplinarian, nutritionist, counselor, psychologist, risk taker, and others too numerous to mention. And did I mention teaching? Teachers deal with minimum competencies, maximum standards; nurturing and nourishing; theory and practice; techniques and strategies; language differences and safety issues. The tasks, like the roles, go on and on.

We looked earlier at quality and Glasser's theory about survival, belonging, power, freedom, and fun. Stress and post-Columbine anxiety has eroded all but the survival stage in many schools. How do we maintain schools that are empowering and enriching, where teaching and learning can be fun?

COACHING ALLEVIATES STRESS

One of the ways a coaching program reduces stress revolves around options. Teachers need as many options as possible to cope, yes, but more importantly to become great teachers. The coach and coachee together collaborate about options, whether in lesson planning or in dealing with stress. Options come from other teachers, videotapes, resources, feedback, shared ideas, and innovations. Coaches and coachees together share resources that assist the coachees in reaching their visions.

Special education teachers know the value of options; they typically use anything they can to reach their students. Teachers have always been a source of ideas for each other. Why not? Despite other responsibilities and distractions the primary goal is to teach. Coaching helps a teacher gain options, and in that process, stress is likely to be relieved, if not dissipated. Great teachers are not great because they know what to do. Great teachers are great because they can always think of something *else* to do.

Stress is alleviated as a trusting relationship grows between a teacher and coach. The days of a teacher handling everything alone are long gone; there are just too many demands imposed by society, parents, and by ever-expanding definitions of the very role of teaching. Coaches are in the teacher's corner. They cheer teachers on, working to help them succeed. Someone once said having a coach is like having someone's strong, supporting hand held firmly on your back, guiding and keeping you from falling backward. The guidance and interest coaches offer teachers allows them to take a deep breath, relax, knowing that someone is there for them.

Ditto for administrators. Those administrators who have undertaken coaching programs report increased energy, enthusiasm for their jobs, reduced stress, a sounder staff, and a district or school with elevated morale. Administrators need coaching too.

Regardless of degree or experience, each teacher or staff member has to discover unique features of his or her job. With a coach they do not struggle alone.

Confronting Change

I could go on and on about the benefits of coaching, but all those would be moot without a coaching program to back me up. So, how do you begin a coaching program in your school or district? How do you implement something you know and the research shows is valuable? Well, one way is to begin, as Margaret Wheatley says, with a conversation.

Change can occur in different ways. Often an interested few begin a conversation about changes they would like to see made. Or two people begin e-mailing a third to explore ways they might save time or create situations where they can be more creative. This threesome grows in number; its members talk about what they would like to see occur, and eventually this effects change. Like grassroots causes, change occurs from the bottom up. This is how many professional learning networks develop on Twitter.

Change from mandate or legislation occurs more rapidly, and it often doesn't garner support as strongly as the groundswell approach. In some situations change doesn't happen until the pain of making the change overrides the pain of the status quo. Finally, change can occur as an outgrowth of circumstances or shift in consciousness of an individual or group. The perception might be that it "just happened."

Resistance to Change

Beginning a coaching program where none existed before represents a change in your school, district, or organization. Regardless of how it's presented, change inevitably is met with resistance. Human beings, and groups in particular, don't like to be prodded out of their comfort zone.

Beyond instinctive resistance to initiating a coaching program that comes from fear of change, there are assumptions that there's not enough time or money, plus the false perception that coaching is a double for evaluation. Beyond that, there is ego-related and territory-related resistance. Resistance comes in a variety of forms:

"There is not enough time to do that."
"I'm hesitant to make any more changes."
"I don't need coaching or mentoring; I'm a tenured teacher!"
"My classroom is my terrain; I don't want others in there telling me what to do."
"What if we start it and it doesn't continue? Then what?"
"I'm afraid of another layer of evaluation."
"The whole idea of coaching scares me."
"There's no one to cover my class if I go coach someone else."
"Stress: just one more thing added to my already-full plate."
"Stay out of my classroom!"
"Who does this coach think she [or he] is?"
"This teacher is younger than I am! How can he [or she] coach *me*?"
"What if I don't measure up?"
"This sounds like another way for the principal to check on me."
"This teacher graduated so long ago, how would she know anything?"
"This is not in my comfort zone."
"I'm not good enough or confident enough to be a coach."

These responses represent real concerns, real fears. They reflect earlier experiences and unpleasant circumstances. Having worked with coaching programs and seen the benefits, however, I know resistance can be overcome. When coaching programs are launched, resistance is often gladly traded in for enthusiasm and those participating wonder why they did not include coaching in their staff development before.

Resistance serves a purpose. Rather than causing dismay, these responses should be embraced. They need to be out in the open. Resistance to change is a sign that change may be in order, and the specific reasons for resistance may turn into starting points to look back on after the program is in place and possible changes have occurred.

Resistance also slows down the process a bit. This serves to ensure that the change benefits the culture and those involved in it.

Speedboats and Barges

Picture your school, district, or organization as a large bay. Within the bay are boats. Some are speedboats; some are barges. Large rocks jut out from the bottom of the bay, solid reminders of an earlier volcanic eruption. Those wanting to immediately introduce a coaching program in the school or district are the speedboats. "Wow. I just read this book by Steve Barkley and we *have* to have coaches in our school *now!*" Six months later, the barges, having heard the cry, finally turn their bows toward the speedboats. "What do we want with coaches? They are velvet things on wheels. Coaches went out with Cinderella!"

"No, no," cry the speedboats. "Coaches are people. We need coaches for teachers! Coaches for administrators! We need a coaching program in our school. It will help us. It will improve student learning. It will improve how we do things. We need this *now!*"

The barges carry a lot of the load at schools, districts, and in other organizations. They hold the system, the regulations, the rules, the peer pressure, the parents, the curriculum, the administration, the budget, the funding—they weigh a lot! Change will not effectively occur until the barges agree to it. The speedboats, then, need to keep approaching, reminding the barges of the benefits. (Remember the Needs/Benefit Statements from chapter 7? Barges need them too.) Eventually, with sound arguments, meaningful conversation, and a growing number of speedboats, the barges will budge, and the program will be put in place.

The rocks, however, will never budge. They are the holdouts. They are stuck in the mud, and no amount of waves washing over them will change that. The moral of the story is to keep the speedboats from running into the rocks! Don't waste a good speedboat. The speedboats need to pool their energy and work on respectfully effecting change with the ones who carry the load—the barges. Rocks can't turn around but they will watch quietly until the proof is in. Eventually, they may come to offer solid support.

MAKING TIME

Coaching programs require time to establish, particularly if trust and rapport are the first priority. Pre- and postobservation conferences need to be held and time set aside for coaches to observe coachees in classes or in other settings. Like the thought of added stress, the thought of spending more time brings up significant resistance when introducing the concept of a coaching program. Time *is* precious. How we use and allocate time concerns not only how we "get things done" but also how we nourish and take care of ourselves and how we grow professionally.

So how do we introduce the concept and practices of coaching to teachers whose lives already seem filled to the brim? Well, as the saying goes, where there's a will, there's a way. In Addison Elementary School in Marietta, Georgia, for example, after several tries at other strategies, those involved decided that the school day would begin ten minutes earlier and end ten minutes later than in other elementary schools. To offset this additional time, students are released at 1:30 P.M. every Wednesday, giving teachers until 3 P.M. to meet in study groups, meet with coaches, or otherwise work on their professional development.

Iowa City Community School District in Iowa City, Iowa, took a similar tack by releasing students one hour early every Thursday. Teachers enjoy a block of time from 2 to 4 P.M. for staff development.

Hefferan Elementary School in Chicago created a Resource Day where regular instruction begins as usual with class time devoted to reading. At 10:30 A.M. on any given day, however, a group of students attend art, music, and gym classes or visit the library or computer lab. Every day a different group gets its Resource Day, so groups are rotated, usually two grades at a time. The second-grade teachers, for example, can work together on staff development when their student group enjoys a Resource Day. To accommodate the frequent Monday holidays, the schedule changes every ten weeks. Teachers have time to reflect, learn, and coach; students see their Resource Day as special and look forward to it.

High school days are long at Fremont High School in Sunnyvale, California, beginning at 7:30 A.M. and going until 3:15 P.M. The state of California reduced the number of preservice days and instead teachers spend more time in the classroom. In addition, there is a substitute teacher shortage so that, even with grant money to hire subs, there are not enough to go around. The school opted for Late Start Fridays as a way for teachers to undertake staff development training and coaching, considered a high priority at Fremont. On Fridays, teachers still assemble at 7:30 A.M., but students do not start school until 9 A.M.

Needless to say, students at Fremont High do not object to Late Start Fridays, but Fremont also received support from the staff and community. Everyone knows teachers need some professional development time. Each of the schools noted here had to work through issues of scheduling, communication, explanation to parents and the community, and shuffling of teacher classrooms.

There were false starts, resistance, and some failed plans, but each school is now achieving the seemingly simple yet very complex task of finding 90 to 120 minutes a week for teachers to talk, learn, and support one another for the betterment of teaching. For many, that represents the equivalent of a good workout at the gym, getting oneself physically fit. It is obviously more than fair that teachers have at least that much time becoming professionally fit.

Each of the schools mentioned here is discussed in *Finding Time for Professional Learning* published by the National Staff Development Council (Pardini, 2008a, b, c, d), which can be found in the reference list.

I suggest we do not find time; we make time. I frequently see educators give up on a program because they are unable to find time for it. However, when some school districts I worked with added a fifteen-hour CEU (continuing education unit) or graduate credit to a coaching program, they found teachers somehow managed to create the time. Still, it was a task for the teachers to squeeze another activity into a very tight schedule.

One teacher lamented that she began a peer coaching program with only three colleagues, and the program died within two months because they were unable to find common time to observe and confer. How can teachers engage in collaboration when no sustained blocks of time are available and work must be accomplished in short bursts of intense effort, and often alone? And where can school leaders find the time for these activities?

I do not believe they can. Instead they need to develop strategies to make or bank time, similar to the schools highlighted earlier. Creativity and risk taking can produce more time. Our existing "boxes" of schedules, classrooms, periods, groups, and job descriptions may be obsolete. In fact, rather than think "out of the box," consider there may not *be* a box! What follows are some box-less ways to make time for coaching.

Box-Less Coaching Time

A rural school superintendent involved students in the schedule when most of the staff were needed to work on a plan for restructuring. There were 250 K–12 students working with twenty-three staff members. Five staff members remained to work with the students for one week while the other eighteen went to a retreat site to restructure the district. By pairing older and younger students, the five faculty members were able to plan an exciting, educational week for the entire student body. Community volunteers assisted when needed.

DVD technology offers another strategy to create time. Instead of in-class observation, video recording increases our flexibility and, therefore, creates more time. Other faculty members can schedule their own time to review a teacher's videotaped lessons for staff development or coaching. Such lessons can even be viewed at home at a time more convenient for the coach.

High school science teachers discovered they could record directions on DVD for their students and a substitute while the teachers were in coaching sessions. On the DVD, the teachers modeled the procedures necessary for the assigned work. Such modeling increased the substitute's effectiveness, and teachers felt more comfortable leaving their classes to attend a coaching session.

The teachers began to build a library of their own instructional DVDs for students who had been absent and for substitute teachers as well. They began trading DVDs with other colleagues, thus maximizing the use of time and, as a side effect, creating a culture of openness among educators.

Team teaching is another way to make time. Three teachers can work together on a K–3 team to teach students from four or five classrooms. The teachers who are freed up by this approach can easily participate in their pre- and postobservation coaching conferences.

Finally, here's a strategy for creating a fifteen-hour block of time for school faculty to take part in planning, coaching, or training. Divide the student population by the total number of certified staff in the building. Be sure to include administrators, guidance counselors, specialists, nurses, and others. (My experience shows a typical range of nine to twenty students per staff, with the average being thirteen.)

Have each staff member plan a five-day, two-and-a-half-hour (per day) seminar that could be taught to twice the number of students assigned to each staff member, or an average of twenty-six students. In the morning, half of the staff (staff A) would teach while the second half (staff B) would have time for planning, staff development, or coaching sessions. They reversed tasks in the afternoon. At the end of one week, students had completed two quality learning experiences while staff gained fifteen hours of time. This was accomplished with no extra cost for substitutes.

To achieve success with this plan, school leaders need to educate, inform, and share results with school boards and parents to assuage the concerns that time spent in coaching that is outside of direct contact with students is of ultimate value to students.

COACHING IS NOT EVALUATING

The importance of basing a coach-coachee relationship on trust is paramount. Remember that evaluators work for the system; coaches work for the coachee. Coaching is entirely nonevaluative and is based on what the coachee has revealed that he or she wants to improve. The content of comments, observations, or feedback is solely between the coach and coachee.

Checking in and reframing the relationship as it evolves often occurs at the beginning of a coaching program. We are all so ingrained with the mentality of judging that coaching seems almost too good to be true. The coach is there to work with the coachee on whatever the latter wants, not what the coach wants. That represents a shift in perception and behavior from the dynamics within an evaluative relationship.

Trust means saying what you're going to do and then doing it. Saying you're going to coach and then offering unsolicited advice, opinions, or judgment disrupts the trust established in the relationship. To ensure that coaching remains separate from evaluating, it's useful to establish norms and guidelines about the coaching relationship, as mentioned in chapter 5.

Norms are established with full participation of all involved in the coaching program. I recommend that they be written and, where possible, posted. As others join the program, they buy into the norms or agreement and may even suggest new ones. Mutual agreement to norms solidifies the coaching program as separate from evaluation so that when someone leans toward evaluation, one needs simply point to the norm and say, "We have agreed not to do that in this program."

IDENTIFYING THE PROBLEMS COACHING CAN RESOLVE

As well as dealing with issues of stress, time, and the fear that coaching may be like evaluation, it's important to refer back to the circumstances that originally led staff and administration to consider implementing a coaching program. Identifying problems that exist and gaining agreement as to what those problems are leads to a discussion of coaching as a solution. There are a couple of ways to open a conversation that lead to the development of a coaching program.

Susan Scott's (2002) *Fierce Conversations* provides a technique of probing for what she calls "mineral rights"—the underlying issue or issues—through asking Probing Questions. The probe is directed to an individual as well as to a group; the process uncovers an issue and its impact, while also paving the way for creating action plans to resolve it. Using the probing technique to advance the cause of a coaching program not only highlights the need for the program but solidifies how people are feeling and how they are impacted in the school generally. Here's what the Probing Questions might sound like:

Step 1: *Identify the most pressing issue.* "The issue that we most need to resolve is . . ."

Step 2: *Clarify the issue.* "What's going on?" "How long has it been going on?" "How bad are things?"

Step 3: *Determine current impact.* "How is this issue currently impacting me?" "What are the effects of this situation?" "What is the impact on others?" "When I consider the impact on myself and others, what are my feelings or emotions?"

Step 4: *Uncover future implications.* "If nothing changes, what's likely to happen?" "What's at stake for me relative to this issue?" "What's at stake for others?" "When I consider the possible outcomes, what are my emotions."

Step 5: Examine personal contributions to this issue. "What is my contribution in this situation?" ("How have I contributed to the problem?")

Step 6: Describe the ideal outcome. "When this issue is resolved, what difference will that make?" "What results will I enjoy?" "When this issue
is resolved, what results will others enjoy?" "When I imagine this
resolution, what are my emotions?" "What is the payoff for everyone
concerned?"

Step 7: Commit to action. "What is the most logical and useful step I could
take to move toward resolution?" "What's might get in my way and
how will I get past it?" "When will I take this step?"

After considering these questions, make a contract with yourself and with
others:

Contract with myself: Here Scott suggests that you identify what you are
willing to do to move things along, starting with making a contract
with yourself.

Contract with others: What do others indicate they are willing to do to
resolve the problem or make needed improvements?

After all this probing and soul searching, Scott suggests, "Take a break.
Walk around. Breathe. Breathing is good" (2002, p. 89).

Using a Force-Field Analysis

Another way problems can be identified and thus lead to the goal of implementing a coaching program relies on employing a simple instrument
called a Force Field Analysis developed by Kurt Lewin (1943), figure 8.1.

An identified problem—possibly uncovered through probing questions—
is written in the top box. This reflects the current state of affairs, or the Current Situation. Desired Change, the second box, represents a goal, such as a
schoolwide coaching program.

In figure 8.2, we have identified a problem for Current Situation as *not
enough time or money for needed, off-site staff development training for teachers.*
That is summarized in figure 8.2 as "Not enough teacher training."

The Desired Change is *to bring in a consultant to develop an in-house training on coaching that provides the opportunity for the school or district to carry on
with the coaching program without having to resort to frequent off-site staff development.* The goal is succinctly stated in figure 8.2 as "Implement in-house
coaching program."

The left column below the two boxes lists Forces for Change. These
represent driving forces that would encourage movement toward the goal.
These forces encourage change to occur. The forces may include available

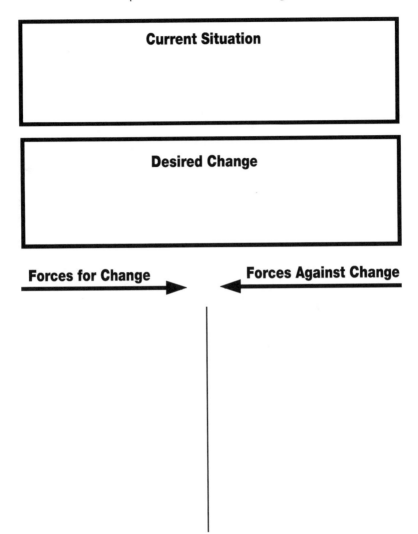

Figure 8.1. Force Field Analysis

resources, readiness and desire of staff, flexibility of schedules, agreement between administration and staff, support by parents, availability of grant funding, and the research we explored earlier that points to improvements in teaching and learning when a coaching program is in place.

The Forces Against Change column lists obstacles or restraining forces that may prevent change from happening. All the factors that may impede the desired change should be listed here and broken down into individual elements if they look too broad based. These forces may consist of insufficient

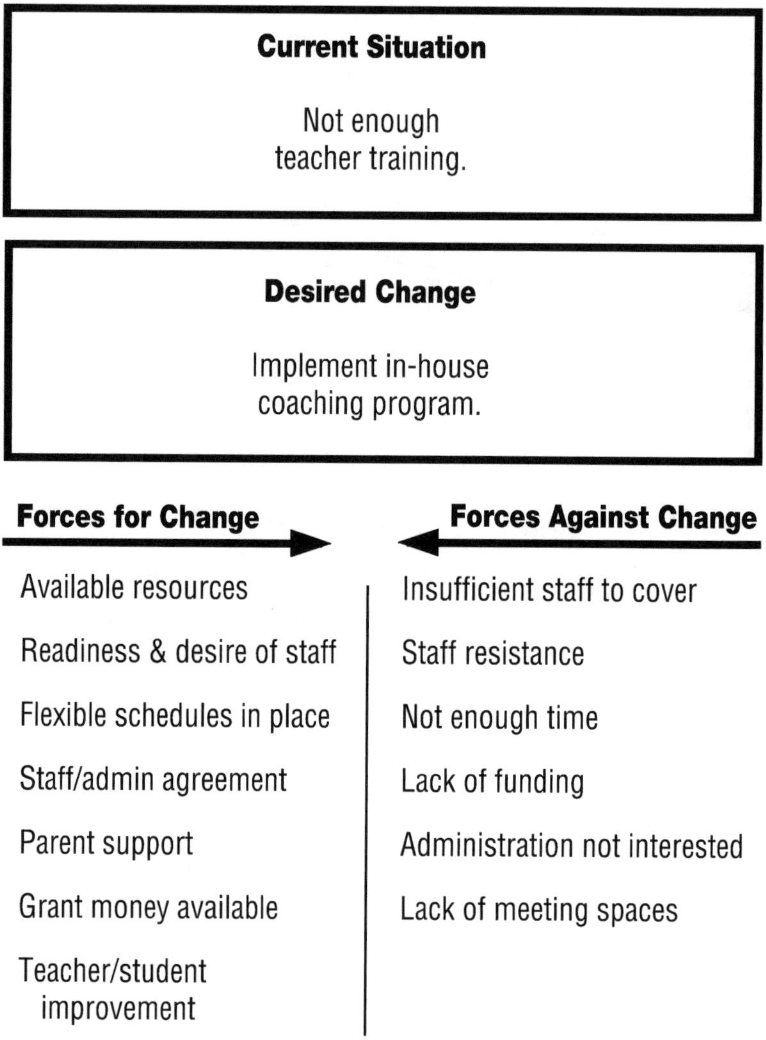

Current Situation

Not enough
teacher training.

Desired Change

Implement in-house
coaching program.

Forces for Change ➡	⬅ **Forces Against Change**
Available resources	Insufficient staff to cover
Readiness & desire of staff	Staff resistance
Flexible schedules in place	Not enough time
Staff/admin agreement	Lack of funding
Parent support	Administration not interested
Grant money available	Lack of meeting spaces
Teacher/student improvement	

Figure 8.2.   Force Field Analysis Implementing Coaching

staff to cover teachers doing coaching, staff resistance to coaching, time and schedule constraints, lack of funding, lack of interest by the administration, lack of available rooms to conduct conferences, and so on.

Next, you rank the Forces Against Change according to those that are strongest and thus most difficult to change as shown in figure 8.3. You do the same prioritization with the Forces for Change as to their strengths—what are your most potent forces advancing changes?

A little hint here: The benefits of coaching can be included on the Forces for Change side. Each Force Against Change can be offset by a Force for

---

Current Situation

Not enough
teacher training.

Desired Change

Implement in-house
coaching program.

Forces for Change ➤   ◀ **Forces Against Change**

Forces for Change	Forces Against Change
Available resources	Insufficient staff to cover
✔**Readiness & desire of staff**	Staff resistance
✔**Flexible schedules in place**	Not enough time
Staff/admin agreement	✔**Lack of funding**
Parent support	✔**Administration not interested**
Grant money available	Lack of meeting spaces
Teacher/student improvement	

Figure 8.3.   Force Field Analysis Coaching Solution

Change. For example, a Force Against Change may be lack of time. As we know from considering ways to "make time," the strongest Force for Change may be a willingness to be flexible in scheduling.

As you identify and prioritize the forces for and against the change, a solution often appears. In the example in figure 8.3, there is readiness among the staff and flexible schedules are already in place, yet there is a lack of interest by the administration and insufficient funds. Those were identified as the strongest forces on either side, for and against the Desired Change (indicated by the bold-face lines and check marks in figure 8.3).

What this reveals, however, is the possibility that the readiness and desire of staff might be capitalized upon to convince the administration of the value of the program. On the plus side, parent support is not in question and grant money is available to fund the program.

Each Force Field Analysis will tell its own tale, and the process serves as a useful model to identify the real factors involved in making a positive change. Since all coaching programs are customized to the circumstances of the school or district, this model can also help identify the kind of program that might work for yours. If the Forces against Change outnumber the Forces for Change, rather than scrap the idea of a coaching program, reframe its format to fit your situation, then complete the chart again and see if the Forces against Change diminish.

INTRODUCING COACHING

Armed with tools to counteract resistance to a coaching program, there remains the step of introducing it. This can take the form of a conversation between two teachers willing to help one another, which might evolve into a group of teachers meeting to create a program. The principal may wish to start a coaching program, or the teachers might present the administrator with an outline of the program, state why they desire it, and include ideas for implementation.

In schools with more experienced staff, it may be time to implement coaching as an alternative to evaluation. If most teachers have skill levels above the system's minimum competence covered in traditional evaluations, the school or district is ready to transfer to a coaching program.

In my experience as a trainer, a coaching program usually gets off to a good start with peer coaching training.

TWO SCHOOLS

Improving school for students is the practical reason for incorporating coaching, and therefore empowerment, into a teaching environment. Let's look at how students receive ultimate benefit from having a coaching program in place.

In a school where one teacher is responsible for a set number of students with no possibility of help from others—a situation we'll call School 1— coaching takes a back burner if it exists at all, as there is no help available. This represents the standard school of the past, where the teacher is isolated in his or her classroom. The teacher welcomes a group of students at the beginning of the school year, then teaches them throughout the year until they leave in the spring, to come back in the fall to a higher grade. The teacher then welcomes a new group, and the cycle begins again.

In School 1, teachers have no responsibility to assist other colleagues; they are in charge only of their individual students. If a teacher has a problem with low-performing students, he or she struggles alone. Low performers get ignored, transferred, or put into a negative category that will mark them for the rest of their school life, if not their whole lives. If the teacher does not know how to keep a high-performing student engaged, he or she does not receive suggestions or options from other teachers.

School 2 does things differently. Rather than follow the model of individual teachers responsible for a group of individual students with no possibility of support, in School 2 every student belongs to every teacher. Each teacher is responsible for the success of every classroom. Teachers work not as individuals but as a team. Students who are having trouble get the full support of the teaching team, and they feel it. In School 1, teachers and students are isolated. In School 2, teachers are part of a team that works together to ensure the success of all students.

In reality, individual teachers can no longer take a group of kids into a classroom and be successful by themselves. They must have an intimate involvement with teachers who taught those students the previous year, the ones they will teach the following year, and others involved with them, from other teachers to parents to sports coaches, counselors, and so on.

One option in a school that affirms everyone's responsibility for all students is to create a vertical team. Let's say the team consists of first-, second-, and third-grade teachers in an elementary school. A beginning teacher teaches second grade. The scaffolding for teamwork is coaching. Let's say the second-grade teacher has every student who was previously in the first-grade class. It's only natural for the first- and second-grade teachers to collaborate and for the first-grade teacher to assist the beginning second-grade teacher—ditto for the second- and third-grade teachers. Every student will pass through each of their classrooms, so it is in their best interest to help one another. Teachers benefit from each other's knowledge and support, and three guesses who benefits the most—the students.

Sometimes there is crossover from School 1 and School 2. A staff of teachers—the teaching team—may focus on a whole group of students, such as sixth-grade teachers focusing on all sixth-grade students. Or it may go the other way—an individual teacher may take care of individual students.

For the most part, however, teachers in the model of School 2—with a teaching team responsible for all students—benefit from coaching, and all benefit from the synergy that occurs when a team of focused educators takes every student into account. You will know when your school is moving to the School 2 model by the number of times individual student names appear on the agenda of your staff meetings. The more often the agenda lists names of students who may need help or input from all on the teaching team rather than simply on curriculum or system issues, the more it is evident that your school is focused on individual students and the closer you are to arriving at School 2 status.

Large-School Solutions

Is your school too big to have every teacher responsible for every student? Here's an example of how a model similar to many advisor/advisee programs can be implemented in a large high school. Take the number of students in the high school and divide that number by the number of faculty. Each faculty member takes responsibility for a team of kids, often only sixteen students. One of those teachers—we'll call him Josh—would attend parent conferences for each of the students on his team. Josh would be the person the student goes to for guidance, assistance, and support. Let's say Josh teaches English and a student is having a lot of trouble in chemistry. In the model of coaching and collaboration, Josh simply consults the student's chemistry teacher, and together they work on a plan to help the student.

This model can work in reverse as well. The chemistry teacher has 120 students, so there is no way he or she can know every one of them. If there are a couple of students acting up in chemistry class, usually at the instigation of a student named Vince, the chemistry teacher goes to Josh, who is the advisor for Vince, and they consult.

What we're really talking about is creating small learning communities within a large school. Those teachers responsible for a set number of students have their own communities of students. Unlike having these individuals in a classroom, however, the advisor gets to know them in all aspects of their learning. The advisors—the "Joshes"—always have access to the other teachers who teach or otherwise work with the same students.

Small Learning Communities

Today many schools look at creating small learning communities to increase the focus on individual student success. Some middle schools form sixth-, seventh-, and eighth-grade "houses" where teams of teachers have a three-year responsibility for a group of students. Teachers coaching colleagues within these houses experience an increased sense of collaboration and at the same time provide a model of cooperation for students.

Let's say one house of advisors consists of math teachers from each grade. They would help students as they travel from sixth to eighth grade, minimizing repetition of content. This system allows the students to build on their math skills from year to year with a common and familiar language, and it gives students the full support of their teachers throughout their middle school years.

In my estimation, School 1 is obsolete, although sadly many schools still operate in that model. To move from School 1 to the model of School 2, coaching is vital. Coaching creates the teamwork necessary to serve students. The trust associated with coaching allows teachers to "let go" of their individual classrooms, seek options, gain support from others, and share in failures and successes. By "let go" I mean share in the wealth of ideas generated in the classroom. The teacher needs no longer be possessive and protective of the students; they belong to all the teachers.

Professional Learning Communities

Professional learning communities—PLCs—extend the concept of small learning communities to embrace the whole learning organization. Gaining traction throughout the country, PLCs offer teachers an opportunity to collaborate with each other, with others in the school community, and with the neighborhood in which the school resides.

Schools working with PLCs apply the concept of coaching in a variety of ways. Teachers in work or study groups might call them learning communities. Some schools bring community members in to work with teachers and staff on certain curricula or special events. Still others limit the PLC to teacher staff development. In each, a commitment from the administrator and school leadership supports the community's willingness to collaborate and share norms and values for student learning.

At the heart of PLCs is a shift from a concentration on teaching to one that focuses on learning. While that might sound flippant, at its core is a real change in perspective that helps to ensure that student learning—or lack of learning—drives teacher behavior and is the focus of professional development. Beyond that, PLCs' focus is on shared learning among teachers in any given PLC. At the same time, PLCs call on collaboration and support from other professionals, parents, coaches, administrators, and staff with a shared vision of assisting students to learn.

The idea of PLCs carries a lot of power and possibility, not only for the advancement of coaching and training for teachers, but for a quantum shift in the focus on student learning and in developing a culture of learning throughout the school organization and community beyond.

Peter Senge, director at the Center for Organizational Learning and author of *The Fifth Discipline: The Art and Practice of the Learning Organization* (1999), coined the term "learning organization," creating a significant shift in the field of organizational development. Relying on his background as a scientist and aerospace engineer, Senge applied *systems thinking* to the concept of learning within an organization. According to his theory, organizations should have a continuous system of learning that is always adapting and forever improving. Within that system—and within PLCs—there exists a shared vision, arrived at in the community, rather than dictated by management in a top-down style.

Likewise, PLCs offer teachers the opportunity to collaborate, analyze issues, and discuss ways to improve their classroom practice. Isolation disappears with improved morale and support of others. Within this arena, the coaching relationship flourishes as teachers grapple with techniques to both improve teaching and to work more successfully with their students in a collaborative culture of their own. Teachers are accountable to one another and to their commitment in a shared and focused vision of their success with students and the viability of their PLC.

Once again, however, there looms the issue of finding—or making—time to commit to a thriving PLC. Richard DuFour, a recognized national expert in PLCs and retired superintendent of Adlai Stevenson High School in Lincolnshire, Illinois, makes this comment in his *Educational Leadership* article "What Is a 'Professional Learning Community'?": "Faculties must stop making excuses for failing to collaborate. Few educators publicly assert that working in isolation is the best strategy for improving schools. Instead, they give reasons why it is impossible for them to work together" (2004, p. 10).

DuFour (2004) then cites Roland S. Barth from a 1991 *Phi Delta Kappan* article "Restructuring Schools: Some Questions for Teachers and Principals": "Are teachers and administrators willing to accept the fact that they are part of the problem? . . . God didn't create self-contained classrooms, 50-minute periods, and subjects taught in isolation. We did—because we find working alone safer than and preferable to working together" (DuFour, 2004, p. 126–27).

Teachers discover early on that when a student is not learning or not learning well enough, the choices are difficult. Do they move ahead anyway to cover content, hoping the student will catch up? Do they dumb down the lessons? Should they suggest remedial classes? Or do they simply leave the student behind, against the mandate and their own integrity as teachers?

PLCs offer a forum for teachers to collaborate with one another on a coordinated strategy for student success. They drop possessiveness about whose student is whose and encourage others to step in to pose or answer questions, help in formulating ideas, and provide additional time and support as needed and available. In the process they turn their collective energies toward the original intent of the PLC: a focus on learning.

Rather than a fad or another gimmick for education, PLCs reflect a shift in how we approach not only teaching but also management of people in the workforce. Employees, like students, have access to more information than ever before. Transparency is not only sought; it is required to achieve successfully functioning teams. Collaboration is far more effective than a top-down exchange where one gives instructions and the other works to comply. There's just too much to know at school and in the workplace. And there's too much at stake at both.

If you aim for a culture of coaching, PLCs are an excellent way for a group to focus on the overall vision and develop and encourage schools and teachers in techniques of excellence in teacher performance. This in turn creates leaders to move well beyond the "box" of teaching to embrace options for learning, coaching, and other staff development for teachers and administrators alike.

Certainly there is more to be said about PLCs than we have space for here—how to start them, ways to overcome obstacles to their formation, how they are applied, and examples of their success. For our purposes, working within a PLC delivers tremendous opportunities for coaching. Sometimes a coaching observation in a single teacher's classroom or perhaps one in each of the PLC members' classrooms stems from a conversation held earlier in the PLC. Other times, an observation from a single coaching experience develops into a topic for conversation at a future PLC session.

PLCs also allow time and space for celebrations and for collaboration among teachers, each of whom are focused on the success of every student. As an individual teacher succeeds in getting a student to read or to stop acting up or to engage in a lesson, the whole team can celebrate the success of that student as "our" student.

SUMMARY

Over the years I have seen countless ways coaching has benefited educators, whether teachers, administrators, principals, or staff members. I have seen how students benefit from the work of teachers who are confident, effective, highly skilled, and yes, *happy* because they have coaches to rely on for support and encouragement.

The addition of a culture of coaching increases the quality of a school environment. Teachers and students alike can move beyond survival mode into the freedom and fun of learning, collaborating, and creating together. Teachers can move from good to great. Time can be freed up through creative solutions that not only allow for the structure of the coaching process but also bring much-needed time to reflect and innovate.

Following the process of a preobservation conference, where the teachers' vision and agenda are uncovered, observing, and then giving feedback in the postobservation conference becomes a natural and smooth process with time. Eventually, those being coached are unable to conceive of teaching without the benefit of coaching. The coachee is the focus, yet the coach also learns, improves, and is rewarded by the successes of his or her protégé. In the process, student learning improves. What's not to like?

To implement a coaching program, one needs to identify issues and goals and then just begin. All change begins with a conversation. There are lots of ways to format a coaching program and many applications for it.

In chapter 9, you will see case studies and examples of coaching programs in the United States and in other countries as well. If you are not already inspired to benefit from the positive impact that coaching can have on your school, district, or organization, perhaps you'll find additional motivation in actual success stories.

RESEARCH SHOWS

Professional Learning Communities

- The National Commission on Teaching and America's Future writes that "it's time to end the practice of solo teachers in isolated classrooms. . . . [Teaching needs to change from] the 20th century culture of solo teaching to a transformative 21st century model in which new teachers become a part of a community of learners" (Fulton, Yoon, & Lee, 2005, p. 6).
- "Clearly, mentoring programs help school districts create these nurturing environments which reduce teacher isolation, and, in turn, inspire new teachers" (Heider, 2005, p. 1).

9

Who Has Coaching Programs?
How Are They Working?

BUILT TO LAST: READING PROGRAM, HILLSBOROUGH COUNTY, FLORIDA

When we published our first edition of this book in 2005, the Hillsborough County, Florida, K–3 Reading First program had already been underway for several years. Fast forward to the present, and it has taken on a life of its own. It has expanded to encompass coaching teachers of kindergarten to fifth-grade students and is known as the K–5 Reading First program. Coaching has spilled over into other content areas and is destined to continue in that direction.

As Assistant Principal Mary Vreeman pointed out in chapter 1, once the concept and process of coaching gets underway, it often permeates the approach to teaching and communicating throughout the school or district. "This was career changing for me," admits Mary. "Being a teacher holds a certain honor, and when the world of coaching opened up to me, it made me a better teacher. Now I am a lifelong learner and have developed an obsession about becoming better with everything I learn!"

Similar to educators in other coaching programs underway throughout the country and now the world, those in Hillsborough grappled initially with the gap that occurred between staff development and actual application in the classroom. The seminal research conducted by Joyce and Showers in 1993 mentioned in chapter 1 shows the powerful impact of feedback and coaching on skill transfer (see table 9.1). This and other research about the value of coaching set the stage for support and administration of the coaching program in Hillsborough County and elsewhere.

Table 9.1. Transfer of Learning by Types of Training

Training Provided	Skill Development	Accurate Use in Class
Theory/Knowledge	5%	0–5%
Theory/Modeling	50%	5%
Theory/Modeling/ Practice and Feedback	90%	5%
Theory/Modeling/Practice/ Feedback and Coaching	90%	75–90%

Source: *The Coaching of Teaching* by Joyce and Showers (1993)

"Coaching keeps staff development training in place," says Mellissa Alonso, one of the originators and now supervisor of the Elementary Reading Coach Project in Hillsborough County. "The staff development information learned in the past often loses direct translation to the classroom. Teachers can hit a brick wall. If it fails, they revert back to old practices, not having the time to recreate the training that occurred earlier. With coaching, a new practice just learned—or improvement of an existing strategy—becomes easily ingrained."

At Hillsborough, the coaching is rooted in student achievement. They began their coaching program with the youngest students to create the most impact and offer early intervention in reading. Apparently it paid off, as the state added another level of funding to the Reading First initiative.

To become a coach in Hillsborough County, one has to go through four layers of review. Coaching applicants are recruited through districtwide advertisements. Initially, they undergo a rigorous screening process designed to assess their level of content knowledge and interpersonal skills, particularly their ability to work with adults. The interview is often followed by classroom observations and discussions with the applicant's principal. Applicants who pass this screening process are accepted into the training program.

Training in coaching begins during the school year with bimonthly after-school meetings of the training cadre. Coaches receive assignments that help them implement the techniques and strategies learned in training, specifically related to reading strategies they can try immediately with students. District personnel who are members of the elementary language-arts team conduct classroom observations of the reading coaches during this process in order to better understand each coach's strengths and weaknesses. They use this information to help customize the training to better meet the coaches' needs.

A mandatory summer institute conducted in June follows the year of training. It includes programs at several school sites that accommodate the Reading Coach practicum—applying the coaching skills in classrooms with students attending summer school. Coaches work in pairs each morning to deliver classroom instruction that reflects their training and allows them to practice their coaching skills by coaching their partners. Each afternoon they attend additional training. Then they conduct exit interviews at the close of the institute to summarize each coach's progress, debrief their learning and that of their students, target areas for continued growth, and receive feedback about the effectiveness of the training program.

Finally, those who have gone through the institute are assigned an experienced coach or mentor whom they can shadow, visit, or work with as another line of support. At that point they have become site-based trainers, enter into "coach-the-coach" sessions, and become certified as district trainers, able to train across the district for the program.

Teachers are able to see the development of coaches as a result of this program, and their level of respect for them increases. Being a coach or working with a coach is now perceived not as a deficit, needing to be coached to "get better," but as a chance for greatness. "Teachers have begun to understand that, as coaches, they can reach more students than in their classrooms," says Alonso. "Not directly teaching in the classroom does not mean you are missing students. All coaching is student-focused. Everything we do is about the students."

Administrators in Hillsborough County have embraced the program, and every school now has a reading coach—a substantial change from when the program began. And the coaches are not picked by the principal; they are preselected by leaders administering the coaching program. These coaches, then, often step into other leadership roles, such as that of assistant principals, media specialists, or resource teachers.

To accommodate the growing cadre of coaches, these area leaders meet monthly to share ideas, celebrate, work on their video feedback, review testing data, discuss methods of communicating with students, and otherwise work toward the common goal of better teaching and increased student achievement. A position description of the role of coach has been approved by the school board and is found in the appendix.

There is now a waiting list for teacher applicants who want to become coaches. As a response, Hillsborough County has piloted a "fast track" program to accommodate more coaches into the system and comply with the superintendent's request that there continually be a coach at every school site. Applicants are teachers who have had the experience of being coached, so they can learn about coaching as they themselves are coached. "This would not have happened in our initial years," admits Alonso. "Now these teachers understand the coaching process because they have been through it and want to embrace coaching for themselves."

So all in all, I think it's fair to say that the "culture of coaching" is alive and well in Hillsborough County!

ROLE REHEARSAL: SALEM-KEIZER, OREGON

As with Hillsborough County, the Salem-Keizer School District in Oregon found it became important to develop a clear and specific job description for coaches in their program. Initially, defining the position was important to assuage the stigma that coaches were there to "fix" someone. Later, "coach" developed into a role that has become a vital part of their learning community.

Started in 2004 as a program funded through Title 1, the Salem-Keizer coaching program had to deal with the perception held by some teachers was that coaching was an extension of the administration. While that was never the case, many teachers feared that coaches would only be working with struggling teachers.

Michael Miller, who served as director of elementary operations for twenty-five schools and then as director of professional development in the Salem-Keizer School District, came to Performance Learning Systems, Inc., coaching training in 2004. What startled him was the shift in approach and perspective that said coaching was for good teachers; coaching was not based on a deficit model but on one that encouraged continuous improvement.

Miller was instrumental in broadening the Salem-Keizer coaching program to non-Title I schools. He enlisted the assistance of Gretchen "Boo" Rayburn to serve on his newly created "coach cadre" and serve as a grassroots organizer, facilitating collaboration and communication among coaches.

The coaching program at Salem-Keizer is now districtwide and federally funded for Titles I and II and general coaching.

Miller brought in training for all coaches, using the first edition of this book as a base. A truncated training session was developed with principals to give them the idea of what coaching and its training entailed, and to let them discover the differences between collegial and technical coaching models.

Now retired, Miller recalls the coach cadre had to "emphasize with the coaches and the principals that coaches were not to be used as assistant principals, after-school organizers, testing coordinators, recess monitors, reading group leaders, or otherwise given additional duties." They even delivered presentations to principals to help them realize the value of allowing coaches to serve exclusively as coaches and taught some "push back" skills—ways teachers could dialogue with principals and defend the roles and responsibilities of the coach. Miller and his team learned to emphasize a coach's focus on student achievement over being recruited to fill in as needed in other capacities. If these coaches were filling in, they were not coaching, thus diluting the effectiveness of their position.

Defining and redefining the role of a coach was ongoing in the early years, and it continues today as teachers fear the coaching program could disappear and that they will again be left in isolation. New teachers fresh from a student-teaching experience with a mentor teacher are eager to have a coach in their classrooms. Boo Rayburn, now an instructional coach at Salem-Keizer, recognized the shift from the "fix-it" model to one that emphasizes coaching the best teachers first, and she understood it was one that made sense. It took time for teachers to believe that the coaching program was really designed to enhance teaching rather than fix problems. Moreover, Rayburn found a need to amplify training about coaching with more real-time collaboration.

"We had great training, read the book, used the manuals, and did the role plays," said Rayburn. "But when we went back to our schools, something was missing. We needed a better way to share with staff what coaching really meant—they had to see the role of coach rehearsed to move them away from what they saw in our earlier coaching days—a Title I teacher fixing problems rather than using the model of coaching a teacher on how to improve what he or she already does."

Salem-Keizer has since developed the "Instructional Coach Guidebook," which clearly defines roles, models, and support systems for instructional coaching; it also includes a log for tracking a coach's progress and follow-up with teachers, a feature that was requested by the coaches. A copy of this guidebook is found in the appendix.

Meanwhile, Boo Rayburn realized that beyond the coaching and training, she needed to provide a forum for coaches to get together to work on each other's skills, ask questions, and receive support. Rayburn also knew she and the other coaches had to sell teachers on the coaching concept and brought that to the fore in their group sessions. "We were chosen to be coaches because we were good teachers," she said. "Now we had to show the teachers how coaching 'pays it forward' to allow them to move from good teaching to great teaching."

When asked why he thought teachers needed a coach at all, Miller responded he felt everyone needs a coach. Principals from various schools coach one another from other schools; there is group coaching. In Salem-Keizer, coaches are in every high school. Coaching is offered as a resource, and many teachers request to have a coach.

As to whether it's working, Miller says they tried to get some quantitative data to make the point that schools with coaching are in better shape than those without. But he admits, "It's hard to get that longitudinal data. Now that we have more coaches, however, we have a better sense of improvement. And there is a lot of anecdotal data, such as 'having a coach in my room has saved my career,' 'coaching has turned my career around,' 'coaching has energized my teaching,' and so forth."

"Besides," he adds, "coaching forces you to be introspective, to look at your own practice. None of us do that enough."

Amen to that.

CULTURES WITHIN A CULTURE:
ENKA SCHOOLS, ISTANBUL, TURKEY

More than half way around the world as the crow flies are teachers and coaches working together in a program at the Enka Schools in Istanbul, Turkey.

Enka Schools are both international and national. The national aspect of Enka Schools is comprised of students who are predominantly from Turkey and whose parents have enrolled them in this type of private school to receive a Western-style education. Enka Schools are approved by the Turkish Ministry of Education and are also accredited by the International Baccalaureate Organisation whose Primary Years Programme and Diploma Programme have been adopted by Enka Schools. Enka Schools belong to the Council of International Schools and the European Council of International Schools (ECIS). The curriculum, designed to groom students for acceptance at universities worldwide, combines both national and international content and methodology, providing an interesting mix—not dissimilar to the mix teachers are creating in the coaching program itself.

Enka Schools' director Darlene Fisher was born in New Zealand and raised in Australia and in multicultural Singapore, an international mix all by herself. She arrived in Turkey via India, Thailand, and Oman with over ten years in international education; eighteen years in Melbourne, Australia; and a one-year stint in the state of Connecticut.

Most recently, Darlene was dean of students in Thailand and the head of a high school in India before taking her current position in Istanbul. She and her strong leadership team launched the coaching program at Enka Schools in 2007. They have been thrilled at the opportunities it provides to capture best practices from many cultures that enhance teacher growth and student learning. The coaching program includes 165 teachers, many of whom speak both English and Turkish. Approximately a quarter of the cadre of teachers is international and the rest national.

In November 2006, Darlene and some of her Turkish leadership staff undertook a Performance Learning Systems training course in coaching at ECIS in Madrid that included many of the concepts, processes, and skills discussed in this book. Empowered by the experience, an executive committee formed to support the program and provide a platform for Enka Schools to become an example of best practices in Turkey. Armed with that support and the collaboration of her principals, Darlene went forth with passion, funding, and determination to offer her services to launch and run the coaching program.

Then came the hard part.

The Enka Schools leadership team was faced with introducing a concept that was foreign to many teachers, and most particularly to those whose culture eschewed the appearance of vulnerability, of showing any weaknesses. As someone who has spent her whole life in multicultural environments, Darlene needed to rely on her knowledge of diverse cultures and speak to the teachers' level of comfort and understanding. She and her Turkish leadership team clearly understood this need and worked together to extol the benefits and value of coaching as a way to improve teaching. They used their own coaching skills to give encouragement and to pave the way for teachers to share with other teachers, to express concerns, to be a little vulnerable themselves.

Referencing the work of Geert Hofstede, a Dutch psychologist who analyzed multiple cultures from five perspectives, Darlene pointed to the concept of "power distance ratio" to explain how she worked with Western and Turkish cultures to achieve a blend. In shorthand, power distance ratio refers to a continuum with top-down hierarchy on one side, and full equality on the other. "We needed to respond differently to different levels of openness as we modified a concept of teaching by incorporating a level of coaching," Darlene explained. "Cultures in an organization are reflections of the hard-wiring of our brains. We can't help how we are wired, but we can change how we behave."

Once the training and the coaching programs were launched, however, many teachers at Enka Schools showed immediate interest in coaching as a way to achieve best practices. Already a highly developed faculty, the teachers of Enka Schools attended professional development programs and workshops offered both live and online through a variety of sources, including workshops provided through the International Baccalaureate program. Coaching, however, offered an ongoing relationship to support professional development.

As some teachers became more accepting and willing to share their needs and requests with other teachers—shedding some of their reluctance and deciding to share at their own pace—they saw how coaching offered a way of continuous improvement. To shore that up, Darlene stressed that teachers who were best served by coaching were those who were good teachers to begin with—that they were moving from "good" to "great"—which went a long way to alleviate the sense of a "deficit model" that existed in the past.

In addition, the leadership team decided that coaches could not also be involved in evaluation, and this decision helped teachers to relax about sharing their thoughts and concerns. Beyond that, the students, raised in a culture of open borders through technology, already tended to be collaborative and international in perspective. In a sense, the students set an example for teachers to risk openness, and teachers modeled the value of collaboration and support as they learned to work together in an open environment.

For now, the international teachers tend to form coaching relationships with other international educators and the national teachers coach one another. Mixing the cultures in coaching relationships is one the goals of Darlene and her leadership team, but they admit that, as a regular process, it is down the road a bit.

"We want to reach every child and develop his or her potential rather than rely on the old concept of teachers filling up an 'empty jug,' " says Darlene. "Our coaching program will never be implemented the same in any two schools, and it can only work in schools where there is a positive attitude toward self-development." And to ride with those variations, Darlene adds, "If you remain flexible and determined and focused on outcomes for students, then coaching is presented as a wonderful tool teachers can use to help their students. It certainly has incredible potential for enhancing student achievement through better teaching. It has a tremendous impact."

As to the future, Darlene expects a 20 to 30 percent increase in participation, training, and growth in the realm of coaching among national and international teachers. Throughout the school year, she will collect ideas and feedback and will support and encourage more coaching relationships and training. Assessment of progress comes in the form of reports teachers and coaches complete throughout the year, recounting their coaching experience. These reports are posted on the Enka Schools Intranet, and while they remain anonymous (at least of this writing), Darlene is counting on an increase in postings and methods to continually adjust her own dance of honoring two cultures at varying places on the "open sharing" continuum. A sample of this report, "Coaching Feedback: Enka Schools, Turkey" is found in the appendix.

Darlene's advice to others formulating a coaching program within another culture is to pay attention to the normal behavior around authority, those who evaluate teachers. Can a worker analyze and question a boss? If so, can he or she do that with colleagues as a normal part of life? The answer reveals at what level the culture may be in terms of opening up to airing of ideas, thoughts, and feedback. Likewise, can a teacher admit to not being the "boss," a fount of knowledge and skills, but open to sharing or asking for support from others? Depending on what is found, Darlene suggests, you begin the coaching program by first working within the culture that exists, and then move toward opening it up to a school culture that will accept the concept of coaching.

This advice sounds valid for many coaching programs being launched in the United States and elsewhere. Yet in Turkey, Darlene and her leadership team are mixing two cultures as they create yet a third culture of coaching, certainly a challenge. And what motivates Darlene to take on this challenge?

"Coaching is the *only* thing that will help a school maintain ongoing development as a part of its culture," she answers. "Otherwise, new ideas can be seen as 'change,' yet another thing to deal with, and will always run into resistance. With coaching in place, we can develop a mentality of 'how can I do something better?' It's continuous improvement and dynamic stability that we seek, and it makes for better teaching. It's the strongest and most wonderful thing you could ever do with a school."

Hats off to the Enka team!

WHAT IF? THE INSTRUCTIONAL FACILITATORS COACHING PROGRAM: ARKANSAS STATE DEPARTMENT OF EDUCATION, LITTLE ROCK, ARKANSAS

When asked why a teacher would even need a coach, Debbie Coffman, Arkansas State Department of Education associate director of professional development, offers a quick response by drawing an analogy. Many teachers used rotary dial telephones in college, she points out, and they are now managing their communication and their schedules on Blackberries and iPhones. In short, the role of teacher has changed as dramatically as technology and, like technology, will continue to do so. Beyond being instructors in classrooms, teachers have had to become multifaceted, highly talented experts in a variety of roles.

"Just as experts in other fields benefit from another set of eyes and ears to improve their practice," Debbie explains, "teachers likewise benefit and even require continual learning, practice, a honing of skills, and reflection with other colleagues to improve as a teacher. And in the end," she adds, "it's all about helping the student."

The coaching program at the Arkansas State Department of Education (DOE) began in 2004 as a literacy program. The state's focus was on literacy content. Then the program manager, Debbie, offered literacy content knowledge that coaches could take back to their schools. Later promoted to lead professional development for the state, she brought in Karen Taylor in 2007 as a literacy specialist with the official title of public school program advisor.

Together, Debbie, Karen, and their instructional facilitators (as they call their instructional coaches) core team masterminded the instructional coaching/facilitating focus, working long and hard to launch a program in response to the need expressed by many schools in the state that they wanted quality training in the skills and art of coaching. Back then, there was nothing available at the state level or from the university. While Karen, Debbie, and their instructional facilitators (IFs) core team learned about coaching as an opportunity to advance teacher learning by reading books and taking part in programs popping up all over the country, no systematic plan was in place for professional development.

Now their coaching program has been endorsed by the Arkansas State Board of Education, and IFs have the opportunity to be licensed by the state after eighteen hours of university study. These licenses can ultimately lead IFs to become curriculum program administrators. Principals now have finally accepted and embraced the IFs' function; even in times of budget-cutting, the role of IF has been left untouched.

Obviously, the road from a lack of available coaching and training—or even an awareness of its value—to full authorization and endorsement of the IF program by the Arkansas State Board of Education was hardly smoothly paved or fast paced. Change creates resistance, and resistance offered obstacles to be overcome.

First, the teacher-coaches had to receive training in the skills of coaching. Their initial coaching had been focused on content: literacy, science, math, and so forth. But what they began hearing was a need for training in how to work with other adults. The coaches needed to know how to gain buy-in from other teachers; to learn and practice collaboration and facilitation skills. What techniques should they use? How, where, and when could they practice them? What does it mean to lead a team? And how do we build a system within the school for reflection, building leaders within that team?

To answer these questions, IFs worked in coaching relationships with individual teachers on specific instructional strategies. While teachers were very successful in the classroom with students, the IFs wanted to expand teacher improvement in other ways, helping to clarify impact on other teachers. Teachers did not always understand the role of the IFs. Neither did the principals.

Frustrated at first, the professional staff development team and the IFs already in place at the Arkansas DOE discussed, briefed, debriefed, and brought in research to shore up belief in what they were doing with other teachers, administrators, and prospective coaches. They studied and shared books on instructional coaching, such as this one and the work of Dr. Jim Knight, as well as books by Joellen Killion of the National Staff Development Council and others. They expanded the amount of training time, brought in experts to assist, crafted a common language, and worked on organization of time and priority. "We were ready with all the right problems," recalls Debbie.

"Setting up a coaching program does not happen overnight; it is not a quick fix," Karen admits. "Change takes a lot of work. It is messy. People cry. You need to do a lot of thinking through what you're going to say, do, and know what you're going to talk about before pushing a coaching culture. And you need to be open to learning, to failing, and to succeeding too."

They persevered and were able to tap and keep good educators willing to expand into coaching roles. Learning the language of coaching from the training they received from Performance Learning Systems, Inc., and its model, *Questions for Life*, the coaching cadre began to grow. Key to overcoming resistance was making a clear distinction between coaching and evaluating; to use language that adults recognize as that of a peer coach, an equal, rather than an authority with judgment and evaluation.

IFs now serve full time; there is a state-approved job description, and administrators have seen their impact on teachers and ultimately students. At this writing, they also have an Arkansas Instructional Facilitators Ning, an online platform and social network where IFs can share vital information with one another. (Check out the Arkansas Instructional Facilitators Ning website at http://www.arkansasif.ning.com or e-mail them at invitations@ arkansasif.ning.com.)

One of the pitfalls that occurs in coaching happens when a coach takes on a teacher's problem as his or her own. A better approach is to continue to focus on the concerns, desires, and agenda of the teacher, else he or she may shut down and resist. IFs within the Arkansas system work with learning specialists and each other to think and rethink how they approach the teacher, the curriculum, and the specific schools. They have formed co-op groups where coaches train with specific learning specialists to better grasp the teachers' areas of expertise. Then the IFs return to the school better armed to coach on teachers' terms. They receive an IFs tool kit—a notebook filled with various handouts from instructional coaching training, materials, and tools downloaded from the Internet, which serve as a reference tool for specialists when they go into the schools for support visits with the coaches/facilitators.

"We entered into this work because our schools were requesting training and coaching," reflects Karen. "We thought we would pull together a professional development learning opportunity. But now, not only have we done that, we have learned to embrace it, to fully live it. Our whole team has pulled together. We work together in a different culture. And the one-on-one coaching has nourished us even as we deliver more of it to teachers throughout the state."

As to what advice the Arkansas DOE team of learning specialists and IFs would give to others launching a coaching program, they all chimed in to say, "Start with the administrators first!"

Echoing that sentiment is a coaching program underway in the Caribbean island of Aruba. Next stop!

IF WE BUILD IT, THEY WILL COME:
THE CARIBBEAN ISLAND OF ARUBA

There is only one teacher-training institute in the lovely island of Aruba in the Dutch Caribbean. The Center of Professional Development and Lifelong Learning of the Instituto Pedagogico Arubano (IPA) serves the 1,500 teachers currently on the seventy square miles of island and is headed by the dynamic and high-spirited Ingrid Kuiperdal. Originally a psychologist by profession, Ingrid has directed professional staff development within the IPA since 2000.

"Our dedicated team and our department started with the coaching-program when we discovered that our in-service training fell short of results in terms of real implementation of the innovations in the classroom practices or schools," Ingrid recalls. "We sought a coaching concept that could meet the needs of the teachers and also support our way of thinking about education, and we found it in the book *Quality Teaching in a Culture of Coaching*. Right now," she adds, "we are striving to create that culture within our own institution first and then in the rest of the educational field of Aruba."

Formerly a colony of Holland, Aruba obtained separate status in 1986 and boasts its own governor and government. Recently, their Ministry of Education, Social Affairs, and Infrastructure created *A Strategic National Education Plan*, which launched a new vision for the development of students into global, responsible, and satisfied citizens who are also lifelong learners and contribute to the community's quality of life.

With about 120,000 inhabitants made up of an international mixture of well-educated, hospitable people, modern Aruban ancestry mixes Caiquetio Indian, Latin American, African from the Caribbean, and European. It has a strong economy, excellent living conditions, and prime weather attracting tourists from all over the world. Today, the island claims over seventy-nine different nationalities that live and work together peacefully on the island.

While Aruba has broken away from colonization with Holland, effects of this heritage are still felt, especially in education, according to Ingrid. She cites as an example: "The Ministry of Education and the Minister have to decide first on much of the content within the staff development and training that the IPA facilitates: a top-down model." And just as others have expressed in some of the programs highlighted in this book, shifting the vision and the implementation of an open culture of coaching from one that is more hierarchical and guarded takes the three p's of passion, patience, and perseverance.

Once the professional staff development team at the IPA latched onto the concept of coaching, however, the three p's served them well. Now schools are coming to them to see about training in coaching.

Training in the concept and skills of coaching began with a conference in 2006 involving the entire field of education in Aruba: the department of education, the inspectors, the school boards, and the ministers. Follow-up workshops involved training in coaching skills for teachers within the IPA, some mentors, and others.

Teachers and other educational professionals then formed work groups to implement the different forms of coaching within the IPA. In short, they began by creating the culture of coaching at IPA in order to model it for others. They undertook various activities for those within the IPA, such as the following:

- Every teacher was motivated to find a coach and serve as a coach.
- Teachers who in the past were supervised in their work were now also coached.
- A teacher became the coach of a group of IPA alumni from secondary schools.
- The IPA team trained teachers, administrative, and facilities workers of the IPA who were not able to participate in the first coaching training.

"This was a great success," shares Ingrid. "Now we can say that everyone in the IPA has heard and participated in coaching sessions in one way or another. We continue to work at motivating everyone in the IPA to continue using the knowledge, to continue to develop their competencies, and to continue to help create this culture of coaching in the IPA."

Each teacher and staff within the IPA has his or her own peer coach, and as they learn more about themselves, they continue to see innovations that would work for teachers. Indeed, the staff development team within the IPA has even altered their approach to how they offer training and staff development to teachers.

Rather than provide a list of options for teachers to choose from, they have modeled the coaching environment and turned to the teachers to allow them to share what they need, what kinds of training would work best for them. Then they endeavor to provide it. It's more open-ended and focused on the teachers; much as coaching is focused on the coachee.

When they believe all or most of their IPA community is sufficiently involved in coaching, those well versed in the process expand beyond the IPA to become models for teachers, educators, mentors, and others throughout the full educational community of Aruba. Already they have seen teachers coming in eager to work toward becoming a professional coach within the education system.

Obstacles in the way of IPA's push to create a culture of coaching, which they currently call Project Coaching IPA, are similar to those in programs in other places: the need for more time and money. They need the time to devote to coaching and the money to provide training, books—not readily available in Aruba—and other materials. They also seek opportunities to extend their education about coaching through conferences and seminars. Those on the leadership team are taking online graduate courses. Many coaches document their own experiences so that they can share and learn from one other.

"As the only teacher training institution in Aruba," says Ingrid, "we have high aspirations, little support from the ministry, and only a few who can commit the time and dedication needed for this cause. Everybody agrees with the idea," she adds, "but there are also other priorities. We work step by step and celebrate small successes."

One of the IPA's ideas consists of organizing a "coaching café" to allow informal presentations about coaching experiences. Anyone who wants to participate, share, or receive information is welcome. They plan to use the café idea as a springboard for a more formal structure in their educational development in Aruba.

"What we envision is an environment where teachers do not feel alone and teach in isolation," Ingrid shares. "We want them to feel—to know—that they are free to visit each other, give each other feedback, help each other, support each other, and create a higher quality of teaching for themselves and others. And we would like to achieve this goal throughout the whole field of education in Aruba—from kindergarten to university."

Three p's and a vision—I'd say that's a formula that's bound to succeed!

COACHING TRUMPS EVALUATION:
WALTON HIGH SCHOOL, MARIETTA, GEORGIA

Whenever Walton High School principal Judy McNeill interviews prospective employees, she inevitably makes the point that Walton High School enjoys a culture of collaboration throughout the school. She explains that coaching is part of school culture from the classroom to the faculty room to staff development classes. And she proudly declares Walton has its own "conversion charter," a document that allows the school to tailor procedures differently from other schools in Cobb County.

The most significant change entails a shift from standard performance assessment to an opportunity for teachers to go through a coaching process where they analyze with their coaches and principal the improvement and growth they experienced throughout the year, based almost entirely on the areas they most wanted to work on.

An issue recognized by Walton early on was that the state's evaluation process did not provide a real learning document or valuable feedback to teachers. "Our evaluation system attempts to verify that you are at least average, and you may stay that way," according to Suzanne Schott, a lead teacher at Walton and a major fixture in Walton's coaching initiatives. "Our Performance Report, on the other hand, asks if teachers met the focus they agreed upon. That they improved and grew in the areas they wanted to achieve."

Dr. Tom Higgins is a former principal of Walton High School and now a member of the teacher recognition team at the Georgia Professional Standards Commission. He has been credited with spearheading the coaching culture that exists at Walton based on his belief that leaders must create environments that allow empowerment of individuals and feedback by colleagues. He quotes Harvard professor Richard Elmore, "Privacy of practice produces isolation; isolation is the enemy of improvement."

"We already had a great start on the creation of this type of environment when I came on board in 2001," says Tom. "Walton has been a really special place for a long time. Our belief is that this approach to training and the model of coaching promoted in the coaching training and material included in the book *Quality Teaching in a Culture of Coaching* created the opportunity to move us to another level."

Because of the rather complex arrangements of a conversion charter involving the state of Georgia and Cobb County as well as smart maneuvers on the part of the Walton leadership, Walton was able to dramatically increase the amount of professional development resources they received from the district. This allowed for an up-tick in training and gave them the option of making peer coaching and peer collaboration a central feature and an option for teachers to use in lieu of a traditional evaluation process.

With the coaching program in place for about three years, the option of offering teachers an alternative to their typical performance evaluation seemed a natural progression. Rather than being evaluated on their regular Performance Assessment Instrument (PAI), teachers who had been coached could opt to become part of a coaching team to work on a specific focus of improvement. They then undertook a conference with their evaluating principal to analyze to what level they had grown and improved.

"It started as a pilot program," says Suzanne. "We accepted twenty teachers to see if they would truly grow and what administrators in charge of evaluations would think of their growth. 'Did I grow?' was actually a major criterion," she adds. "Not surprisingly, the most successful teachers were the first to sign on for the program."

The idea was an instant hit. Coaching teams worked together to assist teachers through feedback, additional coaching, and observation as they went through this pilot performance-improvement process. There were rules, of course. Each person going through the coaching process had to be a teacher at Walton for at least a year, they had to have three or more years teaching experience, and they had to have participated in peer coaching training. Other criteria were added later. The pilot program soon became a permanent program. The following year, there were thirty applicants. (A copy of the "Peer Coaching Teacher Performance Report" is included in the appendix.)

Teams within this performance improvement process would each have a preobservation, observation, and postobservation conference, and then each team held a final conference with the team's evaluating administrator. Principal Judy McNeill and her assistant both worked with the various teams.

"One of the reasons we were interested in peer coaching," says Tom, "is that advice from a colleague is often the biggest source of influence on another teacher's professional practice. Peer coaching offers colleagues a framework to better understand what the teacher wants to accomplish. Peers observing peers and giving feedback should be a critical aspect of any learning community," he concludes.

So why not involve everyone in the school's professional-improvement-through-coaching model? Several reasons surfaced. Some people had been evaluated the same way for thirty years and received proficient marks each time. They would not want to change that process or their records. Others were still cautious and skeptical about the peer coaching program, similar to those in other programs we have covered in this book. Because the PAI was tied to the district, some were concerned that it might not be accepted at other schools should they transfer. To address these issues, Cobb County School District is implementing a new evaluation instrument, and, as of this writing, Suzanne is creating a coaching assessment document to line up with the district's new teacher evaluation standards.

The synergy that occurred within coaching teams who formed for the purpose of "evaluation" was a highly dynamic and unexpected outcome. Teams met with administrators to share what focus each or all were taking (most teams were from common subject areas—math, history, etc.). In lively discussions, they found one focus shifted to the next; one led to another and then another. "We have a high-achieving faculty," admits Suzanne. "But even with the teachers who were less strong, the collaboration alone was worth everything. It helped those on the fence to move past 'I'm not good enough' and 'what will I look like teaching?' It developed trust," she concludes.

Teams that opt for the coaching assessment process do two rounds of coaching throughout the year before the final conference with their administrator in February. Individuals serve as coach and are coached a minimum of two times. And the team discussions and the focus, refocus, and feedback continue throughout.

Endemic to coaching programs and their various processes are opportunities for teachers to deliberately practice the art and performance of teaching—to engage in what psychology professor and author K. Anders Ericcson calls "deliberate practice." Ericcson says that what gets in the way of "deliberate practice" is not receiving an instant objective response. (Ericeson, Krampe, & Tesch-Romer, 1993).

In other words, practice exists in a vacuum without the observation and feedback that peers can provide to assess the impact of that practice. Walton enjoys a strong foundation for a highly successful culture of coaching, one that has all the underpinnings for continued growth and success. With these elements in place, they have built an ongoing process for continuous improvement.

"Our wish was for peer coaching to take a big step forward by providing the right feedback at the right time, frequently and well, in a job-embedded form of professional learning," reflects Higgins.

To paraphrase an American proverb, "The wish is father to the thought, as the thought is father to the deed."

I agree.

SUMMARY

As you can see, highly successful coaching programs are embedded in schools around the country and around the world. By every account, the programs work. These programs have trained teachers who are now doing a better job of teaching students, and they continue to create programs customized to their individual needs.

In the introduction to this book, I pointed out that I have experienced the tremendous boost a culture of coaching provides professional educators. This benefit ultimately transfers to students, who enjoy a heightened passion for learning. Coached teachers are fiercely alert to their practice. They reflect on how they achieve learning in their students with other professionals, whose focus and desire is to support them in achieving success.

For those who have not yet begun, I trust this book will provide you with a framework to incorporate a culture of coaching into your own educational environment. And for those who have coaching programs under way, I hope you have been inspired to continue moving from good to great and to share the benefits of your culture of coaching with as many other educators and administrators as you can.

Appendix

CONTENTS

Rochester School District, Rochester, New York

Application for Lead Teacher
Confidential Reference for Lead Teacher Applicant
Lead Teacher Interview Questions—For Panel Use
CIT Mentor Reapplication

Hillsborough County Public Schools, Hillsborough, Florida

Position Description

Salem-Keizer Public Schools, Salem-Keizer, Oregon

Instructional Coach Guidebook (see its own table of contents.)

Enka Schools, Istanbul, Turkey

Coaching Feedback

Walton High School, Cobb County, Marietta, Georgia

Peer Coaching Teacher Performance Report

APPLICATION FOR LEAD TEACHER

Career in Teaching Program
Rochester School District
Rochester, NY 14614

You are applying for: Lead Teacher/_____

Name: _____Employee ID no. _____

   Home address: _____ Zip code_____

   Home telephone: _____

   Summer address (if different from above):_____

Current tenure area: _____ Tenure date: _____

Permanent/professional certification(s) held: _____

During the selection process, the Selection Committee may request to review your annual performance evaluations as reference material.

Circle one: I do consent.   I do not consent.

Teaching Experience:

List most recent teaching first. Minimum requirement is 7 years with at least 5 full years in the Rochester City School District as of the date that the Lead Teacher position begins. A resume of up to two pages may be submitted with this application.

Inclusive Dates		School	Subject Area or Grade Level	No. of Years	Name of Principal or Supervisor
From Mo./Yr.	To Mo./Yr.				

Six confidential references are required to complete this application. Please include teachers within the same discipline or from the same teaching level (primary, intermediate, same cluster, etc.) who are knowledgeable about your professional performance. List the names and phone numbers of individuals who will be completing confidential reference forms below.

Position	Name	Telephone Number
Principal		
RTA Faculty Rep		
Teacher		
Teacher		
Teacher		
Other		
Other Supervisor (Optional)		

Applicant's Statement:

Please include in your statement why you desire this position of Lead Teacher/_____ and how your experience and training have qualified you for this position. Indicate in your statement how professional development has expanded your knowledge and skills in ways that support your interest in guiding beginning teachers. If possible, refer to evidence that you have incorporated the Professional Standards and Expectations for teachers in your work with students, colleagues, and parents.

Signature of Applicant: _____ Date: _____

All applications and references are confidential. Applications will be reviewed by the CIT Panel where decisions are made on who will be interviewed. The CIT Panel may request to observe your teaching performance. Applications must be received in Human Resources on or before the close of business on the date specified in the job description.

The Rochester City School District is an equal opportunity employer. By Board of Education policy, and in accordance with Title VII of the Civil Rights Act of 1964 and 1972 amendments; with Title IX of the Education Amendment of 1972, and section 504 of the Rehabilitation Act of 1973; the district prohibits discrimination on the basis of national origin, race, sex, religion, age, and handicapping condition in its hiring and promotional procedures.

CONFIDENTIAL REFERENCE—
FOR LEAD TEACHER APPLICANT

Career in Teaching Program
Rochester School District
Rochester, NY 14614

Dear _____ :
I am submitting an application for the position(s) of:
Lead Teacher/ _____ .
I would appreciate your taking the time to fill out this reference report. You were
my _____ at _____
from _____ to _____

Sincerely,

_____

(Sign *and* print your name)

Directions:

Please evaluate this applicant in relation to other teachers that you have known by writing comments in the space provided that supports your overall rating as written on the lines provided. Specific information about this candidate's experience and qualifications for a Lead Teacher role is essential in determining suitability for a position. Please attach any supportive materials to this page.

1. Success in classroom instruction or other professional responsibilities to engage students of different backgrounds in successful learning environments as evidenced by meeting or exceeding professional standards for:

   Pedagogy: *Teachers are committed to their students and provide for effective, worthwhile, student-centered learning.*
   Content: *Teachers know the subjects they teach and how to develop content-related skills, knowledge, understanding, and attitudes in students.*
   Rates with Lowest 25% _____ Rates with Middle Group _____
   Rates with Highest 10% _____ No Data _____
   Example/Evidence:

2. Ongoing professional development and growth as evidenced by meeting or exceeding the professional standard for:

Professional Development: Teachers think systematically about their practice and are members of learning communities.

Rates with Lowest 25% _____ Rates with Middle Group _____
Rates with Highest 10% _____ No Data _____
Example/Evidence:

3. Interpersonal skills including judgment, tact, interaction with colleagues and parents, and school leadership qualities as evidenced by meeting or exceeding the professional standards for:

   School Quality: Teachers have a professional, collegial responsibility to contribute to the improvement of school quality and to student learning.

   Home Involvement: Teachers reach beyond the school to make connections with students' homes and families in order to provide a school experience which addresses the needs and interests of each child.

   Rates with Lowest 25% _____ Rates with Middle Group _____
   Rates with Highest 10% _____ No Data _____
   Example/Evidence:

4. Ability to communicate orally and in writing:

   Rates with Lowest 25% _____ Rates with Middle Group _____
   Rates with Highest 10% _____ No Data _____
   Example/Evidence:

5. Candidate's suitability to this specific Lead Teacher role:

   Rates with Lowest 25% _____ Rates with Middle Group _____
   Rates with Highest 10% _____ No Data _____
   Example/Evidence:

Comments:

Signed: _____Date:_____

Position: _____Work Location: _____

LEAD TEACHER INTERVIEW
QUESTIONS—FOR PANEL USE

Career in Teaching Program
Rochester School District
Rochester, NY 14614

Date: _____ Applicant's name: _____

Interviewers: _____

Panel recommendation: _____

Interview Questions for Lead Teacher/Mentor

1. Please provide us a snapshot of your classroom by sharing with us the evidence that you have brought which shows your use of the following:

   - instructional strategies: _____
   - formative assessment to drive learning: _____
   - data-driven instruction: _____
   - cultural responsiveness: _____
   - inclusiveness: _____

2. What has been the focus of your professional development during the past year?
3. Describe a PD opportunity taken within the past 2 years that has impacted your students' learning?
4. What attributes do you associate with a successful co-teaching model?
5. Please share any co-teaching and/or coaching experience you have had.
6. Why do you want to be a mentor?
7. If your intern's philosophy is different from your philosophy, what will you do?
8. For a beginning teacher, which do you believe is more important to master: classroom management or effective lesson plan design and delivery? Please explain.
9. What criteria will you use to determine your recommendation for an intern's continuation?
10. What do you consider harmful practice?
11. Questions asked by applicant.

General Guidelines for Interviewer

1. Remind each applicant of his/her responsibility to attend Lead Teacher/Mentor training on: _____
2. Include date of interview and all notes about the interview along with the names of the interviewers.
3. Review written application and references.
4. Application, interview materials and discussion are considered confidential. Put all notes in application folders and return to _____ _____.

CIT MENTOR REAPPLICATION

Career in Teaching Program
Rochester School District
Rochester, NY 14614

Applicant's name: _____ Date: _____

Directions:

Mentors whose terms expire in June, 2009, should complete the reapplication. PART I should be completed on this form. PART II *should be completed on a separate sheet of paper.* Please base your answers on your experiences with interns and with your own classroom practice. Please be specific and provide concrete examples. Using a rubric, the CIT Panel members will review the mentor reapplications and mentor records to determine whether or not a mentor has been selected for another term. The CIT Panel may determine that an interview is necessary before making a final decision. *If you have not been activated throughout your 2-year term, you should complete Part I only. In order to be considered for a second term, you will be invited to an interview.*

Part I

Please complete the information below.
1. Besides mentoring, what is your current assignment? _____
   _____
2. How many years have you been a mentor? _____
3. How many years have you been activated as a mentor? _____
4. Are you currently an activated mentor? _____
5. Were you activated last year? _____
6. If you have not been activated during the past 2 years, are you interested in being interviewed and considered for another term as a mentor?
   _____yes
   _____no
   _____not applicable

If you have not been activated at some point during the past 2-year term, stop here. If you have been activated at some point during the past 2-year term, go on to Part II.

Part II

Please complete the questions below on a separate sheet of paper and attach your answers to this form.

1. You are an experienced mentor. What evidence exists that demonstrates you are making a difference with new teachers?
2. How do you establish your relationship with your interns and how do you develop your relationship throughout the year?
3. What advice do you give your intern regarding establishing collaborative relationships with key stakeholders?
4. How have you handled, or how would you handle working with a thriving intern?
5. How have you handled, or how would you handle working with a struggling intern?
6. Explain how you determine whether or not to recommend an intern for continued employment in the RCSD?
7. Describe your approach in working with administrators. Please include a description of how you introduce yourself and how you maintain regular communication throughout the year.
8. What has been the focus of your own professional development during the past 2 years? How does your professional development align with the CIT Mentor Goals discussed in the fall?
9. Describe examples of strategies you have employed to apply best practices in your classroom and its impact on your students' performance. Be specific on the measure of student performance and the growth that has occurred.
10. What is one question that you believe is important to ask an intern? Why?

POSITION DESCRIPTION FOR
HILLSBOROUGH COUNTY K–5 READING COACHES

Hillsborough County Public Schools
Hillsborough County, FL

Primary Responsibilities: K–5 Reading Coach—Elementary Education

The K–5 Reading Coach will provide assistance to K–5 teachers in meeting students' educational needs by performing the following functions:

1. *Curriculum Implementation:*

   • Assist K–5 teachers in implementing the Florida *Standards and Benchmarks.*
   • Assist K–5 teachers in connecting the Florida *Standards and Benchmarks* with their reading materials and instructional planning.
   • Assist K–5 teachers in developing an understanding of grade level benchmarks, appropriate assessment of the benchmarks, and instructional strategies to teach grade-level benchmarks.

2. *Instructional Support for the Classroom:*

   • Train K–5 teachers in effective instructional strategies and use of materials to increase reading achievement.
   • Model and Coach effective shared and guided reading lessons.
   • Assist teachers in planning and selecting appropriate text and teaching points for Read Alouds, Shared, and Guided Reading Instruction with continued support in Independent Reading strategies.
   • Model and Coach effective instructional strategies for intensive reading instruction and interventions.
   • Assist teachers in organizing classroom and time for reading instruction.
   • Provide follow-up support to district and site-based training.

3. *Instructional Support for Assessment:*

   • Train teachers in the use of a variety of reading assessments.
   • Model and Coach how to administer assessments and collect data.
   • Assist teachers in selecting appropriate assessments.
   • Assist teachers in using assessment data to plan appropriate instruction to accelerate reading achievement.

4. *Coaching and Conferencing:*

- Coach K–5 teachers to facilitate changes in instructional practices, behaviors, attitudes, and expectations that include pre- and post-conferencing.
- Conference with K–5 teachers to interpret assessment data and plan instruction.

5. *Site Support:*

- Provide support at school sites by providing modeling/training/follow-up sessions for K–5 teachers and parents of K–5 students.
- Conduct book studies related to reading.
- Serve as a resource to the school for ideas to increase reading achievement.

6. *Professional Growth:*

- Continue participation in ongoing training and support sessions for Reading Coaches provided by the district and the state.
- Receive coach-the-coach support from a mentor coach.

INSTRUCTIONAL COACH GUIDEBOOK

Salem-Keizer Public Schools
204 Lancaster Dr.
Salem-Keizer, Oregon 97305

Table of Contents

Foreword from Superintendent
Purpose of Instructional Coaching
Research on Instructional Coaching
Roles and Responsibilities
   Instructional Coach
   School Administrator
   Central Office Administrators
   Classroom Teacher
Coaching and the Salem-Keizer Delivery Model
Coaching Models and Establishing Relationships
Support Systems for Coaches
Record Keeping
   Instructional Coach Log
Suggested Coaching Bibliography

Foreword

In Salem-Keizer Public Schools we recognize that the number one factor in reaching our goal of improved student achievement for every student is a quality teacher delivering first class instruction with fidelity, consistency, and intensity every day.

In order to meet our goal it is critical that we support our instructional staff with meaningful, relevant, and job-embedded professional development. This means professional development that occurs not just in the training environment, but also in the actual classroom. We support this effort with the collegial and facilitative guidance and modeling of an instructional coach in each school in order to achieve the level of follow-up work and assistance that research demonstrates is necessary to achieve a positive result.

This manual defines our mission for instructional coaching and the roles for each of the supportive district players and participants in the process, the project management model that guides our instructional program and training initiatives and insures reciprocal accountability, the data collection tool for coaches and supportive professional references for coaches.

We have invested significant resources in our instructional coaching program over the past two years and we are confident that through our efforts we will positively impact student achievement and reach our goal of a quality teacher delivering first class instruction for every student every day.

—Dr. Sandy Husk
Superintendent
Salem-Keizer Public Schools

The Purpose of Instructional Coaching

Teachers primarily work with students in isolation. Interaction with their colleagues is often limited to social contact, planning, and informational meetings. The work of teaching students is most often done without the benefit of collegial feedback or observation. Administrators observe and give feedback, but these are fairly formal and happen infrequently. Administrators often work on creating more time in the day to be in classrooms and provide meaningful feedback to teachers, but with one administrator to every 10–30 teachers, the reality is that there is simply not enough time in the day. This is where coaches come in.

The purpose of coaching is to provide: opportunities for teachers to observe effective teaching practices; observations of teachers practicing strategies that are research-based and proven to improve student achievement; support for the classroom teacher in the important job of educating students by facilitating professional discussions about instructional practice, student work, and data.

The coach is not part of the evaluative process and is a confidential partner for teachers as they try out strategies, implement new programs, and manage the many complex tasks of teaching.

Research on Instructional Coaching

Coaches participated in training with Stephen Barkley who wrote the book *Quality Teaching in a Culture of Coaching.* In his book Barkley cites the research of Bruce Joyce and Beverly Showers. This research illustrates the power of coaching in the process of embedding professional development into effective classroom instructional practice. Table A.1 shows that when teachers learn something new, they may or may not try it out in the classroom. If they do try it, they most likely will abandon the new practice before it is implemented with fidelity. Without support and coaching, professional development can be a waste of time and money and research-based practices that are showing gains for students are abandoned before they are transferred into the classroom.

Professional development that focuses only on theory, knowledge, and limited opportunities for practice and feedback may create high levels of knowledge, but rarely translates into classroom practice. When a coach comes along side the teacher, supports him/her, gives feedback, models new techniques and knowledge, and experiments together with the teacher, there is a much greater chance that the new techniques will be firmly embedded into the teachers instructional practice.

We know from change theory outlined in McREL's Balanced Leadership Framework Reference that teachers may perceive a new initiative as a second-order change. This means they see it as a break from the past, inconsistent with their value system or the norms of the school or team, and requiring new skills and knowledge. Think of a time when you learned a difficult new skill. There is the initial excitement, what Gordon's Skill Development Ladder would call being "unconsciously unskilled." In terms of the implementation of the skill, you don't know what you don't know.

In table A.1 participants demonstrated 90 percent proficiency in skill development after theory/modeling practice and feedback, but only 5 percent accurate use in class. In the artificial work of the professional development training, they feel confident, but once they try it in the classroom, with real students and all of the other pressures and constraints of the real world, they abandon the practice for one that is more familiar. They become consciously unskilled and they go back to practices that are more familiar and comfortable.

Continued practice and coaching move the practitioner through the stages to unconsciously skilled, i.e., the new skill becomes part of their repertoire of strategies to help students become more successful. As we learn more about how the brain works and how children learn, it is more important than ever for educators to keep up with advances in technology, instruction, curriculum and assessment. Without the collegial and facilitative support of a coach, this becomes even more difficult.

It is critical that the classroom teacher get the support that he/she needs in order to meet the needs of today's students. In the pages that follow we have outlined the various roles of school personnel as they apply to the work of the instructional coach.

Table A.1

Training Provided	Skill Development	Accurate Use in Class
Theory/Knowledge	5%	0–5%
Theory/Modeling	50%	5%
Theory/Modeling/ Practice and Feedback	90%	5%
Theory/Modeling/Practice/ Feedback and Coaching	90%	75–90%

Source: *The Coaching of Teaching* by Joyce and Showers (1993), as shown in *Quality Teaching in a Culture of Coaching* by Steve Barkley (2010).

Roles and Responsibilities

Instructional Coach

1. Develop supportive interpersonal relationships with your school(s) teaching team.
2. Keep a laser focus on your work as a coach and support to teachers as you are one of the most important resources in helping us reach our goal of improved student achievement. Remember you are a coach, not an administrator, counselor, or classroom assistant.
3. Work with the district licensed professional development coordinator to plan, implement, and evaluate training for instructional coaches.
4. Implement the coaching model (technical, collegial and/or facilitative) depending on the needs of the site and the teachers.
5. Schedule and commit to regular classroom visits in the school(s) where you are assigned.
6. Work with teachers as they plan and implement lessons in order to provide opportunities for thoughtful teacher reflection and professional growth.
7. Consult with teachers on matters relating to instructional strategies, instructional delivery, and analysis of results.
8. Model and demonstrate strategies and methods for teachers.
9. Find ways to support teachers and share those ideas as they work to differentiate instruction and integrate math and literacy into the curriculum.
10. Network frequently with the coaching cadre to improve your skills, reflect on your practice as coach and share ideas for everyone's benefit.
11. Keep your contact records and logs up to date and accurate, and use the information to make decisions about your further interactions with teachers.
12. Continue to model lifelong learning.
13. Maintain confidentiality and professionalism in your relationship as coach to every teacher you serve and other professionals with whom you interact.
14. Assist your administrator in building and sustaining the leadership team in your school.

School Administrator

1. Support the coaching model and encourage all teachers to view it as a resource to improve their individual practice. Probationary teachers or teachers needing assistance should be asked how they will use the coach as part of their plan for professional growth.
2. Utilize and support your coach as he/she supports teachers, embed professional development into the building's instructional program,

and provide assistance with facilitation of the leadership team in the building.

3. Meet frequently with the coach to close the communication loop in order to increase situational awareness related to school culture.
4. Establish a school culture that models and expects reciprocal accountability for student achievement, with the coach as a primary resource for making this happen.
5. Do not ask or imply that the coach should provide information to you regarding teacher performance that could be evaluative. Respect the teacher/coach confidential relationship.
6. Monitor the implementation of adult learning.
7. Model the process of coaching. Be publicly coached yourself to demonstrate the importance of this process for your staff.

Central Office Administrators

1. Support the coaching model as a resource for improving instruction and embedding professional development in a sustained, focused manner.
2. Make provisions for ongoing training based on needs assessment, results data, and the need to sustain the coaching model and the program.
3. Identify District nonnegotiable initiatives that require the attention of the coach, i.e., implementation of the district literacy model.
4. Make instructional coach reports part of the Continuous Improvement Plan for the district.
5. Conduct frequent accountability check-ins with coaches via onsite visits and with school administrators through onsite visits and academic conferences.
6. Be willing to revise and modify instruction based on data, teacher and coach feedback, and best practice research.

Classroom Teacher

1. Develop an understanding that everyone can benefit from a coach (Susan Boyle has one).
2. View the coaching/teacher relationship as proof that you desire to be the best teacher you can be and are willing to accept suggestions and ideas that you can embrace and employ in your teaching.
3. Recognize that working with a coach is *not* evaluation—it is part of your resource/toolkit.
4. Schedule classroom visits, observations, and time for instructional dialogue either individually with your coach or with your PLC, in order to move from professional isolation to a culture of collaboration.
5. Translate your new learning into practice with the coach as an integral part of the feedback loop.

6. Reflect and dialogue with your coach to revise and make changes that you feel are needed.
7. Monitor the effectiveness of your instruction using student performance data through formative assessments or your own evaluation procedures.
8. Provide quality learning experiences for your students based on their learning needs, the district curriculum, your lesson plans and assessments for learning.

Coaching and the Salem-Keizer Support Delivery Model

In an effort to provide support for classroom teachers and school-based administrators and instructional assistants, Salem-Keizer has created a multi-tiered network of support personnel. These instructional coaches, program assistants, English Language Acquisition specialists (ELAs), and mentors are supported primarily through federal and state funds. Curriculum developers are a part of this process. Figure A.1 on the next page presents a visual organizer:

Coaching Models and Establishing Relationships

Stephen Barkley talks about three types of coaching: Technical Coaching, Challenge Coaching, and Collegial Coaching. The Salem-Keizer coaching model employs all three of these types of coaching. Barkley says that technical coaching assists teachers in applying their staff development training in the classroom. It relies on the concept that objective feedback can improve teaching performance. The focus of technical coaching is to help the teacher implement a specific strategy. Although it is not intended to be evaluative in nature, sometimes teachers can perceive it as such.

Challenge coaching involves a group effort. A group of teachers or other professionals may work together to address a specific issue that is presenting problems for the team. The members of the team brainstorm strategies that may work, suggest ways to measure success and work together to implement agreed-upon processes. Professional Learning Communities often benefit from participating in "challenge coaching."

Barkley says that collegial coaching focuses on giving teachers time and support to think metacognitively about their work in a safe atmosphere with plenty of support. Its intent is to improve teaching practices, enhance relationships with colleagues, and increase professional communication about teaching practices. Barkley maintains that the research indicates that teachers will acquire and deepen teaching strategies, habits and reflection about his/her teaching when given an opportunity to develop and practice skills with feedback from peers delivered in a collegial model.

The bottom line about coaching is that it is all about relationships. Coaches need to work hard to build trust and establish relationships with

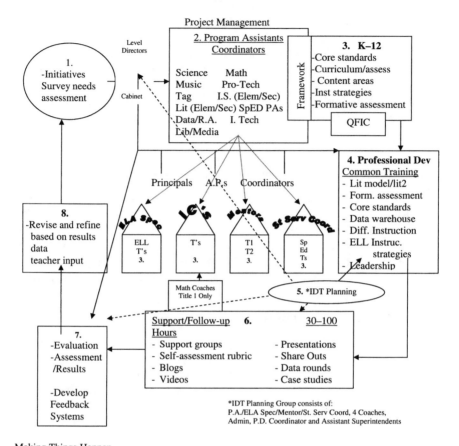

Making Things Happen
Reference: Kellogg Logic Model

Figure A.1.   Project Management

teachers. Teachers need to open up to the idea that they can improve their practice by working collegially with a coach. Administrators need to encourage teachers who are struggling to seek the coach as a support system. Coaches are not looking to "fix" anyone. Coaches are looking to be a support to the teacher who recognizes that given the complexity and importance of teaching, there is always room to grow and get better.

There are many different ways that coaches can give valuable feedback to teachers. Classroom management, instructional strategies, questioning strategies, teacher-student interaction, planning, curriculum work, assessment . . . the list goes on. Many other professions view collaboration and collegial feedback as a natural part of improvement and professional growth. The culture of isolation that permeates American education reinforces the misguided belief that teachers need to fear collegial feedback. The Salem-Keizer Instructional Coaching program is an effort to make this cultural paradigm shift in order to increase collaboration, improve instructional practice, and through improved teaching quality increase student achievement.

Support Systems for Coaches

Coaches are teachers. Yet because they do not work every day in a classroom with students they are often seen as neither teacher nor administrator. In fact, their role is somewhat unique and for this reason it is important that they have their own support system. The District recognizes this and has designed a year-long schedule for coach training that focuses on the major initiatives of the strategic plan: Instruction that works for ELL students, the District Literacy Model, Literacy Squared, Formative Assessment, Core Standards, Differentiation of Instruction, and the Data Warehouse. In addition to this training coaches work with other coaches on better ways to coach teachers, support each other, and sharpen their training relationship and communication skills as they participate as trainers alongside program assistants and coordinators. Coaches have developed a blog and get together regularly to share ideas and discuss ways to better help the teachers they serve.

Record Keeping

Instructional Coach Log

Each coach will be asked to complete a log of their daily activities. This is not intended to be a justification of their time or a report for their administrator. It is intended to be a tool for the coach to use to track growth, see patterns, reflect on their work, and help with planning and organization. The log should not contain specific names of teachers, and will not be shared with the administrator under normal circumstances. Guidelines and a sample log follow (Table A.2). See table A.3 for the template.

1. The log and training record should be kept in order to give the coach perspective on the kind of work he/she is being asked to do, as well as themes/ideas for professional development purposes.
2. Work with teachers should be recorded, but the coach should develop a system to protect teacher confidentiality. (See sample log.)
3. Transitional activities, casual conversations, breaks, lunch, etc. should not be recorded. Not every minute needs to be accounted for, just major activities. A sample two-day log follows.

Table A.2. Instructional Coach Log

Date	Time	Activity/Training	Category	Follow-up
T 5/12	8–9	Worked with teacher on planning lesson for formal observation	TS	Meet after formal to debrief- 5/13 at 3:00
T 5/12	9–11	Planned for staff meeting presentation on word study	PD	Meet with Prin. at 3:00 to review
T 5/12	11–12	Covered teacher's class while she observed reading lesson	TS	Schedule time to debrief
T 5/12	1–2	Went on OAKS to pull data and organize for 3rd grade team	D	Send to team members for PLC meeting on Thursday
T5/12	2:15–3	Met with teacher re: the class she observed	TS	Schedule time to help her with word wall
T 5/12	3–4	Met with Principal to review plan for staff meeting on Monday	PD	Organize materials tomorrow
W5/13	8–12	Coach training on GLAD at LPDC	T	Schedule visit to GLAD library
W5/13	1–2	Finished materials for staff meeting Presentation on word study	PD	Make sure DVD player is available on Monday
W5/13	3–4	Met and debriefed with teacher re: formal observation	TS	Bring chocolate

Codes:

PD:	Coach-lead professional development;
T:	Training for coach
TS:	Teacher support
ML:	Modeling lessons
TO:	Teacher Observation/feedback
D:	Work with Data
PLC:	Work with professional learning communities
O:	Other

Table A.3.   Instructional Coach Log and Training Record

Coach:

School:

Month:

Date	Time	Activity/Training	Category	Follow-up

Codes:

PD:	Coach-lead professional development;
T:	Training for coach
TS:	Teacher support
ML:	Modeling lessons
TO:	Teacher Observation/feedback
D:	Work with Data
PLC:	Work with professional learning communities
O:	Other

Suggested Coaching Bibliography

Barkley, Stephen G., *Tapping Student Effort, Increasing Student Achievement*, Performance Learning Systems, 2007.*

Barkley, Stephen G, *Quality Teaching in a Culture of Coaching*, Performance Learning Systems, 2005.*

Bloom, Gary, Castagna, Moir and Warren, *Blended Coaching*, Corwin Press, 2005.

Duncan, Marilyn, *Literacy Coaching*, Richard C. Owens Publishers, 2006 (companion DVD).*

Hasbrouk, Jan, Denton, Carolyn, *The Reading Coach*, Sopris West Publishers, 2005.

Knight, Jim, *Instructional Coaching: A Partnership Approach to Improving*, Corwin Press, 2007.

Robbins, Pam, *How to Implement a Peer Coaching Program*, ASCD, 1991.*

* Multiple copies available to loan through Professional Development.

COACHING FEEDBACK

Enka Schools, Istanbul, Turkey

1. What have you learned from the coaching interactions? This can be from coaching and/or from being coached.
2. How would you see students gaining from your investment in coaching?

Other questions that might be of interest to note so that the school can see how we can best encourage and support the enthusiastic spread of coaching among staff are:

3. What was the goal of this particular example of coaching?
4. How were your coaching sessions and discussions structured? When? Where? How did it work?
5. How did your coaching occur: between peers in one department, different departments, different grades, or other groups or relationships?
6. How can the administration encourage coaching across departments and grades?
7. What professional staff development would further support your coaching skills?
8. In what other ways could the program support more quality coaching?
9. What PD would support further skills in coaching?
10. What other developments might support more quality coaching happening?

PEER COACHING TEACHER
PERFORMANCE REPORT

Walton High School
Cobb County
Marietta, Georgia

I. Identification

Name _____, _____ _____

            Last Name   First   M.I.

SS#_____ Location _____

Years Teaching

Period of Report:

From _____ to _____

This School _____

Other School(s) _____

In CCSD _____

Reason for Report (check one): Annual _____ Departure _____ Directed _____

Outside CCSD _____

Total Years Teaching _____

II. Job Description

Teaching Responsibilities:

Significant Additional Duties and Responsibilities:

III. Overall Performance Assessment

_____ Meets or exceeds standards in all five performance areas and has undertaken and successfully complete a collaborative peer coaching experience that has resulted in professional growth and an enhanced awareness and understanding of his/her teaching practices.

IV. Signatures

Evaluator _____ Date _____

Position _____

Principal (if not the evaluator) _____ Date _____

Teacher _____ Date _____

(Receipt acknowledged. Signature does not indicate agreement or dis-agreement.)

V. Teacher's Comments

(Optional. Principal must receive comments, if provided, within 10 school days of receipt date above.)

References

Agnes, M. (Ed.). (1999). *Webster's new world college dictionary* (4th ed.). Hoboken, NJ: John Wiley and Sons.

Baker, R. G. (1983). *The contribution of coaching to transfer of training.* Unpublished doctoral dissertation, University of Oregon, Eugene.

Barth, R. S. (1991). Restructuring schools: Some questions for teachers and principals. *Phi Beta Kappan, 73*(2), 123–128.

Block, P. (1990). *The empowered manager.* San Francisco: Jossey-Bass.

Baron, L., & Morin, L. (2009). The coach-coachee relationship in executive coaching: A field study. *Human Resource Development Quarterly, 20*(1), 85–106.

Browne, M. N., & Keeley, S. M. (2009). *Asking the right questions: A guide to critical thinking* (9th ed.). New York: Pearson Prentice Hall.

Bowman, C. L., & McCormick, S. (2000). Comparison of peer coaching versus traditional supervision effects. *Journal of Educational Research, 93*(4), 256–262.

Caccia. P. F. (1996). Linguistic coaching: Helping beginning teachers defeat discouragement. *Educational Leadership, 53*(6), 17–20.

Coates, J. (2007). *Generational learning styles.* River Falls, WI: LERN Books.

Cooperrider, D. L., Whitney, D., & Stavros, J. M. (2003). *Appreciative inquiry handbook: The first in a series of appreciative inquiry workbooks for leaders of change.* Brunswick, OH: Crown Custom Publishing.

Covey, S. R. (1990). *The 7 habits of highly effective people.* New York: Simon and Schuster.

Diamond, J. (1979). *Behavioral kinesiology.* New York: Harper and Row.

Dougherty, D. C. (1993). Peer coaching: Creating a collaborative environment for change. (Doctoral dissertation, University of Oregon, 1993). *Dissertation Abstracts International, 54*(1), 71A.

Downs, A., Downs, R. C., & Rau, K. (2008). Effects of training and feedback on discrete trial teaching skills and student performance. *Research in Developmental Disabilities: A Multidisciplinary Journal, 29*, 235–246.

DuFour, R. (2004). What is a "professional learning community"? *Educational Leadership, 61*(8), 6–11.

Dunn, K., & Villani, S. (2007). *Mentoring new teachers through collaborative coaching.* San Francisco: WestEd.

Eiszler, C. F. (1983). Perceptual preferences as an aspect of adolescent learning styles. *Education, 103*(3), 231–242.

Ericsson, K. A., Krampe, R. T., & Tesch-Romer, C. (1993). The role of deliberate practice in the acquisition of expert performance. *Psychological Review, 100*(3), 363–406.

Esquith, R. (2003). *There are no shortcuts: How an inner-city teacher—winner of the American Teacher Award—inspires his students and challenges us to rethink the way we educate our children.* New York: Pantheon Books.

Fulton, K., Yoon, I., & Lee, C. (2005). *Induction into learning communities.* A paper prepared for the National Commission on Teaching and America's Future. Retrieved from http://www.nctaf.org/documents/NCTAF_Induction_Paper_2005.pdf

Garmston, R. J. (1987). How administrators support peer coaching. *Educational Leadership, 45*(5), 18–26.

Glasser, W. (1992). Quality, trust, and redefining education. *The Educational Forum, 57*(1), 37–40.

Glasser, W. (1998). *The quality school: Managing students without coercion* (3rd ed.). New York: HarperCollins.

Glasser, W., & Dotson, K. L. (1998). *Choice theory in the classroom.* New York: Harper Collins.

Goleman, D. (1995). *Emotional intelligence: Why it can matter more than IQ.* New York: Bantam.

Goodlad, J. I. (1984). *A place called school.* New York: McGraw-Hill.

Goodlad, J. I. (1994). *Educational renewal: Better teachers, better schools.* San Francisco: Jossey-Bass.

Gordon, W. J. J. (1961). *Synectics.* Cambridge, MA: Synectics.

Granitz, N. A., Koernig, S. K., & Harich, K. R. (2009). Now it's personal: Antecedents and outcomes of rapport between business faculty and their students. *Journal of Marketing Education, 31*(1), 52–65.

Grinder, J., & Bandler, R. (1981). *Frogs into princes.* Moab, UT: Real People.

Hanson, S., & Moir, E. (2008). Beyond mentoring: Influencing the professional practice and careers of experienced teachers. *Phi Delta Kappan, 89,* 453–458.

Harriman, S. G. (1992). An evaluative study of teacher portraiture. (Doctoral dissertation, University of Connecticut, 1992). *Dissertation Abstracts International, 53*(9), 3093A.

Hart, L. A. (1998). *Human brain and human learning.* Kent, WA: Books for Educators.

Hasenstab, J. K, Barkley, S. G., & Flaherty, G. M. (1996). *Coaching skills for successful teaching.* Emerson, NJ: Performance Learning Systems.

Haskell, R. E. (2001). *Transfer of learning: Cognition, instruction, and reasoning.* San Diego, CA: Academic.

Heberly, J. (1991). A comparison of the use of the peer-coaching format with the workshop format in changing teacher skills. (Doctoral dissertation, University of Idaho, 1991). *Dissertation Abstracts International, 52*(7), 2505A.

Heider, K. L. (2005, June 23). Teacher isolation: How mentoring programs can help. *Current Issues in Education, 8*(14). Available at http://cie.ed.asu.edu/volume8/number14/.

Jenkins, J., & Veal, M. L. (2002). Preservice teachers' PCK development during peer coaching. *Journal of Teaching in Physical Education, 22*(1), 49–68.

Jensen, E. (1997). *Completing the puzzle: The brain-compatible approach to learning* (2nd ed.). Del Mar, CA: Brain Store.

Jensen, E. (1998). *Teaching with the brain in mind.* Alexandria, VA: ASCD.

Johnson, S. M., & Kardos, S. M. (2002). Keeping new teacher in mind. *Educational Leadership, 59*(6), 13–16.

Jones, C., & Vreeman, M. (2008). *Instructional coaches & classroom teachers: Sharing the road to success.* Huntington Beach, CA: Shell Education.

Joyce, B., & Showers, B. (1982). The coaching of teaching. *Educational Leadership, 40*(1), 4–8, 10.

Joyce, B., & Showers, B. (1990). *Staff development and student achievement.* White Plains, NY: Longman.

Joyce, B., & Showers, B. (2002). *Student achievement through staff development* (3rd ed.). Alexandria, VA: ASCD.

Joyce, B., Wolf, J., & Calhoun, E. (1993). *The self-renewing school.* Alexandria, VA: ASCD.

Joyce, B., Wolf, J., & Calhoun, E. (1996). The evolution of peer coaching. *Educational Leadership, 53*(6), 12.

Knight, J. (2007). *Instructional coaching: A partnership approach to improving.* Thousand Oaks, CA: Corwin Press.

Knight, J. (2009). Coaching: The key to translating research into practice lies in continuous, job-embedded learning with ongoing support. *Journal of Staff Development, 30*(1), 18–20.

Koballa, T. R., Edison, S. D., Finco-Kent, D., et al. (1992). Peer coaching: Capitalizing on constructive criticism. *The Science Teacher, 59*, 42–44.

Kohler, F. W., Crilley, K. M., Shearer, D. D., & Good, G. (1997). Effects for peer coaching on teacher and student outcomes. *Journal of Educational Research, 90*, 240–250.

Kovalik, S., & Olsen, K. (1997). *ITI, the model: Integrated thematic instruction* (3rd ed.). Kent, WA: Books for Educators.

Lewin, K. (1943). Defining the "field at a given time." *Psychological Review 50*, 292–310. Published in *Resolving social conflicts and field theory in social sciences.* (1997). Washington, DC: American Psychological Association.

MacLean, P. (1978). A mind of three minds: Educating the triune brain. *Science Teacher, 45*(4), 31–39.

Martin, C. (2001). *The life coaching handbook.* Carmarthen, Wales, UK: Crown House.

McGraw, P. (1999). *Life strategies: Doing what works, doing what matters.* New York: Hyperion.

Mehrabian, A., & Weiner, M. (1967). Decoding of inconsistent communication. *Journal of Personality and Social Psychology, 6*, 109–114.

Morrison, G. M., Walker, D., Wakefield, P., & Solberg, S. (1994). Teacher preferences for collaborative relationships: Relationship to efficacy for teaching prevention-related domains. *Psychology in the Schools, 31*, 221–231.

Neufeldt, V. & Guralnik, D. B., eds. (1997). *Webster's new world college dictionary* (3rd ed.) New York: Macmillan.

Nielsen, D. C., Barry, A. L., & Addison, A. B. (2007). A model of a new-teacher induction program and teacher perceptions of beneficial components. *Action in Teacher Education, 28*(4), 14–24.

Orem, S., Binkert, J., & Clancy, A. L. (2007). *Appreciative coaching: A positive process for change.* Hoboken, NJ: John Wiley and Sons.

Pardini, P. (2008a). Fridays for 90 minutes. In V. von Frank (Ed.), *Finding time for professional learning* (p. 133). Oxford, OH: National Staff Development Council.

Pardini, P. (2008b). I have happy teachers. In V. von Frank (Ed.), *Finding time for professional learning* (p. 136). Oxford, OH: National Staff Development Council.

Pardini, P. (2008c). Making time for adult learning. In V. von Frank (Ed.), *Finding time for professional learning* (p. 132). Oxford, OH: *National Staff Development Council.*

Pardini, P. (2008d). One hour early. In V. von Frank (Ed.), *Finding time for professional learning* (p. 132). Oxford, OH: National Staff Development Council.

Park, S., Oliver, J. S., Johnson, T. S., et al. (2007). Colleagues' roles in the professional development of teachers: Results from a research study of national board certification. *Teaching and Teacher Education: An International Journal of Research and Studies, 23,* 368–389.

Pennsylvania High School Coaching Initiative (PAHSCI). *Research highlights.* Retrieved from http://piic.pacoaching.org/index.php/research-and-evaluation

Peters, T. (1994). *The pursuit of wow!* New York: Vintage Books.

Philpott, J. S. (1983). *The relative contribution to meaning of verbal and nonverbal channels of communication.* A meta-analysis. Unpublished master's thesis, University of Nebraska.

Qualters, D. M. (2009). Creating a pathway for teacher change. *Journal of Faculty Development, 23*(1), 5–13.

Raney, P., & Robbins, P. (1989). Professional growth and support through peer coaching. *Educational Leadership, 46*(8), 35–38. Reproduction Service ED 466 461.

Reese, C. (1986, July 11). A guide for assessing public issues: Remember to do it on four levels. *Orlando Sentinel,* p. A10.

Reeve, D. (2009). *Renewal coaching: Sustainable change for individuals and organizations.* San Francisco: Jossey-Bass.

Richardson, J. (2002). Think outside the clock: Create time for professional learning. In V. von Frank (Ed.), *Finding time for professional learning* (p. 34). Oxford, OH: *National Staff Development Council.*

Rock, M. L., Gregg, M., Howard, P. W., et al. (2009). See me, hear me, coach me. *Journal of Staff Development, 30*(3), 24–26.

Rose, J. (2007, April 14). *Designing training for Gen Y: Learning styles and values of generation Y.* Retrieved from http://trainingpd.suite101.com/article.cfm/designing_training_for_gen_y

Sadker, D., & Sadker, M. (1985, January). Is the o.k. classroom o.k.? *Phi Delta Kappan.*

Sagor, R. (2003). *Motivating students and teachers in an era of standards.* Alexandria, VA: ASCD.

Sawchuck, S. (2009). Grade inflation seen in evaluation of teachers, regardless of system. *Education Week*. Retrieved June 1, 2009, from http://www.edweek.org

Schroeder, C. M., Scott, T. P., Tolson, H., et al. (2007). A meta-analysis of national research: Effects of teaching strategies on student achievement in science in the United States. *Journal of Research in Science Teaching, 44*, 1436–1460.

Scott, S. (2002). *Fierce conversations: Achieving success at work and in life, one conversation at a time*. New York: Penguin.

Senge, P. M. (1990). *The fifth discipline: The art and practice of the learning organization*. New York: Doubleday/Currency.

Senge, P. M. (1999). *The dance of change: The challenges to sustaining momentum in learning organizations*. New York: Currency/Doubleday.

Showers, B. (1984). *Peer coaching: A strategy for facilitating transfer of training*. A CEPM R&D Report. (ERIC Document Reproduction Service No. ED271849)

Showers, B. (1990). Aiming for superior classroom instruction for all children: A comprehensive staff development model. *Remedial and Special Education, 11*(3), 35–39.

Showers, B. (2003a). The evolution of peer coaching. In A. C. Ornstein, L. S. Behar-Horenstein, & E. F. Pajak (Eds.), *Contemporary issues in curriculum* (3rd ed., pp. 315–320). Boston: Allyn and Bacon.

Showers, B. (2003b). *Student achievement through staff development* (3rd ed.). Alexandria, VA: ASCD.

Smylie, M. A. (1989). Teachers' views of the effectiveness of sources of learning to teach. *Elementary School Journal, 89*, 543–558.

Storms, B. A., & Lee, G. (2001). *How differences in program implementation influence opportunities for developing reflective practice*. Paper presented at the annual meeting of the American Educational Research Association, Seattle, Washington. (ERIC Document Reproduction Service No. 466 461)

Thomas, H., Cox, R., & Kojima, T. (2000). *Relating preferred learning style to student achievement*. Paper presented at the annual meeting of the Teachers of English to Speakers of Other Languages, Vancouver, BC. (ERIC Document Reproduction Service No. 445513)

Tomlinson, C. A. (2009). Learning profiles & achievement. *School Administrator, 66*(2), 28–29.

Tschannen-Moran, M. (2009). Fostering teacher professionalism in schools: The role of leadership orientation and trust. *Educational Administration Quarterly, 45*, 217–247.

Villar, A., & Strong, M. (2007). *Is mentoring worth the money? A benefit-cost analysis and five-year rate of return of a comprehensive mentoring program for beginning teachers*. Santa Cruz: New Teacher Center, University of California, Santa Cruz.

von Frank, V. (Ed.). (2008). *Finding time for professional learning*. Oxford, OH: National Staff Development Council.

Wang, J., & Odell, J. (2007). An alternative conception of mentor-novice relationships: Learning to teach in reform-minded ways as a context. *Teaching and Teacher Education: An International Journal of Research and Studies, 23*, 473–489.

Wheatley, M. (2002). *Turning to one another: Simple conversations to restore hope to the future*. San Francisco: Berrett-Koehler.

Wiener, G. R., & Mehrabian, A. (1967). Immediacy, discomfort-relief quotient, and content in verbalizations about positive and negative experiences. *Journal of Personality and Social Psychology, 30,* 420–425.

Wineburg, M. S. (1995). *The process of peer coaching in the implementation of cooperative learning structures.* Paper presented at the annual meeting of the American Educational Research Association, San Francisco. (ERIC Document Reproduction Service No. 385528)

Zwart, R. C., Wubbels, T., Bolhuis, S., & Bergen, T. C. M. (2008). Teacher learning through reciprocal peer coaching: An analysis of activity sequences. *Teaching and Teacher Education: An International Journal of Research and Studies, 24,* 982–1002.

Index

abstract vs. concrete communication, 83–84

acknowledging students, 108–9

action-oriented cue words, 70–71

active listening, 61, 75

administrators: coaching and, 153, 181; role switching by, 35, 47–48; wowing teachers, 12. *See also* supervisors

advice giving, coaching as not about, 6, 158–59

affirming coachees' own perceived values/qualities, 131–32

Agenda Skills, 55–67, 76; congruence (authenticity), 55, 59–61, 75. *See also* Confirmatory Paraphrases; questioning skills

agendas, of coachees, 55; aspects, 66–68, *68*; fitting Needs/Benefit Statements to, 129–30. *See also* Agenda Skills; discovering/ uncovering the agenda; vision

agreements. *See* norms and agreements for preobservation conferences

AI (Appreciative Inquiry), 138–40

Alonso, Mellissa, 172, 173

analysis-oriented cue words, 71

Appreciative Inquiry (AI), 138–40

approval adjectives, 132, 133

Approval Statements, 131–34, 138; vs. compliments or praise, 132; fitting to the values of coachees, 131–32, 134, 138, 142; guidelines for, 132– 34; myths about, 137–38

Arkansas coaching program, 4, 179–82

Aruba coaching program, 4, 182–84

assessment: vs. evaluation, 32, 33; "I" messages in, 33–34

assisting vs. helping, 25

attitudes: confirming, 61–62; Confirmatory Paraphrases for, 62, 62–63; vs. feelings, 62

auditory learning styles, 82

"Ban the BMW Club" sign, 66

Bandler, Richard, 61, 118–19

Barkley, Stephen G.: educational experience and wisdom, vi; postobservation conference conversation, 134–36; preobservation conference conversations, 72–74, 89–91

Barth, Roland S., 168

beliefs: about coaching, 17–18; organizational model, 67. *See also* vision belonging, teachers' need for, 40, 50, 51

benefits of coaching, v, xii–xiv, 5, 20–22, 75, 127, 129, 151–53; and Needs/Benefit Statements, 129–30

Big Four teaching techniques, 15

Block, Peter, 87

BMW Club (Bitching, Moaning, and Whining Club), 65–66

body language: in communicating approval, 132, 134, 138; congruence in, 59–61; and emotions, 119; interpreting, 60; monitoring of, 119; percent of communication through, 60; recognizing incongruence in, 60

books on coaching, 180

box-less coaching time, 157–58

Boyle, Susan, 17–18

Career in Teaching Program (Rochester), 25–26

caring for others, and quality of life, 10–11

challenge coaching, 16

change, beginning/confronting, 151, 153

charting teacher responses to student answers, 107–8, 107, 108, 109, *110*

clarity: through listening, 75; in Positive Phrasing, 128–29

classroom, tracking movements of teachers and students in, 111, *117*

Closed-Ended Questions, 56–57; rephrasing as Open-Ended Questions, 58–59, 65, 76

coachees: affirming perceived values/ qualities, 131–32; and Approval Statements, 131–32, 134, 138, 142; as in charge of coaching, 6, 17, 27, 39–40, 80; coaching as not about fixing, 6; conversation between coaches and, 52; great teachers as role models for, 18; instilling confidence in, 118–22; learning and working styles, 82–86, 93; and Needs/Benefit Statements, 129–30;

responsible for own improvement, 6, 16–17, 27. *See also* coaching relationship; teachers

coaches: as cheerleaders, 43; conversation between coachees and, 52; expertise, 103; as not evaluators, 80; "eyes, ears, and skin" observation-only coaches, 103; insight from observation, 88–89; instilling confidence in coachees, 118–22; instructional facilitators, 179–81; learning and working styles, 82, 93; vs. mentors, 23–25; position description statement, 198–99; reflecting of coachee's learning and working styles, 82, 93; responses (answers) required from, 92–93; redefining, 174–75; roles, 6, 27, 43, *44*, 173; success (rewards) for, 6, 41, 47, 75; trust between teachers and, 27–28, 47–48; types, 15. *See also* coaching relationship

coaching: and administrators, 153, 181; beliefs about, 17–18; benefits (value), v, xii–xiv, 5, 20–22, 75, 127, 129, 151–53; books on, 180; and celebration of success, xii, 13–14, 169; coachees as in charge of, 6, 17, 27, 39–40, 80; collegial approach to, 16–17; communication in, 27, 52; consistency in, 92; data as helpful in, 109, 111; deficit model of, 5; discomfort with, 20; effectiveness of, 7–9; vs. evaluation, 34, 48, 48–49, 92, 158–59, 185; on the evaluation/coaching continuum, *23*; expertise of coaches in, 103; as feedback only, 15–16; for good/great teachers, 17–18, 20; group effort, 16; incentives for, 27; instilling confidence, 118–22; international teachers and, 5, 178; introducing, 164; learning elements in, 48–49; as a learning process, 9, 40–47, 49; vs. mentoring, 18–19, 23–28; need for, after mentoring, 25, 26; in negotiated contracts, vi; as nonevaluative, xii–xiii, 27, 32; as not about fixing coachees, 6; as not about making friends, 39–40, 70; as an ongoing process, 98, 111, 122, 143; outcomes (opportunities), 13–14, 40, 41, 66; process of occurrence, 41–47, *41*; power, 6; and practice, 14; psychological, 121; and quality of life, 11; and recognition, 13–14, 18; research on the value of, 20–22, 36; skills, 75; and stress, 14, 152, 152–53; success and the need for more, 17–18; success stories, 3–5; and teaching options, 14, 152–53; team approach, 16; and transfer of learning, 9; types, 15–17; unpredictability in, 92, 99

coaching and teaching process, 125

coaching café idea, 184

coaching environment, 124–34; Needs/Benefit Statements, 129–30; as positive, 124, 126–27; Positive Phrasing, 127–29, 130. *See also* Approval Statements

coaching feedback questions, 211

coaching models, 67–68, *68*, 87–88, *88*, 93–94, 104–5, *104*

coaching programs, 171–87; beginning, 151, 153–54; benefits, 151; concerns about, 154; creating, 151–70; cultural issues in, 5, 177–79; large-school solutions, 166; making time for, 155–58; Probing Questions on, 91, 159–60; in professional learning communities, 167–69; in small learning communities, 166–67; starting, 164, 181; teaching prerequisites, 185–86; in team teaching vs. individual classroom teacher schools, 6–7, 164–66. *See also* resistance to coaching programs; *specific programs*

coaching relationship, 39–40, 40–41, 52, 153; as between equals, 6; conversation as the key to, 27, 52;

role switching, 94; synergy in, v, 5, 19; trust as the basis of, 27–28, 47–48

coaching training, 79–80; PLS program, 174, 181. *See also* staff development training

Coffman, Debbie, 4, 179–80

collaboration, 51

comfort zones: in the BMW Club, 65–66; in knowledge/skills, 19–20

commitment: confirming, 61–62; establishing, Confirmatory Paraphrases for, 64–65

communication: key to the coaching relationship, 27, 52; learning and working style preferences, 82–84. *See also* congruence; conversation

competence model (teacher's triangle), 94, 104–5, *104*

compliments, 131; Approval Statements vs., 132

concrete vs. abstract communication, 83–84

"confer," 79

conferences, terminological considerations, 79. *See also* postobservation conferences; preobservation conferences

confidence, 111, 118; instilling, 118–22. *See also* self-esteem

Confirmatory Paraphrases, 61–65, 75

confirming: attitudes or feelings, 61–62; commitment, 61–62; facts, 61–62; intent, 61–62, 75

congruence: in intonation and body language, 55, 59–61, 75; in Positive Phrasing, 129

conscious practice, coaching and, 14

Consciously Skilled level (Gordon's Ladder), *41*, 44–45

Consciously Unskilled level (Gordon's Ladder), *41*, 42–43

constructive criticism, providing, coaching as not about, 6

continuum of closed and open questions, 56, *57*

contracts, coaching in, vi

conversation: between coach and coachee, 52; "Every change begins with a conversation," 151; fierce, 51–52; postobservation conference, 134–36, 143–45; preobservation conference, 72–74, 89–91, 94–99; as relationship, 52, 79

conversion charter (Walton HS), 184

Cooperrider, David L., 139

Costanza, Marie, 25, 26

Covey, Stephen R., 74

Cranford High School: observation example, 101–3; postobservation conference conversation, 143–45; preobservation conference conversation, 94–99

creative questions, 68, 69; cue words for, 70–71

creativity, uncovering, 69–74

crusader's tale, 67

cue words, 70–72

culture of coaching, 6–7; beliefs useful for, 17–18; creating a, 151–70; in Hillsborough County, 171–73; IPA model, 183; and professional learning communities, 167–69; at Walton HS, 184–87

data, as helpful in coaching, 109, 111

deficit model: of coaching, 5; mentoring as, 25

Diamond, John, on giving directions, 127

directions, giving, 127

discomfort with coaching, 20

discovering/uncovering the agenda, 61–65, 86–91, 88, 105; the focus of activity/observation, 68, 68, 86–88, 88, 90–91; the vision, 68, 87, 89–90. *See also* empowering questions

discussion development by students, 97–98

"don't" commands, 127

drawing diagrams or flow charts during preobservation conferences, 93

DuFour, Richard, 168

DVD technology. *See* videotaping teachers

education: supervisory roles, 23–37. *See also* coaching; evaluation; mentoring; supervision

Elmore, Richard, 185

emotional intelligence, 119

emotions: body language and, 119; conjuring up, 61; flushing out, 62. *See also* feelings

empathy in listening, 74

The Empowered Manger (Block), 87

empowering questions, 68, 69–74;

encouraging teachers, 137–38

energy: from celebration of success, 152; from quality of life, 10

enjoyment, focus of coaching on, 127. *See also* fun

Enka Schools coaching program, 5, 176–79

enthusiasm, creating, 61

Esquith, Rafe, 20

establishing. *See* confirming

evaluation(s), 32–34; vs. assessment, 32, 33; vs. coaching, 34, 48, 48–49, 92, 158–59, 185; collaboration and, 51; and coaching continuum, 23; as ineffective, 129; inter-rater agreement among, 34; learning elements missing in, 49; vs. postobservation conferences, 123, 126; predictability, 92; as undermining trust, 34; "you" messages in, 33–34

evaluation/coaching continuum, 23

evaluative questions, 68, 69; cue words for, 71

evaluators: coaches as not, 80; skill set, 32; trust between teachers and, 33, 34

"Every change begins with a conversation" (Wheatley), 151

excellence in teaching, v

expertise continuum, 103

expertise of coaches, 103

extra credit statement, 92–93

eye contact, and Approval Statements, 134

"eyes, ears, and skin" observation-only coaches, 103

facial expression, percent of communication through, 60

facts, 61–62; Confirmatory Paraphrases for, 62, 62–63

"fake it 'til you make it," 61, 121

feedback: Approval Statements as, 131; coaching as only, 15–16; coaching questions as, 211; from colleagues, 5; as feedforward, 6, 126; and learning, 8; vs. kudos, 111; in postobservation conferences, 125–26; as useful, 7

feedback form. *See* Postobservation Conference Planning Sheet

feelings: vs. attitudes, 62; body language and emotions, 119; confirming, 61–62; Confirmatory Paraphrases for, 62, 62–63; conjuring up emotion, 61; flushing out emotion, 62; good feeling and quality of life, 11

fierce conversations, 51–52

Fierce Conversations (Scott), 51–52; Probing Questions from, 91, 159–60

The Fifth Discipline (Senge), 167–68

Finding Time for Professional Learning, 157

Fisher, Darlene, 5, 176–79

flow charts, drawing during preobservation conferences, 93

focus of activity/observation: discovering/uncovering, 68, 68, 86–88, 88, 90–91. *See also* empowering questions

focus of coaching: on enjoyment, 127; on what the coachee wants, 6, 17, 27, 127–28, 181; on what works or has worked, 138–40

Force Field Analysis, 160–64; form for, 161; implementing coaching, 162, 163

freedom, teachers' need for, 50, 51

friends making, coaching as not about, 39–40, 70

frontal lobe, 119

Full Communication Model, 31–32, 31

fun, teachers' need for, 50, 51. *See also* enjoyment

giving advice, coaching as not about, 6, 158–59

giving directions, 127

Glasser, William: on needs that motivate people, 49; on quality, 9–10

global vs. sequential communication, 84

goals, for coaching: organizational model, 66–67; of preobservation conferences, 68, 87, 88

Goleman, Daniel, 119

good feeling, and quality of life, 11

good teachers, 44, 45, 46–47; coaching for, 17–18, 20; as needed to become great teachers, 19–20; pretty good teacher problem, 19–20; Unconsciously Talented teachers as, 47. *See also* great teachers

Goodlad, John, 108

Gordon's Skill Development Ladder, 41–47, 41

"Grade Inflation Seen in Evaluation of Teachers . . ." (Sawchuk), 32

great teachers, 14, 44, 45, 47, 153; coaching for, 17–18; good teachers as needed to become, 19–20; as role models for coachees, 18; support needs, 66; Unconsciously Talented teachers as not, 46–47

Grindler, John, 61, 118–19

group effort in coaching, 16

guidelines: for Approval Statements, 132–34; for preobservation conferences; for reinforcing and encouraging teachers, 138

Harold and the Emerald bus story, 10–11

Hartford Union High School: mentoring and coaching programs, 27, 31; skill development coaching examples, 45–46

Harvey, Paul, 59

heart/question/light bulb form. *See* Postobservation Conference Planning Sheet

helping vs. assisting, 25

Higgins, Tom, 185, 186, 187

Hillsborough County reading program, 171–73

Hofstede, Geert, 177

"how" questions, 59; caution in using, 58

"I" messages, 33–34

"I should notice . . ." statement, 92–93

IFs (instructional facilitators), 179–81

in-service training. *See* staff development training

incentives for coaching, 27. *See also* benefits of coaching

incongruence in intonation and body language, recognizing, 60

individual classroom teacher schools vs. team teaching schools, 6–7, 164–66

individualism among teachers, school policies and, v

insight: from observation, 88–89; -oriented cue words, 71

Instituto Pedagogico Arubano (IPA), 182; culture of coaching model, 183

Instructional Coaches and Classroom Teachers (Jones and Vreeman), 3

"Instructional Coach Guidebook," 175, 200–10

instructional: coaching, 15; facilitators (IFs), 179–81

Instructional Coaching (Knight), 15

intent: confirming, 61–62, 75; establishing, Confirmatory Paraphrases for, 63–64

internalization of learning. *See* transfer of learning

international teachers and coaching, 5, 178

inter-rater agreement among evaluations, 34

intonation: in communicating approval, 138; congruence in, 59–61; percent of communication through, 60; recognizing incongruence in, 60

introducing coaching, 164

introductory words for Confirmatory Paraphrases reflecting facts, or attitudes or feelings, 62–63

Intuitive Feeler (NF) type, 84–85

Intuitive Thinker (NT) type, 85

isolation, teaching in, v, 168, 170

ITI: The Model (Kovalik), 48–49

Japanese teachers, practice of coaching, v–vi

Jones, Cheryl, 3–4; *Instructional Coaches and Classroom Teachers*, 3

Joyce, Bruce: *Peer Coaching*, xi; *Student Achievement through Staff Development*, 7; on transfer of learning, xi, 7–9

judgment, coaching as not about, 6, 158–59

The Kaleidoscope Profile, 85–86

kinesthetic learning, 82–83

knowledge: comfort zone in, 19–20; and learning, 8

kudos, as of not much help in improving skills, 111

Kuiperdal, Ingrid, 182–84

large-school solutions, 166

lead teacher form: application for, 190–91; confidential reference for, 192–93; interview questions for, 194–95

learning: as a skill, 19; dip in, 43–45, 44; elements of, 48–49; number of trials necessary to learn a new skill, 58; relationship and, 40–41; skill development levels (rungs), 41–47,

41; styles (*see* learning and working styles); vs. teaching, 123–24, *124*. *See also* transfer of learning
learning and working styles, 82–86, 93; PLS survey, 85–86; preferences, 82–84; research on, 99; temperament types, 84–85
learning organizations, 167–68
lesson characteristics, options for observation, 109, 111, 114–15
levels of listening, 74
Lewin, Kurt, Force Field Analysis, 160–64
Life Strategies (McGraw), 129
limbic system, 119
listening levels, 74
listening skills, 74–75; active listening, 61, 75; empathy, 74; neutrality, 75; responses (answers) required from coaches, 92–93; taking notes, 93

MacLean, Paul, 119
mental states. *See* attitudes; commitment; feelings; intent
Mentor, in the *Odyssey*, 24
mentoring: vs. coaching, 18–19, 23–28; coaching after, 25, 26; as a deficit model, 25; on the evaluation/coaching continuum, *23*; models, 28–32; principals in the process, 28, 28–29, 29–30, 30, 31–32; relationship in, 27–28. *See also* mentors
mentors: vs. coaches, 23–25; reapplication form, 196–97; roles, 24; trust between teachers and, 27–28, 29, 30
Miller, Michael, 5, 174, 175–76
mission, organizational model, 66
modeling, and learning, 8
Motivating Students and Teachers in an Era of Standards (Sagor), 40
motivation: collaboration and, 51; needs that motivate teachers, 40, 49–51; strict standards and, 51
movements of teachers and students, tracking, 111, *117*

Myers-Briggs temperament types, 84–85

Ned's story, 119–22, 142–43
needs that motivate teachers, 40, 49–51; fitting Needs/Benefit Statements to, 129–30. *See also* support needs
Needs/Benefit Statements, 129–30
negative phrasing, 127; rephrasing as Positive Phrasing, 128; suggested answers, 147
negativity, 126, 139
negotiated contracts, vi
neurolinguistic programming (NLP), 61, 118–19
neutrality in listening, 75
NF type (Intuitive Feeler type), 84–85
NLP (neurolinguistic programming), 61, 118–19
nonverbal vs. verbal communication, 82–83
NT type (Intuitive Thinker type), 85

observation, by coaches, 101–22; of coachees' body language, 119; example observation, 101–3; frequency, 19; insight from, 88–89; and learning, 8; length, 105; options for, 111, 112–16; of student movements, 111, *117*; of teachers, 105–11, 118–22
observation, by teachers: of other teachers, 109, 111
observation-only coaches, 103
Odyssey, Mentor character, 24
offering opinions, coaching as not about, 6, 158–59
Open-Ended Questions, 56, 57–58; rephrasing Closed-Ended Questions as, 58–59, 65, 76; value, 59, 70
opening day celebrations, 12, 13–14
operations, organizational model, 67
opinions, offering, coaching as not about, 6, 158–59
options. *See* teaching options
organizational preferences, of teachers, 84

paraphrasing statements. *See*
Confirmatory Paraphrases
pause time technique, skill
development levels, 41–46
payoffs. *See* benefits
peer coaching: research on value of,
20–22; staff development training
in, 79–80; teacher performance
report, 212–13; at Walton HS, 185,
186
Peer Coaching (Joyce and Showers), xi
peer review programs, 26
perceptual preferences, of teachers,
83–84
Performance Learning Systems (PLS),
181; coaching training program,
174, 181; learning styles survey,
85–86
personalized questions, *68*, 69–70; cue
words for, 71–72
physiology. *See* body language
A Place Called School (Goodlad), 108
PLCs. *See* professional learning
communities
PLS. *See* Performance Learning Systems
position description statement for
coaches, 198–99
positive adjectives. *See* approval
adjectives
Positive Phrasing, 127–29, 130;
rephrasing negative phrasing as,
128; suggested answers, 147
Positive Reinforcement Model, 30, *30*
Postobservation Conference Planning
Sheet, 111, 140–42, *141*
postobservation conferences, 55, 80,
123–47, 130; data helpful in, 111;
encouraging teachers in, 137–38;
environment, 124; vs. evaluations,
123, 126; example conversations,
134–36, 143–45; feedback/
feedforward in, 125–26; making
suggestions, 90–91, 142, 143;
Planning Sheet (feedback form),
111, 140–42, *141*; planning the
process, 140–43; and preobservation
conferences, 98, 111, 122, 143;

problem solving in, 98; reinforcing
teachers in, 137–38; research on,
146; timing, 126
power, teachers' need for, 50, 51
"power distance ratio," 177
practice: coaching and, 14; and
learning, 8
praise, 131; Approval Statements vs.,
132
predictive cue words, 70
preobservation conferences, 55, 79–99,
130; coaching models, 67–68, *68*,
87–88, *88*, 93–94, 104–5, *104*;
drawing diagrams or flow charts
during, 93; example conversations,
72–74, 89–91, 94–99; goals, *68*, 87,
88; initial meeting, 80; learning and
working styles, 82–86, 93; norms
and agreements, 80–86, 159; note
taking during, 93; postobservation
conferences and, 98, 111, 122, 143;
problem identification in, 81–82,
98–99; problem solving in, 98;
responses (answers) required from
coaches, 92–93; sitting side by side
in, 93, 105; subsequent conferences,
80; topic possibilities, 91. *See also*
Agenda Skills
"Pretty Good" (poem), 20
pretty good teacher problem, 19–20
pride. *See* self-esteem
principals: in the mentoring process,
28, 28–29, 29–30, 30, 31–32;
role identification criterion, 34;
role switching by, 35, 47–48;
coaching vs. evaluating, 34. *See also*
supervisors
problem identification, 159–64;
Force Field Analysis, 160–64; in
preobservation conferences, 81–82,
98–99; Probing Questions on, 91,
159–60
problem solving: avoiding in
Confirmatory Paraphrases, 62; in
pre/postobservation conferences, 98
professional behavior, improving, 111,
118–22

professional learning communities (PLCs), 167–69; research on, 170
Project Coaching IPA, 183
psychological coaching, 121

quality of life, 9–11; coaching and, 11; energy from, 10; Glasser on, 9–10; as going above and beyond, 11–12; Harold and the Emerald bus story, 10–11; recognition and, 13–14, 18
"Quality, Trust, and Redefining Education" (Glasser), 9
The Quality School (Glasser), 49
questioning modes, 106, *106*, 107. *See also* empowering questions
questioning skills (of teachers), 105–6, *106*; observation of, 105–11; research on, 76
questions, wording so the answers are neither right nor wrong, 59
quiz development by students, 95–96, 97

Rayburn, Gretchen "Boo," 5, 174, 175
reapplication form for mentors, 196–97
recognition, coaching and, 13–14, 18
reinforcing teachers, 137–38
relationship: conversation as, 52; and learning, 40–41; in mentoring, 27–28. *See also* coaching relationship
research: on collaboration and trust, 53; on learning styles, 99; on postobservation conferences, 146; on professional learning communities, 170; on questioning skills, 76; on the value of coaching, 20–22, 36; on the value of trust, 36–37
resistance to coaching programs, 154, 155; cultural issues, 5, 177–79; overcoming, 5, 155; Resource Day, 156
"Restructuring Schools" (Barth), 168
Rochester mentoring program, 25–26

Sagor, Richard, 40
Salem-Keizer School District coaching program, 5, 174–76

Sawchuk, Stephen, 32
school days, fitting staff development time into, 156
school policies, and individualism among teachers, v
Schott, Suzanne, 4, 185, 186
Scott, Susan: on fierce conversations, 51–52; Probing Questions from, 91, 159–60
self-esteem (pride), 111, 118, 137; affirming coachees' own perceived values/qualities, 131–32. *See also* confidence
self-reinforcement of teachers, 137
seminars, making time with, 158
Senge, Peter, 167–68
Sensing Judger (SJ) type, 85
Sensing Perceiver (SP) type, 85
sensory preferences, of teachers, 82–83
sequential vs. global communication, 84
Seven Habits of Highly Effective People (Covey), 74
shifting the questioning, 69
Showers, Beverly: *Peer Coaching*, xi; *Student Achievement through Staff Development*, 7; on transfer of learning, xi, 7–9
Silent Mentor Model (for mentoring), 29–30, *29*
SJ type (Sensing Judger type), 85
skills: of coaching, 75; development ladder, 41–47, *41*; of good teaching, 19–20; number of trials necessary to learn new, 58. *See also* Agenda Skills; listening skills; questioning skills
small learning communities, 166–67
solo teaching (in isolation), v, 168, 170
SP type (Sensing Perceiver type), 85
special needs, options for observation, 115–16
specificity: in communicating approval, 138; in Positive Phrasing, 128–29
speedboats, barges, and rocks scenario, 155–58
staff development training (in coaching): in Aruba, 183; gap

between application and, 171, 172; in Hillsborough County, 172–73; in peer coaching, 79–80

standards. *See* strict standards

statements: "I should notice . . . ," 92–93; Needs/Benefit Statements, 129–30; responses required from coaches, 92–93. *See also* Approval Statements; Confirmatory Paraphrases; Positive Phrasing

strategy (for coaching), organizational model, 67

stress, coaching and, 14, 152, 152–53

strict standards (for teachers), and motivation, 51

Student Achievement through Staff Development (Joyce and Showers), 7

student behaviors, options for observation, 109, 111, 113–14

students: acknowledging, 108–9; class assignment quiz and discussion development by, 95–96, 97–98; movements in the classroom, tracking, 111, *117*; pretty good student problem, 19–20; teacher impacts on, observing, 111, 118–22; teacher responses to student answers, 106–8, 107, 108, 109, *110*, 111

success: celebration of, xii, 152; for coaches, 6, 13–14, 41, 47, 75, 169; and the need for more coaching, 17–18; on opening day, 12, 13–14; stories of, 3–5

suggestions, making, in postobservation conferences, 90–91, 142, 143

summarizing what's said, 75

supervision, 34–35; on the evaluation/ coaching continuum, *23*

supervisors, 34–35; responsible for all supervisory roles, 35; role switching by, 35, 47–48; trust between teachers and, 35. *See also* administrators; coaches; evaluators; mentors; principals

supervisory roles in education, 23–37. *See also* coaching; evaluation; mentoring; supervision

support needs (of teachers), 7, 9, 66. *See also* needs that motivate teachers

survival, teachers' need for, 49–50, 51

Susan Boyle syndrome, 17–18

synergy (between coaches and coachees), v, 5, 19

tactics (for coaching), organizational model, 67

Taylor, Karen, 4, 179–81

teacher behaviors, options for observation, 109, 112–13

teacher's triangle, 94, 104–5, *104*

teachers: administrators wowing, 12; competence model, 94, 104–5, *104*; encouraging, 137–38; impact on students, observing, 111, 118–22; international teachers and coaching, 5, 178; Japanese teachers' coaching practice, v–vi; learning and working styles, 82–86, 93; movements in the classroom, tracking, 111, *117*; needs that motivate, 40, 49–51; observation of other teachers teaching, 109, 111; peer coaching performance report, 212–13; on principals as evaluating vs. coaching, 34; professional behavior, improving, 111, 118–22; professional learning communities, 167–69; reinforcing, 137–38; responses to student answers, charting, 107–8, 107, 108, 109, *110*; observing, 106–11; roles, 6–7, 152; role switching by, 35; wowing students, 12, 13–14, 61. *See also* coaches, videotaping

teaching: and coaching process, 125, *125*; enjoyment of, 127; excellence in, v; in isolation, v, 168, 170; learning vs., 123–24, *124*; team teaching, 158 teaching options, coaching and, 14, 152–53

team approach to coaching, 16

team teaching, 158; vs. individual classroom teacher schools, 6–7, 164–66

technical coaching, 15–16

temperament types, 84–85

time, making, for coaching programs, 155–57

tracking movements of teachers and students, 111, *117*

training: types, and transfer of learning, 7

transfer of learning (internalization), 7–9

Triune Brain Theory, 119

trust: evaluations as undermining, 34; research on collaboration and, 53; research on the value of, 36–37

trust between teachers: and coaches, 27–28, 47–48; and evaluators, 33, 34; and mentors, 27–28, 29, 30; and supervisors, 35

Turning to One Another (Wheatley), 151

Two-Way Communication Model (for mentoring), 28–29, *28*

Unconsciously Skilled level (Gordon's Ladder), *41*, 45–46

Unconsciously Talented level (Gordon's Ladder), 46–47, *46*

Unconsciously Talented teachers, 137; as good teachers but not great teachers, 47

Unconsciously Unskilled level (Gordon's Ladder), *41*, 42

uncovering creativity, 69–74

unpredictability in coaching, 92, 99

Urbanski, Adam, v–vi, 25–26

usefulness of experience, and quality of life, 11

values: coaches fitting Approval Statements to, 131–32, 134, 138, 142; organizational model, 66

verbal vs. nonverbal communication, 82–83

videotaping teachers: frequency, 19; making time for, 157–58; value of, xiii, 19, 60, 137

vision, of coaches, 65–74, 87; discovering/uncovering, 68, 87, 89–90; erosion of, 65; making suggestions and maintaining, 90–91, 142, 143; organizational model, 66; rekindling opportunity, 66. *See also* empowering questions

visualizing what we want vs. what we do not want, 128

voice. *See* intonation

Vreeman, Mary, 3, 171; *Instructional Coaches and Classroom Teachers*, 3

Walton High School coaching program, 4–5, 184–87

"what" questions, 58–59

Wheatley, Margaret, 151

"why" questions, 58–59

Whyte, David, 79

Williams, Cheryl, conversation with Steve, 72–74

working styles. *See* learning and working styles

"Wow!" experience: administrators wowing teachers, 12; creating the, 61; getting to the, 11–12; teachers wowing students, 12, 13–14, 61

"you" messages (in evaluation), 33–34

About the Author

Stephen G. Barkley serves as executive vice president of Performance Learning Systems, Inc. He has thirty-two years of experience teaching educators and administrators in school districts, state departments, teacher organizations, and institutions of higher education throughout the United States and internationally. A riveting motivational keynote speaker, trainer, consultant, and facilitator, Steve is known for increasing clients' effort and success by sharing his knowledge and experience, especially his expertise in the field of coaching teachers to excellence.

Steve's other books—*Wow! Adding Pizzazz to Teaching and Learning*; *Tapping Student Effort, Increasing Student Achievement*; and *Questions for Life: Powerful Strategies to Guide Critical Thinking*—have also contributed to teacher and student learning and achievement.